Between Philosophy and Non-Philosophy

Between Philosophy and Non-Philosophy

The Thought and Legacy of

Hugh J. Silverman

Edited by

Donald A. Landes
with Leonard Lawlor
and Peter Gratton

Cover image: *Hugh J. Silverman, Place Monge, Paris, France, 2008*
Image by Donald A. Landes

Published by State University of New York Press, Albany

Printed in the United States of America

For information, contact State University of New York Press, Albany, NY
www.sunypress.edu

Production, Diane Ganeles
Marketing, Fran Keneston

Library of Congress Cataloging-in-Publication Data

Names: Landes, Donald A., editor.
Title: Between philosophy and non-philosophy : the thought and legacy of Hugh J. Silverman / edited by Donald A. Landes, Leonard Lawlor, and Peter Gratton.
Description: Albany : State University of New York Press, 2016. | Includes bibliographical references and index.
Identifiers: LCCN 2016007711 (print) | LCCN 2017015549 (ebook) | ISBN 9781438463377 (ebook) | ISBN 9781438463353 (hardcover : alk. paper) | ISBN 9781438463360 (pbk. : alk. paper)
Subjects: LCSH: Silverman, Hugh J.
Classification: LCC B945.S6484 (ebook) | LCC B945.S6484 B48 2016 (print) | DDC 191—dc23
LC record available at https://lccn.loc.gov/2016007711

10 9 8 7 6 5 4 3 2 1

Contents

Afterword

Acknowledgments

The editors would like to acknowledge a very important debt of gratitude to the faculty and students in the Department of Philosophy at Stony Brook University, and particularly to the chairperson at the time, Eduardo Mendieta. Without their efforts in organizing the Silverman Memorial Symposium (held at Stony Brook University, September 2013), where several of the papers here were first read, this collected volume would not have been possible. In addition, we would like to offer a very sincere acknowledgement to the continuous support and advice from feminist philosopher Gertrude Postl, Hugh's spouse. We would also like to offer our thanks to Hugh's friends and colleagues who offered us advice or support throughout this process, especially those persons who are continuing Hugh's work through the International Association for Philosophy and Literature and the International Philosophical Seminar. Finally, we offer our thanks to all of the contributors to this volume, whose efforts have made possible the timely publication of this collection. This volume itself, of course, stands as its own monument to the debt of gratitude we individually and collectively owe to Dr. Hugh J. Silverman himself.

Abbreviations

DA Roland Barthes, "The Death of the Author," in *Image—Music—Text*, trans. Stephen Heath (New York: Hill & Wang, 1977), 142–48.

ER Hugh J. Silverman, "Excessive Responsibility and the Sense of the World (Merleau-Ponty and Nancy)," *Chiasmi International* 10 (2008): 307–17.

HC Hannah Arendt, *The Human Condition*, 2nd ed. (Chicago: University of Chicago Press, 1998).

I Hugh J. Silverman, *Inscriptions: After Phenomenology and Structuralism*, 2nd ed. (Evanston, IL: Northwestern University Press, 1997).

LN Julia Kristeva, "Life as a Narrative," in *Hannah Arendt*, trans. Ross Guberman (New York: Columbia University Press, 2001), 3–99.

PC Jacques Derrida, *The Post Card: From Socrates to Freud and Beyond*, trans. Alan Bass (Chicago: The University of Chicago Press, 1987).

RR Hugh J. Silverman, "The Mark of Postmodernism: Reading *Roger Rabbit*," *Cinémas: Revue d'études cinématographiques/Cinémas: Journal of Film Studies* 5, no. 3 (1995): 151–64.

RSS Julia Kristeva, *Revolt She Said*, trans. Brian O'Keeffe (New York: Semiotext(e), 2002).

SS Hugh J. Silverman, "The Postmodern Subject: Truth and Fiction in Lacoue-Labarthe's Nietzsche," in *Subjects and Simulations: Between Baudrillard and Lacoue-Labarthe*, ed.

Anne O'Byrne and Hugh J. Silverman (Lanham, MD: Lexington Books, 2015), 47–56.

T Hugh J. Silverman, *Textualities: Between Hermeneutics and Deconstruction* (New York: Routledge, 1994).

W Henry David Thoreau, *Walden*, ed. Jeffrey S. Cramer (New Haven, CT: Yale University Press, 2004).

WT Roland Barthes, "From Work to Text," in *Image—Music—Text*, trans. Stephen Heath (New York: Hill & Wang, 1977), 155–64.

Other Abbreviations

IAPL International Association for Philosophy and Literature

IPS International Philosophical Seminar

SPEP Society for Phenomenology and Existential Philosophy

1

Introduction

DONALD A. LANDES[1]

> It would be presumptuous to claim that a man is essentially one thing or another, that he is social, political, or rational, that he is a tool-maker, or that he is a user of symbols, etc. He is clearly not any one of these, since surely he is all of them. . . . What remains unclear is the particular sense in which he is ambiguous.
>
> —Hugh J. Silverman[2]

Drawn from the introduction to Hugh J. Silverman's doctoral dissertation (Stanford University, 1973), this passage captures something persistent in his thought and in his person. Silverman was never comfortable with a simple answer, and it is hardly surprising that those who know his work best regularly reach for the word "between" to characterize both him and his work. From his first formulation of "the between" in the concept *existential ambiguity* to his rich later characterization of it via the "Silvermanian twist" he brought to the deconstructive term *indecidability*, Silverman's self-conscious efforts were always toward *thinking the between*. In his work, he cultivated the space between phenomenology, hermeneutics, psychoanalysis, structuralism, poststructuralism, and deconstruction; he moved between an enormous range of philosophical guides, from Husserl, Heidegger, Merleau-Ponty, Sartre, and Beauvoir to Foucault, Deleuze, Lacan, Lévi-Strauss, Lévinas, Irigaray, Barthes, Nancy, Kristeva, Lacoue-Labarthe, and Stiegler, and he thereby explored a staggering number of philosophical concepts and deconstructive strategies.

Indeed, Silverman's career was marked by "the between" in several ways, and he always managed to cultivate a between that was between many, and never just between two. At Stony Brook University, Silverman held a joint appointment as Professor of Philosophy *and* Comparative Literary & Cultural Studies, and this between was enriched via active affiliation with the Department of Art as well as the Department of European Languages, Literatures, and Cultures, *and* further punctuated by an incredible international presence as a visiting professor at institutions around the world.[3] Silverman was incredibly active in cultivating places of intellectual exchange that mark continental philosophy and the intersection between philosophy and literature. Not only did he serve as executive co-director of the Society for Phenomenology and Existential Philosophy (SPEP) (1980–1986) and as long-time executive director of the International Association for Philosophy and Literature (IAPL),[4] but he was also the co-founder and director of a much different, more intimate annual seminar (the International Philosophical Seminar [IPS][5] that met at the border between Austria and Italy each year for a week of intensive study of a book written by a living author), and this too was further complemented by Silverman's regular organization of weekend conferences and symposia at Stony Brook and elsewhere. Even his list of awards, grants, and fellowships reveals a "between"—the between of a teacher-scholar who remained committed to both aspects of his academic career. This between of teaching and research was itself further punctuated by various other activities within the core functioning of the university (such as his long service on the Senate at Stony Brook) and the discipline more broadly (such as service on department review boards). If we turn our attention to his publication activities, not only did Hugh author two important books (*Inscriptions: Between Phenomenology and Structuralism*[6] and *Textualities: Between Hermeneutics and Deconstruction*,[7] both of which exist in translation into Korean and the latter also into Arabic, German, and Italian), but he also edited and coedited twenty-two volumes, served as series editor for key international publishing houses in continental philosophy,[8] and was an active

Advisory Board member for a long list of top academic journals and other book series.

Given the sheer weight of Hugh's 120-page curriculum vitae—with its sprawling list of international presentations, publications, graduate dissertation committees, tenure-case committees, review boards, university service, conference organization, courses taught as a visiting professor at other universities, and so forth—it is hard to imagine anyone to be a more connected, a more *networked* member in the fields of philosophy and comparative literature. Indeed, it is hard to imagine any member of these fields to have not been influenced in some way by the presence of Hugh J. Silverman. Surely what Gail Weiss refers to in her contribution to this volume as the "Silverman Network" was a remarkable phenomenon cultivated by a significant academic phenomenon. The essays that make up this volume collectively reveal both the reach of Hugh's influence and the loss felt when the center of such a network suddenly disappears, leaving behind a system that must begin to find a new equilibrium.

Nevertheless, so far we have merely listed accomplishments and named some academic markers. Silverman once himself wrote an "Autobiographical Statement," but placed at its head the following elliptical reminder: "The dates do not trace a chronology . . . epistemological markers of events and discursive developments . . . persons, programs, publications, and places constitute elements of an itinerary . . ."[9] Indeed, as impressive as a review of his CV might be, it risks missing both what Hugh's brother calls (in the afterword to this volume) the "human, caring, and deeply loving person that he was" as well as the subtle and profound influence his philosophical "itinerary" had on the development and shape of continental philosophy in America. In the richness produced *between* these markers we look for "Silverman," a goal that we have trepidatiously set for this volume, which aspires to be more than just a celebration of Hugh's accomplishments in the past tense. The contributions to this volume, personal in tone and deeply philosophical in scope, aim collectively to explore the rich field of possibilities that Hugh cultivated, a field that continues to shape the future of continental philosophy in the voices and gestures of Hugh's colleagues, students, and critics (sometimes all in the same person!).

Taking as our title an opposition that Hugh held to be critical in thinking the future of continental philosophy—what is *between philosophy and non-philosophy*—we hope that this volume serves to open the conversation on Hugh's contribution to continental philosophy (both past and future), to reinscribe and widen the "Silverman Network," and to remind us of the uniquely open practice of contemporary continental thought that Hugh saw moving ever forward toward plurality, reflected in the very title of his posthumous manuscript, *Postmodernisms: Between Ethics and Aesthetics.*[10] Such would be the only appropriate tribute to Hugh J. Silverman—to think death, authorship, hospitality, justice, responsibility, indecidability, subjectivity, the between, and its closely related "the after," and so forth, once again, with and against our collective past and future erstwhile guide, Professor Silverman.

Writing about/for/after Hugh: An Overview of the Content of this Volume

As the news of Hugh's passing disseminated in the weeks and months following his death, many of his colleagues and former students turned to writing, as if instinctively sensing in the creation of text a way of dealing with this particular loss. Whether online or as part of the various memorial events or conference sessions, an entire community felt the surge of memories of the various experiences and events that would bring to presence Hugh's quirks and his kindness, his stubbornness and his sense of humor, his loyalty and his accomplishments. What was striking in the various writings and speeches produced in these moments was the deep resonance between Hugh's personal and philosophical contributions to continental philosophy. It quickly became clear that a personal reflection on the character of Hugh Silverman could not remain isolated from the philosophical content of his thought, and vice versa, because Hugh quite directly lived and practiced his philosophy.

Part 1—Between Inscriptions and Textualities: Silverman's Deconstructive Practice

Recalling a deeply formative philosophical experience from his 1971–1972 *séjour* in Paris, Silverman writes: "I went to Paris as a budding phenomenologist. Everywhere friends and peers in France told me that phenomenology was *passé*, that I would need to learn about structuralism and especially what was forcing itself to be called 'poststructuralism.'"[12] This indeed must have been disconcerting. Ahead of the curve on the American scene with his firm foundation in phenomenology, which he had been studying since 1966, this young graduate student was suddenly made to feel behind the curve, trapped in another era, pursuing philosophical questions with outdated theoretical tools. In fact, and Hugh perceptively sensed this, it was more than simply having the wrong books in his checked luggage. The *bouleversement* named "poststructuralism" threatened to undermine the very philosophical concerns and methodologies that Hugh and many others had been so committed to. After all, Hugh's philosophical leanings were firmly rooted in philosophical anthropology, and his attraction to existential and phenomenological philosophy was animated by the rich potential he found in these traditions for rethinking the idea of human nature (while simultaneously managing to avoid giving up the idea of humanism altogether or falling back into a naive dogmatism). As the epigram to this introduction shows, even several years after his striking personal encounter with poststructuralism in post-1968 Paris, Hugh remained committed to studying human nature via existential phenomenology and its description of the ambiguity of lived experience in Sartre, Merleau-Ponty, and Heidegger.

Yet the upheaval of the poststructuralist moment did not fade for Silverman, and much of his early career found him deepening his knowledge of Saussure, Lévi-Strauss, Foucault, Barthes, Lacan, Derrida, and others. As he learned the subtleties of the poststructural texts that marked the contemporary philosophical landscape, Hugh set for himself the task of evaluating the claim that the phenomenological and existential study of the human subject could not stand in the face of the "developments in structuralism, semiology, and poststructuralism."[13] The confrontation between these two major moments in twentieth-century philosophy culminated in Silverman's first book, *Inscriptions: Between Phenomenology and Structuralism*, which was nothing less than the attempt to think *together* these two seemingly divergent paths:

> The place between phenomenology and structuralism does not occupy any space. It only marks the place between two methodologically parallel yet historically converging paths.

> At the limit of one, signs of the other are already plotted. At the frontier of the other, the former is incorporated and advanced. Yet structuralism does not take over where phenomenology ends. Nor does phenomenology succeed where structuralism fails. Often presented as antipodean ways of thinking, phenomenology and structuralism indicate two very different orientations in recent continental thought. . . . They each build upon a separate theoretical base which allows for and even promotes a philosophical practice or practices in their own right. (*I*, xv)

Stubbornly holding on to the value of the phenomenological tradition, Silverman was and remained interested in the difference *between* because of its potential for bringing together, not dividing.

Arguably two names in particular stand out in Silverman's thought precisely for their ability to move between these two orientations: Merleau-Ponty and Derrida. In Merleau-Ponty, Silverman found an adventurous phenomenologist who dared to take seriously both Saussure (at least beginning in 1947–1948) and the burgeoning structuralist work of his own friends, Lacan and Lévi-Strauss. At the time of his death, Merleau-Ponty was on the verge of demonstrating "the possibility of operating in the place between phenomenology and structuralism" (*I*, xvii). The practice of operating in this space, for Silverman, may have been announced by Merleau-Ponty, but was soon to be "signed by Derrida," and in this light Silverman found himself working toward what he terms a "hermeneutic semiology of the self-language-world complex" (*I*, xviii), at once Merleau-Pontian and Derridean.

For Silverman, the exploration of the place between phenomenology and structuralism sketched out a theory of textuality. His early commitment to rethinking the self found him following to its end the movement of thought that takes seriously the decentering of the subject, and this led to a deepening of his methodology and questions via the notion of *textualities*, the title of his second book. As he writes:

> While *Inscriptions* identifies the places of difference—the slashes, the borders, the belonging-together of alternatives—*Textualities* reiterates the "place between" as the locus of multiple textualities . . . Examples of textualities

> are developed in determinate regions, such as in "autobiographial textuality," "photobiographical textuality," "visible textuality," "scriptive textuality," "philosophical textuality," and "institutional textuality." (*T*, 2)

For Silverman, the seeming closure of the place between phenomenology and structuralism in a theory of hermeneutic semiology needed again to be reopened, and *Textualities* aimed to do just that. The work of this opening was trusted to what Hugh called "juxtapositional deconstructive reading," an evolution in his methodology, questions, and philosophical style.

Part 1 of this volume aims to explore the richness of Silverman's philosophical praxis, both in its overall style and in the various moments suggested by the brief description above. The first essay of this part is offered by Gary Aylesworth, one of Hugh's first PhD students and subsequently a longtime friend and collaborator. As Aylesworth stresses, *Inscriptions* and *Textualities* do not present us with a simple philosophical methodology. Rather, they present a cascading series of "experimental readings in which various methods and discourses of philosophy are exposed to a space of difference, a 'between,' in which something might be said that cannot be said within the limits of one side or another." And indeed, Silverman's various readings are at the heart of defining what has become known as "continental philosophy," a term that Silverman self-consciously adopted and reflected upon throughout his career. Taking Merleau-Ponty and Heidegger as the focus, Aylesworth illustrates how Silverman's philosophical praxis remained deconstructive by eschewing any "center." Aylesworth writes:

> The agency at work in [Silverman's deconstructive praxis] is not that of a self-identical subject or ego. It is, however, enactment of a diffuse and de-centered subjectivity that does not bind agency to identity, that is, to an agent that is formally or substantively "one." There is no proper name for this subjectivity, but it enacts itself in the multiplicity of its effects.

Taking the elusive praxis of deconstructive reading as his focus, Aylesworth explores the very place between *Inscriptions* and *Textualities*.

In the second paper of this section, I (Donald Landes) opt to venture into a blind spot of my own. Despite being a student of Silverman's, I too was and continue to be first a phenomenologist. My own *séjour* in Paris (2007–2009) was marked by many events, but nothing of the theoretical gravity of the poststructuralist shift or the post-1968 social revolution that Hugh encountered in the streets around the *École normale supérieure*. Moreover, I was there to work on the new translation of Merleau-Ponty's early *Phenomenology of Perception*,[14] a work that Hugh would insist remained somewhat incompatible with Merleau-Ponty's later evolutions through structuralism in the late 1940s and 1950s. As such, it was phenomenology that I primarily studied with Hugh, though he subtly (and sometimes not-so-subtly) guided me toward thinkers such as Derrida, Nancy, and Stiegler. A regret, however, that remains on the margins of my own studies is the absence of a concerted study of poststructuralism and deconstruction with Hugh when I had (and missed) that chance. Under the weight of this sense of nostalgia for a path not taken, I set out in this essay to take some steps on that other road, the road of poststructuralism, by exploring with Hugh his own internalization of Barthes's foundational texts, "The Death of the Author" and "From Work to Text." The outcome of this exploration is a glimpse into what I call Silverman's "intertextuality as philosophical method," as well as a reflection on the death of *an* author after the death of *the* Author.

In the final essay of part 1 of the volume, Galen Johnson—again a long-time friend and collaborator of Silverman's, particularly via the International Merleau-Ponty Circle—begins the difficult task of circumnavigating Silverman's rich network of concepts, primarily via Silverman's theory of textuality and autobiography, thereby focusing on the practice and potential of Hugh's second book, *Textualities*. Johnson argues that Silverman's theory of textuality brings together phenomenology and deconstruction in a particular way by drawing out the manner in which Silverman illustrates a "non-transcendent" practice of reading. The text as such is the place of the auto-text and neo-noema, the place where the reader *textualizes*, not a referent to a beyond of the text where the meaning could be found in itself. In a meaningful shift from "Prof. Silverman's" theory of the text to the thoughtful exploration of "Hugh's" own practice within autobiographical textuality, the second part of Johnson's contribution serves to illustrate the link between theory and practice to be found in Hugh's philosophy. Johnson carefully reconstructs Hugh's unique perspective on Thoreau's *Walden* and its relation to the "writing the self" practice of autobiography. As Johnson argues, in writing the self we write not just a story *about* ourselves, but rather we write our self, our body, and our voice. As a result, it is the search and cultivation of "perfect pitch" that autobiography illustrates in seeking that interpersonal tone that is "just right" in writing the self, the discovery of one's own voice. Drawing together Hugh and his subtle readings of Derrida and Barthes, Johnson ventures that autobiography itself emerges as the very voice of philosophy, which would be the profound discovery of philosophy *as* autobiography. The practice of writing the self via autobiography is central to Hugh's contribution, and thus Johnson's text provides an excellent transition to the next two sections of this volume, which resonate with his exploration of Hugh's philosophical method.

Part 2—Silverman and Derrida: Justice/Hospitality/Writing

As discussed above, 1971–1972 were formative years for Silverman in terms of his realization that he would work to think together phenomenology and structuralism. Yet 1972 also marks the year that Silverman first met Derrida. He admits, however, that in 1972 he "knew little of Derrida" when he was invited to a weekend seminar near the end of his stay in Paris. He writes, "Although these lectures occurred near the end of my stay, they marked my subsequent philosophical development."[15] In the second part of this collection, our contributors draw our attention to how influential Derrida was not only on Silverman's "philosophical development," but even more profoundly on his style of questioning and the stakes of philosophical questions that he came to appreciate in words such as hospitality, difference, and responsibility.

The first essay of part 2 is a contribution from Michael Naas, a former student of Hugh's. Naas—a leading translator of Derrida—offers an essay that revolves around what may at first glance seem to be a minor point: the difference between an *in-* and an *un-* in the translation into English of Derrida's use of the term *indécidable*. Of course, Hugh could detect (and exploit) in the smallest of details the most profound consequences. Naas makes a remarkable entry into Hugh's corpus via nothing more than a syllable, a "Silvermanian syllable—a prefix, really—that . . . Hugh signed, marked, or, better, inscribed in a unique and inimitable way." As Naas writes, "That word, *indécidable*, is almost always, indeed pretty much systematically, translated into English as *undecidable* rather than *indecidable*, and yet Hugh insisted on the *in-* of indecidable." The attempt to understand *why* Hugh insisted on this translation takes Naas into the deep thickets of Hugh's relation to Derrida's corpus and to the "Silvermanian twist" that Derrida's ideas received in his work. As Naas argues, the term *indecidable* became for Hugh synonymous with the work of deconstruction itself, and what is indecidable is the establishing of the place between. In short, Naas illustrates just how profoundly Derrida influenced what was arguably Hugh's most pressing philosophical concern—exploring the *between*, thanks to the *in-* of the *indecidable* that he learned from Derrida.

In "Of Philosophy, Friendship, and Justice," Debra Bergoffen explores other deeply Derridean themes in Hugh's thought. Recalling in some ways the tone of the essays from part one of this collection, Bergoffen strikes again for our reader the balance between the personal and the philosophical sides of Silverman. She recalls the profound experience of Hugh's community and democracy at the IPS: "Whether you were a graduate student, a new professor, or the occupant of a named chair, at the IPS you presented your paper and engaged in discussions as an equal. No hierarchies here. The seminars thrived on intellectual differences, challenges, probes." What she sees in this practice was nothing short of a politics of friendship, to allude to the title of one of Derrida's books. Moving to the content of Silverman's thought, Bergoffen explores how these Derridean influences shaped Hugh's understanding of philosophical practice, the role of philosophy in the university, and ultimately the idea of the subject in the postmodern moment, illustrating a "between" of Merleau-Ponty and Kristeva on this latter Silvermanian theme.

The final essay in part 2 is written by Eduardo Mendieta, Hugh's long-time colleague at Stony Brook University. Mendieta explores how the key theme of "autobiography" in Hugh's work emerges from his encounter with Derridean deconstruction and resonates with the characteristics of epistolary texts. Mendieta thus connects Silverman's deconstructive practice to a fundamental aspect of the deconstruction of metaphysics: "metaphysics is written in and through the practice of writing the self. The self is implicated in metaphysics, and thus, the task of deconstruction is to also—or perhaps most primordially—dismantle the metaphysics of the self." As a result, Mendieta draws our attention to the subtleties of part 3 of *Textualities*, "Autobiographical Textualities," and brings to the fore the manner in which autobiographical practice creates the *topoi* of the writing of the self that is the very location of the decentering of the self in writing. Drawing together Silverman's work on autobiography and Derrida's concepts from *Post Card*, Mendieta leads us to the profound questions of the who of the writer and the who of the addressee in the autobiographical gesture and the textuality of letters.

Part 3—Postmodern Heroes, Subjects, and Responsibilities

In 1997, Silverman released a new edition of *Inscriptions*, and in doing so he took the opportunity to modify the book's subtitle—originally *Between Phenomenology and Structuralism*, *Inscriptions* was now understood by Silverman to be heralding an *After Phenomenology and Structuralism*. For the many students and colleagues who published books or edited volumes with Hugh, or organized conferences with him, there is no question that Hugh took titles and subtitles *very* seriously! We can be sure, then, that this change must have resulted from a long reflection upon an important development in his work. No longer committed to the rigor, perhaps, of a new methodology named *hermeneutic semiology*, Hugh now understood *Inscriptions* as the groundwork for a *working into* the postmodern. And indeed, even the more open-ended "juxtapositional deconstructive readings" method that he described in *Textualities* perhaps failed to break fully with schools, movements, and signatures. In short, with this shift in subtitle, Silverman was retroactively announcing in the subtitle of his first book a third book that would have to come after his second book. This third book would be one that was to open up the practice of juxtapositional reading with wild abandon. Silverman writes:

> Yet at the end of *Textualities*, the question of the "end," the "after," the "post-" is articulated. This question of postmodern textuality will have to be the concern of a new study that comes after *Textualities*, one that asks how the postmodern is inscribed in the modern; how the alternatives

> to modernism mark the unpresentable in the presentation; how indecidables are distributed throughout the textures of contemporary culture; and how juxtapositions of differences interrogate the *after*, the *between*, and the *ends* that are disseminated rhizomatically throughout the textures of fin-de-siècle thinking, writing, filming, and textualizing. After phenomenology and structuralism, after hermeneutics and deconstruction, postmodern textualities will need to reinscribe these traditions, but as other, juxtaposed identities, as the fabric of the differences of twentieth-century thought, experience, understanding, bridging, and textualizing. (*I*, xiii–xiv)

It is in this spirit that we find as the final essay in part 3 an invaluable exploration of Silverman's unpublished manuscript, written by someone who knew Hugh better than any of the other contributors: feminist philosopher and Hugh's long-time partner, Gertrude Postl. As Postl reports, Silverman left behind a significant set of chapters for the book that is clearly being announced above in the new preface to *Inscriptions*. In the manuscript, Hugh seems to have settled on the following title: *Postmodernisms: Between Ethics and Aesthetics*. The manuscript itself reveals the expansive view that Hugh took on "the postmodern" and enacts precisely the wild opening up of the juxtapositional deconstructive practice to the very fabric of cultural and social proliferation of textualities. Postl writes:

> Theory, culture, political and social events criss-cross each other in rhizomatic fashion, are presented in their differences and interlinked by (sometimes randomly) chosen topics or themes. Philosophy, literature, films, TV shows, artworks, architecture, music (all from different time periods), but also the European Union or the new Europe, presidential elections, sport events or the state of the university are set up within various patterns of interaction and recurring themes. None of these texts, events, or phenomena are more important than the others, there is no hierarchy or recognizable predetermined decision with respect to impact, influence, or importance. They cover a spectrum from well-known to unknown, from high culture to trashy, from well established to minor contributions.

Moreover, Postl offers us important insights into why Hugh would have insisted on the plural in his title *Postmodernisms*.

The other essays in part 3 illustrate precisely Hugh's evolving philosophical practice, as each turns to explore some of Hugh's late work in relation to just this cultural adventure that he announced as the future of his "juxtapositional deconstructive" practice. The first essay is by Leonard Lawlor, (like Aylesworth) one of Hugh's first students. Here Lawlor explores two essays by Silverman that enact precisely the style announced for *Postmodernisms*. In the first essay discussed, "The Mark of Postmodernism: Reading *Roger Rabbit*," Lawlor identifies how Hugh finds the postmodern notion of the "frame" as articulated in Derrida's theoretical writings also subtly shaping the very unfolding of the movie *Who Framed Roger Rabbit*. In the breaking of the frame and the "counter-anachronism" of the film's plot, Silverman finds that beyond being a playful character in an insignificant film, Roger Rabbit in fact "operates difference" and as such emerges as a "postmodern hero." Even if there is perhaps something arbitrary about the objects of study, the bringing together of the diverse textualities to be discussed allowed Silverman to work through the fabric of postmodernism writ large. Turning his attention to the essay "Excessive Responsibility and the Sense of the World," which invokes the subtitle of Silverman's *Postmodernisms* manuscript, Lawlor finds Silverman again exploring the instantiations of the postmodern in a striking juxtaposition, this time placing the ideas of Jean-Luc Nancy in relation to the film *Crash*. Emphasizing the Silvermanian conclusion of these reflections, Lawlor writes that, despite the necessity of response, responsibility is "so excessive that no response is ever good enough."[16]

In the second essay of part 3, Ewa Płonowska Ziarek takes a posthumously published essay by Silverman as her point of departure: "The Postmodern Subject: Truth and Fiction in Lacoue-Labarthe's Nietzsche." It is striking that in this late moment of his career, the moment shaped by his cascading readings in *Postmodernisms*, Silverman is again returning to nothing other than the question of the "subject." In the essay, Ziarek weaves together personal reflections on Hugh the person and philosophical probing regarding Silverman the thinker, all in order to think through just what becomes of the subject in the postmodern moment. Ziarek focuses on how Silverman follows Lacoue-Labarthe's insistence that the subject is a "fiction," a story that can be (and is) told again and again. Such a story, concludes Silverman, is not one that has an "original" against which the truth of each telling could be measured, and as such we find what we might call an essential connection between philosophy and literature. After all, if the subject that philosophy has been searching for is a fiction, then we had better come to terms with the structures of fiction. For Silverman, a fiction is not necessarily "outside the truth," and as Ziarek observes, such a conception involves nothing less than a reworking of the "Platonic opposition between reality and appearance." This catapults Ziarek into the presentation of a fascinating juxtaposition—Silverman and Arendt on the question of the subject, a productive postmodern juxtaposition that adds the political to the ethical and the aesthetic of Hugh's *Postmodernisms*.

The third essay of part 3 is by Peter Gratton, a former student and longtime collaborator of Hugh's. Gratton offers a study of what we might term "postmodern responsibilities" via an excursion into the responsibilities of autobiographical and biographical textualities in the mode of journalistic writing. This study, venturing into what Gratton calls an "applied textualities," raises a set of cascading questions in relation to the place of responsibility in writing and the incipient return of fiction in any context of aiming for the truth. The ethical weight of Silverman's thought serves to undermine the dogmatic (implicit) claims to power and omniscient knowledge in the voice of a journalistic writer. Moreover, the weight of the texts themselves is critical to a Silvermanian account of responsibility; Gratton writes, "Texts are not something that can refer to us to some extra-textual evil, some ultimate irresponsibility, but are, as Silverman would put it, the *topoi* in which these events happen." With this case study in hand, Gratton turns to explore the Derridean roots of Hugh's notion of responsibility. As Silverman writes: "Responsibility can only happen in the between, in the spaces and gaps, in the chiasms and chasms that link us and separate us."[17]

Part 4—Care/Time/Community: Remembering Hugh J. Silverman

Part 4 of the current volume offers an illustration of the phenomenon of the coming together of the personal and the philosophical, revealing something quite profound about the practice of continental philosophy as not merely a philosophical perspective among others, but rather as a place of care, hospitality, responsibility, and difference. The section begins with a contribution from Kelly Oliver, a former colleague of Hugh's, who writes: "Silverman's work is a testament to the connections between life, memory, and writing." From within a subtle reflection upon how Hugh was a master at bringing together people and traditions in order to "stage encounters" and create memories alongside understanding, Oliver's exploration itself stages for the reader an encounter between time, place, cosmopolitanism, and hospitality. It is precisely this coming together of the theoretical and the personal in the life and work of Hugh Silverman that appears again and again throughout this volume.

In the second essay, contributed by Hugh's longtime colleague at Stony Brook University, Edward S. Casey, this intertwining of the personal and the philosophical again imbues the text. Casey's reflection resonates deeply with all who knew Hugh, because all of us who knew and worked with Hugh have the shared experience of watching Hugh *take his time*. Casey explores how this character trait was hardly isolated from Hugh's philosophical perspective, a perspective marked above all by "care." As Casey insists, Hugh's care stemmed from a deep and "unqualified respect for other human beings, whatever their rank or walk of life." It is through this coming together of time and care, which Casey forcefully argues necessarily belong together, that Casey manages to capture the style of Hugh's person and the philosophical (and ethical) example that Hugh set for all of his students.

The final essay of part 4 is by Gail Weiss, a long-time collaborator with Hugh as a member of the IAPL Executive Committee and various other shared works. Weiss coined a phrase in the title of her essay that reverberated throughout the Silverman Memorial Symposium[11] and that has since sedimented into a term of art among many colleagues around the world: "The Silverman Network." Beyond the illustration of how this ever-expanding network of those influenced by Hugh serves as a genuinely welcoming space within continental philosophy, Weiss describes an essential attribute of Hugh's personal/philosophical style in his remarkable mastery of the "greeting." Drawing from her personal experiences with Hugh as well as her deep familiarity with his work on hospitality and the creation of encounters across difference, Weiss's contribution is a convincing statement of the coming together of the personal and the philosophical in Hugh and in continental philosophy more generally.

Afterword

The final word in this volume is offered by Lee Silverman, Hugh's younger brother, who made the trip from Australia to attend the Silverman Memorial Symposium at Stony Brook University in September 2013, where many of the papers in this volume were read for the first time. For the participants at the conference, Lee's presence was particularly memorable, because Lee is indeed strikingly similar in appearance and comportment to his older brother. Moreover, Lee took a keen interest in engaging with Hugh's colleagues and former students, patiently exploring the ideas being put forth and drawing from his own experiences to contribute a Silvermanian perspective to the proceedings. Although Lee holds an undergraduate degree in philosophy, his training turned to computers, and his career in information technology has kept him from philosophy for decades. We are very pleased that he agreed to write an afterword for this volume of essays honoring his brother's life and work. The piece is genuine, and genuinely Silvermanian. Lee's essay offers the perfect tone to conclude this volume.

After/Post/Beyond the Between

We hope that there will be no end to the exploration and expansion of the Silverman Network. No end—but perhaps a *post-*. The signs of what might be "post-Silverman," of what might follow or come after, lie, as Hugh would have insisted, in the *indécidable* of all the betweens he interrogated throughout his life. The instability, unbalance, and injustice of these plural indecidables demand that we (at least those of us who follow Hugh Silverman, in time and in spirit) make a decision about how to find something stable—we must say something that makes sense—we must establish some balance—we must hear all voices equally—and we must find some justice for all of those who suffer. In short, we must *care* for them. Many of the essays in this volume speak of how much Hugh cared, excessively cared, *about* concepts and questions, titles and subtitles, but above all how much he cared *for* his students, his colleagues, and his friends. His work and life demand from us no less than that we care excessively in return. Anticipated by Hugh's 1973 doctoral dissertation, Hugh's thought of ambiguity demands from us today to seek answers to this question: how are we to think between ethics and aesthetics? Perhaps only by means of the pursuit of the question between ethics and aesthetics can we respond to the demand that we care and care excessively for justice.

Notes

1. I would like to thank Peter Gratton and Leonard Lawlor for their comments on this introduction, particularly Lawlor's significant contribution to the final paragraph.

2. Hugh J. Silverman, "Existential Ambiguity: A Phenomenology of Human Nature" (PhD diss., Stanford University, 1973).

3. Silverman held part- or full-year visiting professorships at the following institutions: Université de Nice, 1980–1981, 1994; University of Warwick, 1980; New York University, 1979–1980, 1986; University of Leeds, 1988, Università di Torino, 1989; Universität Wien, 1993, 1997, 2000, and Fulbright Distinguished Chair in the Humanities, 2001, Fulbright Distinguished Chair in Art Theory and Cultural Studies, 2010; University of Helsinki, 1997, 1999; University of Sydney, 1998; Duquesne University, 2000; Università di Roma-II, 2001; University College Cork, 2002; University of Trondheim, 2002; Universität Klagenfurt, 2003, 2005; University of Tampere, 2004; University of Tasmania, 2004; Distinguished Fellow at La Trobe University, 2008; Tallinn University, 2011; and the National University of Singapore, 2012.

4. The International Association for Philosophy and Literature (IAPL) was founded in 1976, a meeting that Hugh attended and at which he was nominated to take part in the organizational structure of the emerging organization. He would go on to become the secretary treasurer (1979–1982), the executive secretary (1983–1987), and finally the executive director (1987–2013).

5. The International Philosophical Seminar (IPS) was founded in 1990 by Silverman and co-founder and co-Director Wilhelm S. Wurzer (1948–2009) of Duquesne University. After Wurzer's death in 2009, Silverman served as director.

6. Hugh J. Silverman. *Inscriptions: Between Phenomenology and Structuralism* (New York: Routledge and Kegan Paul, 1987). With a changed subtitle, the second edition of this book appears as Hugh J. Silverman, *Inscriptions: After Phenomenology and Structuralism*, 2nd ed. (Evanston, IL: Northwestern University Press, 1997). All references in this volume to this text are to the 2nd edition and are henceforth cited as *I*.

7. Hugh J. Silverman, *Textualities: Between Hermeneutics and Deconstruction* (New York: Routledge, 1994). Henceforth cited as *T*.

8. Silverman edited the following book series, many of which were still active at the time of his death: *Continental Philosophy* (Routledge); *Philosophy, Aesthetics and Cultural Theory [PACT]* (Continuum International/Bloomsbury); *Philosophy and Literary Theory* (Humanity Books); *Contemporary Studies in Philosophy & The Human Sciences* (Humanity Books); *New Horizons for Continental Philosophy* (Rowman & Littlefield); *Textures: Philosophy/Literature/Culture* (Lexington Books/Continuum); *Series in Philosophy, Literature and Culture* (Northwestern University Press); and *Contemporary Studies in Philosophy and Literature* (State University of New York Press).

9. Hugh J. Silverman, "Continental Philosophy on the American Scene: An Autobiographical Statement," in *Portraits of American Continental Philosophers*, ed. James R. Watson (Bloomington: Indiana University Press, 1999), 187.

10. For a discussion of this unpublished manuscript, see chapter 14 in this volume, "Postmodernisms: On a Posthumous Book," by Gertrude Postl.

11. The Silverman Memorial Symposium was held at Stony Brook University, September 13–14, 2013. Several of the essays in this volume were first shared during this memorial event.

12. Silverman, "Continental Philosophy on the American Scene," 189.

13. Ibid.

14. Maurice Merleau-Ponty, *Phenomenology of Perception*, trans. Donald A. Landes (New York: Routledge, 2012).

15. Silverman, "Continental Philosophy on the American Scene," 189.

16. Lawlor himself is at grips with the question of a sufficient response in his book *This is Not Sufficient: An Essay on Animality and Human Nature in Derrida* (New York: Columbia University Press, 2007).

17. Hugh J. Silverman, "Response-abilities for Legacies: Jacques—on vous suit à travers vos texts," *Mosaic: A Journal for the Interdisciplinary Study of Literature* 40, no. 2 (2007): 305.

Part I

Inscriptions and *Textualities*

Silverman's Deconstructive Practice

2

Enacting the "Between"

Silverman and Continental Philosophy

Gary E. Aylesworth

> καί γὰρ πᾶν τὸ δαίμόνιον μεταξύ ἐστι θεοῦ τε και θνητοῦ ("For the whole of the spiritual is between divine and mortal").
>
> —Plato, *Symposium* 202e [202d–202e]

I open with this passage from Plato in recognition that the "between" (το μεταξύ) has long been a place of concern for philosophy. In light of its importance in such a key text as the *Symposium*, one might rightly say that it has been *the* place of concern, even when it remains unacknowledged. Plato tells us, for example, that love (*eros*), which is ultimately love of the unconditionally real and true, which is to say philosophy, can only happen when there is a spiritual (*daimonic*) passage between the mortal and the divine, the apparent and the real, the many and the one, the sensuous and the ideal. Where there is no passage and no movement, there is no philosophy, not among the gods who are fully wise and do not pass between wisdom and ignorance, nor among those mortals who think, in their ignorance, that they are already wise, and therefore need not subject themselves to the demands of philosophy. In its purest sense, as Plato suggests, philosophy is not a doctrine, but a movement of spirit that is always "*metaxu*," always *between* established alternatives and distinctions. It cannot settle upon a particular theory, method, or approach, but always moves in a space of difference that has no final closure.

In this spirit, which is, after all, the spirit of philosophy, I would like to commemorate the philosophical praxis of Hugh Silverman. It cannot be said that Silverman's published texts, *Inscriptions* and *Textualities,* present or develop a particular philosophical method or school of thought, phenomenology or semiotics, for example, but they provide us with a series of experimental readings in which various methods and discourses of philosophy are exposed to a space of difference, a "between," in which something might be said that cannot be said within the limits of one side or another. In this sense, Silverman writes in the 1987 preface to *Inscriptions* that the volume "was written at the end of phenomenology and structuralism; hence it can write the differences between them" (*I*, xiii). But what is his sense of "end"? First of all, it would be a certain situated-ness in relation to the discourses and institutions of philosophy, as well as a recurring motif *within* them. Heidegger, for example, attempts to think the "end" of metaphysics, Foucault imagines the "end" of the concept of "man," and Derrida writes of "the end of the book and the beginning of writing." In each case "end" means a certain limit, but also a place where something new may be said. It is not a mere termination of metaphysics, or "man," or "the book," but a space *between* in which another step may be taken.

As to the difference between phenomenology and structuralism, specifically, Silverman states that "[w]hile Merleau-Ponty stands at the opening of the place between, Derrida formulates its closure" (*I*, xviii). But again, we must recall that "closure" for Derrida is also not a terminal limit, but a turning point or a reversal, perhaps a doubling back that shifts and displaces the sense of a text. The chapters of *Inscriptions*, therefore, are not to be read as exercises in phenomenology, structuralism, or Derridean deconstruction, but as experimental attempts to write the differences between them. We do not find in these texts extended phenomenological descriptions, systematic structural analyses, or the iteration of marks and traces, but we find, instead, attempts to open a space of difference in which *another* writing can take place. One of Silverman's names for this space is, to be specific, "continental philosophy."

The fact that Silverman chooses this name is indicative of his own situated-ness in relation to certain discourses, institutions, and practices that Anglo-American philosophers have gathered together, perhaps quite arbitrarily, under this appellation. While movements such as structuralism, phenomenology, and deconstruction are of European provenance, the term "continental philosophy" is mostly an American invention. It signifies "exotic" texts and concepts that do not conform to a paradigm that is standard for the official elites of a certain profession. Silverman, however, seeks to rewrite this term, so that it signifies, instead, a space of operation that did not previously exist, thus introducing an appropriative gesture that would shift the sense of what so-called "continental philosophy" could mean and what its possibilities could be. Insofar as it challenges the prevailing norms and practices of institutional, or "professional" philosophy, this gesture is not abstractly theoretical, but is essentially and unavoidably political.

Silverman is quite explicit on this point in his introduction to *Philosophy and Non-Philosophy Since Merleau-Ponty*, which inaugurates a book series bearing the name "Continental Philosophy" as its title. "[C]ontinental philosophy calls out for a space of its own," he says, and further, "continental philosophy operates in terms of an orientation toward openness."[1] The twofold sense of this call is worthy of exploration. First, it is a call for a space that has not already been delineated and marginalized as a space allotted to an "other" who is not acknowledged within the space of a dominant paradigm and its institutions. Silverman calls us to claim this space as our *own*, that is, to write the name "continental philosophy" in another space, one that is neither the space of "analytic philosophy" nor the space analytic philosophy designates for its marginalized "other," but a space opened by a practice that invents itself. Furthermore, this practice is to be directed or oriented toward openness, which means that the term "continental philosophy" is fundamentally about this space and not about any particular thing that is said, heard, or written within its dimensions. Silverman does not, therefore, call for another orthodoxy that would oppose itself to the one already prevailing in institutions of professionalized philosophy, but orthodoxy *itself* is the gesture he is calling us to oppose and to submit to the rigors of difference. Hence, "continental philosophy" would be a way, a manner of philosophizing, whose horizon is always open to alternatives and previously unheard-of possibilities. Indeed, it must seek out or even invent these alternatives in order to maintain the openness of its space, and to convey a sense of this space as the matter of its concern.

In this regard, Silverman declares, "we are not as concerned to propose a name as to have an effect, to expand the space for writing."[2] Writing, or "inscription," is his term for the practice of philosophizing, a practice that opens, and situates itself within, the space "between." This could be the space between phenomenology and structuralism, or between hermeneutics and deconstruction, or between philosophy and art, or the modern and the postmodern. It is also, as he writes, a space in which the "self" is inscribed in autobiography, painting, photography, literature, and institutions such as the university. As he says in *Textualities*, inscription *textualizes* the self or the subject in its world. It situates and locates the self "here" and "there" in relation to a world that it inherits as already existing, but inscription also exposes the self to what is other, and to what might be, to what cannot be reduced to the world as we find it. Inscription opens a space for the new, for the other, and for the different.

Here, there is an irreducible ambiguity between the self that *is* an act of inscription and the self that is inscribed. Silverman calls attention to this ambiguity, for example, in his account of Husserlian phenomenology. In *Inscriptions*, he notes that while Husserl criticizes Descartes for not distinguishing between the psychic ego and the transcendental ego, it is still the case for Husserl that the empirical ego must perform the initial *epochē* that shifts consciousness from the natural attitude into the phenomenological attitude *before* this shift is authorized by the "things themselves," which appear only after the shift has been made. As Husserl himself insists, phenomenology requires an institution, a method of instruction and effectiveness, within the scientific and cultural world that would bring about the motivation for the required shift in consciousness that would then "bracket out" the real existence of that world. In other words, that existence that must be suspended for the sake of phenomenological "seeing" must *enact* this seeing as a practice, a practice whose moment of intervention must always remain invisible and unseen, but whose effects present themselves in experience. As Silverman would say, transcendental consciousness can only arise as a difference of inscription, as the effect of a practice that is, strictly speaking, neither transcendental nor empirical, but that operates in the space between.

This essential indecidability recalls, but also distinguishes itself from, Heidegger's characterization of *Dasein* as being-in-the-world. On Heidegger's account, *Dasein is* the totality of possibilities that constitutes its world, but, on the other hand, as an ek-sistence, it is also a projection toward the world and the possibility of death as its unsurpassable limit. In this regard, death is that *for the sake of which* we are involved with the world and everything in it. Silverman's encounter with Heidegger is particularly illuminating, in that the opening or clearing of being and the "there" of *Dasein* are associated with Silverman's attempt to thematize the "space between" in his inscriptions of continental philosophy. However, there is a fundamental difference between Heidegger's thinking and Silverman's practice. This difference has to do with the *anamnesic* project that underlies all of Heidegger's philosophical efforts, from *Being and Time* to *Time and Being*. For Heidegger, the "there" of *Dasein* is an *already there*, a *schon Gewesen sein*, that he seeks to recover by bringing to light *Dasein*'s facticity. The lesson of the existential analysis of *Being and Time* is that all of *Dasein*'s possibilities are already bound and limited by the possibility of death, a possibility that is projected out of *Dasein*'s past insofar as Dasein *has been* thrown into its world. As Heidegger would say, I do not throw myself into the world, but find myself already thrown. However, Silverman suggests, in reference to Heidegger, that "when I constitute myself . . . I perform an act" (*I*, 40), and (citing Heidegger) that "man as such situates himself in the relation to Being" (*I*, 50). Hence there is a perhaps irreconcilable difference between Silverman's insistence upon human agency in the act of situating the self in the world and Heidegger's declaration of *Dasein*'s essential receptiveness in relation to being and to its own existence as thrown-being-toward-death.

This difference comes to a head in Silverman's rewriting of Heidegger's statement in the "Letter on 'Humanism'" that "(l)anguage is the house of Being."[3] Silverman says in *Inscriptions* that "man is the presence of that which is present," and that "that which is present in man is given by thinking," which leads him to conclude that "(t)hinking constructs the house of Being" (*I*, 57). This, of course, stands in contradiction to Heidegger's own declaration that "thinking never creates the house of Being" (*Gleichwohl schafft das Denken nie das

Haus des Seins),[4] which denies to human agency the leading role with regard to being and language as well as being and thinking. While Heidegger would agree that particular utterances are human constructions that build *upon* the house of being, the power of language to say something *about* something, its *significance*, is granted by being, and the granting of significance is the matter of thinking. In other words, Heidegger's thinking is always directed toward the recovery of an event that has *always already* happened, as is the case with the ek-static opening of *Dasein*'s temporality and with the *Ereignis* of being (*Seyn*). For Heidegger, Silverman's assertion that "man as such situates himself in relation to being" would no doubt fall under the "subjectivism" that Heidegger believes to announce the end and closure of metaphysics, but which would perhaps open the possibility of recovering *another* event of being and another mode of thinking.

By way of denying primacy to human agency, and thus to the inescapable subjectivism it entails, Heidegger is keen to distinguish thinking from praxis. As he remarks: "thinking is a deed. But a deed that also surpasses all *praxis.* Thinking permeates action and production, not through the grandeur of its achievements, . . . but through the humbleness of its inconsequential accomplishment."[5] Indeed, its humbleness entails a de-subjectivized "saying" for the sake of being. Silverman, to the contrary, states that the ambiguity of the self's situated-ness with regard to being and to the world arises because we are both in the world *and* "an originating source of the whole world order" (*I*, 66). The question is, then, whether this "originating source," which *is* an action and a practice, and which *does* produce effects, can be written in such a way as to escape the snare of subjectivism *and* to open possibilities of *subjectivization* that Heidegger's thinking cannot anticipate. For Silverman, it is not Heidegger who points the way here, but Merleau-Ponty, particularly with the concept of the *chiasm* as he develops it in *The Visible and the Invisible.*

For Merleau-Ponty, the chiasm, the reversibility of the visible and the invisible, is not simply "thought," something carried out in reflective consciousness, as in Hegel, or in commemorative meditation, as in Heidegger's *andenkendes Denken.* We recall that for Merleau-Ponty, the lived body and its "flesh" is the locus of the chiasm, and the body itself is not objectively or empirically found in the world, but is the very way and opening to the world. It is also essentially a praxis, and an enactment of praxis, as the origin of the relation between experience and ideality. As Merleau-Ponty remarks: "the 'pure' ideality already streams forth along the articulations of the aesthesiological body, along the contours of the sensible things, and however new it is, it slips through ways it has not traced, transfigures horizons it did not open."[6] The chiasm is thus the performance of an intertwining that always brings ideality to an experience it did not initiate, but from out of which it arises. In reference to this, Silverman remarks in *Inscriptions*: "*Praxis*, for Merleau-Ponty, *is* the absolute; and the absolute is nature, visibility, the phenomenal field" (*I*, 119). This means that, "[f]or Merleau-Ponty, [philosophy] must initiate a movement in the direction of actual lived experience" (*I*, 129–30). In his rewriting of the chiasm, the difference between the visible and the invisible is repeated in the difference between meaning and significance, where meaning is the being of the self and significance is the *enactment* of being (*I*, 83). Another way of expressing it might be that there is no effecting without thinking and no thinking without effecting, which means the essential difference is not "there" for thinking alone, but it is initiated in praxis, and in a space that requires human agency or subjectivization to bring about the event of its opening.

In his experimentation with what he calls "a hermeneutic semiology of the self," Silverman attempts to show that the chiasm, and its praxis, also holds between hermeneutical understanding and the semiotic linking of signifiers. The signs of the self are inseparable from the understanding that reveals and interprets them. The only question, then, is how to characterize their difference, which can be neither hermeneutical nor semiological. Silverman is clear on this point: their difference is made through acts of doing and effecting. As he says in *Inscriptions*:

> This ambiguity is the perplexity of western philosophy and has motivated not only the subject/object dichotomy, but also the separating of soul and mind from body, being-for-itself from being-in-itself, and knowledge from what is to be known. A hermeneutic semiology of the self will show that the separation is artifice. (*I*, 342)

We can also extend this artifice to Heidegger's ontological difference and his separation of thinking from acting. In this regard, Silverman could be read to see in Heidegger a performative contradiction; the separation between thinking and effecting that Heidegger insists upon is itself enacted by the writing of texts that are released into a space of *reading*, and that means a space that is public, effective, and political. Hence, as a writer of texts, Heidegger himself cannot evade *inscription* or subjectivization.

In *Textualities*, Silverman reformulates his notion of hermeneutic semiology to say that it could also be characterized as "a juxtapositional deconstructive reading" (*T*, 2). Juxtapositional deconstruction could, in fact, characterize Silverman's practice in all of its dimensions. First, "juxtaposition" is the act of placing methods, texts, and institutions next to one another to open up a space between them. There is, in principle, no limit to the differential spaces that can be explored, to the angles, tangents, and lines that can be drawn through this gesture. It is the how and the way, the manner and the style, for constructing the artifice of difference, such that the space of difference itself is never closed off or gathered into a totality. Hence the writings that make up the content of *Inscriptions* and *Textualities* are not so much about the texts that Silverman is reading as they are about the space or spaces that can be created by juxtapositional experimentation. Their intent is not so much to add to the accumulation of scholarly knowledge and commentary on, say, Merleau-Ponty or Derrida, as it is to draw us into this space of experiment, interrogation, and exploration.

Silverman's practice is deconstructive because its acts of juxtaposing, separating, and differing are not initiated from a focal point, a nucleus, or a center (*I*, 49). The agency at work in it is not that of a self-identical subject or ego. It is, however, the enactment of a diffuse and de-centered subjectivity that does not bind agency to identity, that is, to an agent that is formally or substantively "one." There is no proper name for this subjectivity, but it enacts itself in the multiplicity of its effects. Its gesture is repeatable and is recognizable as a particular quality or tonality of experience, and it opens and operates in the space that could just as easily be called "Hugh Silverman" as "continental philosophy," or "the space between." Furthermore, this subjectivity intends no delimitable effect or set of effects as its terminal goal or purpose; rather, the openness of its space is its ultimate concern. In this respect, Silverman's practice falls under a description given by Merleau-Ponty: "*Praxis* is not an empirical action in this respect. Properly speaking, it has no *goal*; rather is a 'manner.'"[7] Silverman's practice is precisely a manner of opening and reopening the differential space he calls "the place between." The urgency of this openness is so compelling that he will insist upon it even at the risk of misprision, as is the case in his reading and rewriting of Heidegger. For him, expanding the space for writing is paramount, while remaining "true" to Heidegger, perhaps because it would introduce a radical passivity into inscription, is an expendable consideration.

Nor is Silverman's "between" a place only to be found in his writings. For him, it also extends into institutional inscriptions, most notably into venues such as the International Association for Philosophy and Literature and the International Philosophical Seminar. These institutions are places for the practice of difference, and, as such, they are realizations of the "between" in actual lived experience. They are also places in which we experience the same quality and tone of juxtapositional deconstruction. In these instances, the spaces at issue are geographical, institutional, cultural, linguistic, personal, social, and political. They are places bearing such names as "Freiburg" and "Strasbourg," "Basel," "Melbourne," "Helsinki," "Rotterdam," "Tainan," "London," "Syracuse," "Regina," "Tallinn," and, most recently, "Singapore." They represent cities, nations, continents, hemispheres, and passages between their boundaries. There is no hierarchy among these places, no consideration of "major" or "minor," and no preference for metro-pole or province. Likewise, the content and structure of the event; its themes and topics; the persons, disciplines and traditions that are invited in, are not subject to an orthodoxy of selection and exclusion. The IAPL is a space that repeats itself in different locations but welcomes everyone into the practice of difference, into the spaces between the established boundaries separating disciplines, methods, and institutions, so that something may be said that has not been said before. This, too, is the practice of inscription, a writing that has no single "author" and no planned or preordained outcome other than the opening and expansion of its space.

For the sake of the new and the different, the International Philosophical Seminar operates with one guiding rule: only texts of living writers will open the readings that are thematically presented and discussed. In addition, the authors themselves are not present, for the aim of the seminar is to create a space free of authority and distinctions of rank and position. Like the IAPL, the space of the seminar is open to experiment, risk, and invention, without hierarchy or orthodoxy. In this regard, the spontaneous movement of discussion is matched only by the wanderings and striking vistas of the mountain trails. The mountains, too, are experienced and "read," in their ever-changing perspectives, and they constantly surround and frame the exchanges that take place in the seminar room, on the terrace of the hotel, and in the cobbled streets of Kastelruth and St. Ulrich. However, our current situation puts into question the rule of living authors, if the seminar itself is indeed one of Silverman's inscriptions. For how can we not read Silverman every time the seminar convenes, no matter which texts are thematically announced? And let us not forget the history of this inscription and the authorship of Wilhelm Wurzer, who, with Hugh, co-inaugurated the seminar in 1991. Neither is now among the living, and yet "who" they are is still a matter of continuing enactment, for this "who" is not restricted to a specific *one*, but is also a space of praxis that has no reference other than to itself.

I stated earlier that Heidegger's insistence upon death as the possibility binding all possibilities into a totality is deeply foreign to Silverman's commitment to agency as a power that can break through the totality of what has been in order to write what is yet unwritten. This breakthrough would only happen in the place between, which means that there can be no limit that has no other side, which is to say, which cannot be juxtaposed with another boundary or another edge. For Heidegger, the other side of death, if there is one, could only be being as such (*Seyn*), which withdraws from all juxtaposition, and whose difference cannot be brought about by human agency or effectiveness. Hence, it remains for us only to wait for the event, to make ourselves ready to receive it, if it grants itself to us—"*Nur noch ein Gott kann uns retten*" ("Only a god can save us"). But does Heidegger's "only a god" forget the lesson of Diotima? Is there not, after all, the possibility of a *daimonian* immortality that passes *between* divinity and the mortal lives of individual humans? Silverman has said that difference is artifice. Plato has written ταύτῃ τῇ μηχανῇ, ὦ Σώκρατες . . . θνητὸν ἀθανασίας μετέχει—"by this device, Socrates . . . a mortal thing shares in immortality" (*Symposium* 208 B). The device, the *mechanē*, Diotima is describing is the movement by which what is passing or has passed is replaced by the new, by something resembling what is passing but is not identical to it. It is, in other words, a movement of difference.

In Ancient Greek, *metaxu* (the place between) and *methexis* (sharing or participating) are closely related. The space between is the place for sharing, as in the Greek theater, where *methexis* is the practice of improvisation and audience participation, where divisions of status and rank are dissolved and the unscripted and the unexpected are allowed to happen. For Plato, philosophy itself is the passage of *daimonian eros* between the visible and the invisible, and between the mortal and the ever-unchanging divine, a passage that is only possible because love is *metaxu*, belonging neither to what perishes nor to what never allows the new. For Silverman, the *metaxu* is also the place of a self, an agency that opens the space of difference and allows the yet unsaid to be said and the unwritten to be written. Who is it, then, this self who has passed, but whose *daimonian* presence still shares itself out by inviting us into the place between? By way of an answer, I return to Hugh's introduction to *Continental Philosophy I*: "we are not as concerned to propose a name as to have an effect . . ."

Notes

1. Hugh J. Silverman, ed., *Philosophy and Non-Philosophy Since Merleau-Ponty*, Continental Philosophy I (London: Routledge, 1988), 1.

2. Silverman, *Philosophy and Non-Philosophy*, 7.

3. Martin Heidegger, "Letter on 'Humanism,'" trans. Frank A. Capuzzi, in *Pathmarks*, ed. William McNeill (Cambridge: Cambridge University Press, 1998), 239.

4. Ibid., 272.

5. Ibid., 274.

6. Maurice Merleau-Ponty, *The Visible and the Invisible*, trans. Alphonso Lingis (Evanston, IL: Northwestern University Press, 1968), 152.

7. Maurice Merleau-Ponty, "Philosophy and Non-Philosophy Since Hegel," trans. Hugh J. Silverman, in *Philosophy and Non-Philosophy Since Merleau-Ponty*, ed. Hugh J. Silverman, Continental Philosophy I (New York: Routledge, 1988), 67.

3

Between Inscriptions

Intertextuality as Philosophical Method

Donald A. Landes

> In the multiplicity of writing, everything is to be *disentangled*, nothing *deciphered*; the structure can be followed, "run" (like the thread of a stocking) at every point and at every level, but there is nothing beneath: the space of writing is to be ranged over, not pierced.
>
> —Roland Barthes[1]

This passage from Barthes captures, I would like to suggest, the spirit of Hugh J. Silverman's philosophical method.[2] A mere glance at any article or chapter by Silverman reveals an artful navigation through some of the densest thickets of contemporary continental philosophy—Silverman was a master of *disentangling* rather than of *deciphering*. He was an explorer, not a code breaker. The titles of his lectures and chapters rarely fail to announce at least two fields or two thinkers to be explored, and when two names are absent, one always finds words such as "difference," "between," and "responsibility," that is, words of relations that invoke rhizomatic rather than arboristic thinking. As

Silverman self-consciously declares at the outset of *Textualities*, he was committed to "thinking the between," and the body of work he produced was an engagement with this endless task (*T*, 1). The "between" serves the role in Silverman's thought of the non-empty negative—a necessarily slippery concept, an ambiguous one, that cannot be closed through a precise and analytic definition. For Silverman, the between is not something *discovered*; it is something *produced*, and so can only be explored through various "strategies and examples" (*T*, 1). And explore the between he did. His chapters and lectures have the feel of a journey into the between, like his beloved *Ausflug* into the intervals of the Dolomites that he would embark upon each summer at the International Philosophical Seminar (IPS). Between the mountains, the production of the meaning of the journey occurs *in the walking*, and between the monuments or "works" of our tradition, the production of meaning occurs *in the reading*. Silverman's philosophical method was an exercise of lingering in the intervals, in *intertextuality*, with the textuality of continental philosophy (broadly construed) as his primary landscape for his exploratory walks.

If the between marked Silverman's philosophy, then he was one of a rare breed of philosophers whose life and work shared in a single authentic style. He relished the between, relished in the between, and had the courage to linger there. Between philosophy and comparative literature, between Port Jefferson and Vienna, between writing and facilitating, between reading and teaching, between phenomenology and structuralism, between hermeneutics and deconstruction, between writing and film, between exegesis and exhortation, between the IAPL and the IPS, between Merleau-Ponty and Derrida, between *Texts and Dialogues*,[3] between *Inscriptions* and *Textualities*.

I would like to suggest in this essay that Silverman's philosophical method—an approach he coined "hermeneutic semiology" or, later, "deconstructive juxtapositional reading"—sketches out as much a method as a call to responsibility. From his first lectures right up until his second book, *Textualities*, Silverman sought to understand the "self" in light of the cascading insights of continental and postmodern thought. Human subjectivity, as he might well have said if he were more prone to offer definitions, is *the incessant production and holding open of a between*. Or if he would not have said it this way, it nonetheless captures what I have learned from him. Thus, his theory of *textualities* suggests that each human is a unique *between* that holds open a place of difference for the fleeting duration of a lifetime. Death is the collapse of a between, and the event weighs upon all those who remain behind. As I said in my memorial address, which is a moment of thinking that lingers beneath the current essay, in the memorializing of death we "promise to hold open the between for the one who can no longer hold it open for themselves, knowing full well that we are inadequate to this task, since all that could really have held open just this unique between is no longer." As such, this reading of Silverman's philosophical method is at once a study of the postmodern self and a humble effort in the face of an impossible responsibility. "Silverman" is, like all writers, to be found *between inscriptions*, that is, in the fleeting glance of a reading.

Because Silverman, the ever conscientious teacher, would have wanted me to learn something new from this reading, I'll venture beyond how he influenced my reading of Merleau-Ponty. Here I would like to provide a reading of Silverman in a Silvermanian style—a reading *between two*, in this case between Roland Barthes and Hugh J. Silverman. Barthes announces the death of *the* author, but today we mark the death of *a writer*. How can we deal with the death of a writer after the death of the author? Our only pathway is a reading, a journey into what Barthes calls the "space of writing," a space that we can at best range over and never pierce, for as Silverman surely would have insisted, there is nothing beneath waiting to be discovered; but there is, he would continue, so much to be *produced*. (Hugh always felt the weight of there being so much to be produced.) The epigraph to Silverman's first chapter in *Textualities* is from Robert Frost's "The Road Not Taken" (1915), in which a person lingers before two roads; we too must always take a road, a pathway, and, as Frost tells us, that will *make* all the difference because the meaning will be produced in the *walking/reading*. The road that I have "less traveled" with Hugh is the pathway forged by Barthes, so I'll choose this road now in order to explore some of what remains for me to learn from Silverman.

Toward a Theory of Intertextuality

In his 1968 essay "The Death of the Author," an essay that surely weighs upon Silverman's philosophy in many subtle and far-reaching ways, Barthes suggests that the writer of the text always discovers him- or herself to be too late to be original. When the figure of "the author" is dead, "the writer" certainly survives, but is left without an interior and without an anterior; when the myth of the author-God or author-genius is withdrawn, the writer is left with nothing to do but practice the absurd skill of the "copyist," to become the imitator of the gestures of those who came before. The writer—in the age of the death of the author—is the site of a concrete and limited function. As Barthes says: "[The writer's] only power is to mix writings, to counter the ones with the others, in such a way as never to rest on any one of them" (*DA*, 146). As Silverman might have interjected at this point, the writer is a *restless function of intertextuality*.

In fact, the mode of *intertextuality* is already at work in the original preface to Silverman's first book, *Inscriptions*, which is a study, or better, a patient exploration of the relationship between structuralism and phenomenology. Silverman writes the following:

> The place between phenomenology and structuralism does not occupy any space. It only marks the place between two methodologically parallel yet historically converging paths. At the limit of one, signs of the other are already plotted. At the frontier of the other, the former is incorporated and advanced. (*I*, xv)

We can see already at work, then, notions of *limits* and *frontiers*, *anticipations* and *incorporations*. These notions are *produced* in the exploration and do not preexist it. There is no frontier on the edge of phenomenology when phenomenology is taken *in itself*; the frontier looms up in the production of the between. The "edge" of phenomenology will be different in every production of a "phenomenology *and* X," and only a modern prejudice would lead us to think that there is such a thing as phenomenology *in itself*. So there is no "space" where we find "the between"; the between is the establishing of a place, and a place is a function of an encounter. The between is experienced in the event in which the limit and intertwining between two separate trajectories *takes place*, and this happens in a reading.

Silverman's task, then, is the attempt to present a reading that would at once exude a phenomenological textuality and a structuralist textuality, and to thereby create the Text in which they intertwine and yet remain distinct. This "between" appears because Silverman, expert in phenomenology, *reads structuralism*, and Silverman, expert in structuralism, *reads phenomenology*. Here we have a writer able to take up and creatively repeat the gestures of phenomenology and of structuralism, producing the intertwining by paradoxically responding to the felt urgency of the production of this emerging future relation. Because of *this* reader, structuralism weighs upon every phenomenology, and vice versa. The "phenomenology/structuralism Text" is produced in the reading, the site of "Silverman," and is reinscribed by each new reading. This Text lingers *between inscriptions*, and the inscriptions remain as an open invitation to new performances.

As Barthes famously concludes, "the birth of the reader must be at the cost of the death of the Author" (*DA*, 148). The writer is not the Author, but is the *first reader*. The reader, then, is the site of the production of meaning, and yet not an authorial power. The between comes about *through* the reader, it *happens* in this intertwining between the text on the page and the past brought to the event by the reader (explicitly and tacitly); a *reading* is each time unique for precisely this reason. Pursuing this thread of the influence of Barthes, we catch sight of the place of Silverman's philosophical method. Silverman's reading is a reading of texts, not of works; of lines of force, not of registries of accomplishments; of *fields* rather than *objects*. And this is what shapes his theory of *textualities* as a genuine philosophical methodology and a call to responsibility.

Silverman/Barthes: Between the "Death of the Author" and "From Work to Text"[4]

There is no simple story to be told about Barthes/Silverman, and a place of difference is perhaps detectable *between* Silverman's studies of the "self" and Barthes's most famous declaration: the "*death of the author*." Barthes argues that removing the author (as any preexisting authority) is to render the practice of "deciphering" a text futile. Our attempt to uncover the author so as to *explain* the work is the attempt to "impose a limit on that text, to furnish it with a final signified, to close the writing" (*DA*, 147). Barthes suggests that writing is "that neutral, composite, oblique space where our subject slips away, the negative where all identity is lost, starting with the very identity of the body writing" (*DA*, 142). For Barthes, writing is the event wherein the author "enters into his [or her] own death" (*DA*, 142). The error, born of a romantic psychology and modern individualism, is to seek out an "explanation" of a work by the details of the life of the man or woman who produced it. Indeed, a work cannot be explained by the life, because the work is what *establishes* the life and produces it, and this is why the writer is the first reader of the work being born *through* him or her. Silverman's wager is that the death of the author reveals the birth of the decentered self as the site of the intertwining of multiple textualities. Indeed, for Barthes, this shift to Text and textualities seems essential, because the death of the author is also the death of the "work," and the birth of the reader is the birth of the Text. In short, we must distinguish between a "work" and a "text." Silverman's theory of intertextuality, *Textualities*, is born through a reader taking up the death of the "work" into a postmodern philosophy of the decentered self. For Silverman, the self is not a work, but a Text.

In his 1971 essay "From Work to Text," Barthes identifies a shift in the conception of a literary work through the subtle and evolving influence of the interdisciplinarity of contemporary humanities (including movements in linguistics, anthropology, Marxism, and psychoanalysis). Approaches to literature from these fields represents a productive moment within literature and criticism, the production of a "new object and a new language," a genuine *mutation* (*WT*, 155). The new object produced in interdisciplinarity and post-romantic literature is what he calls the "Text." Barthes distinguishes between the work and the Text through seven intertwining propositions concerning "method, genres, signs, plurality, filiation, reading and pleasure" (*WT*, 156). For example, the work is something that we might hold in our hands, whereas the Text is rather "held in language" (*WT*, 157). We can extrapolate from this by suggesting that, as "held in language," the Text structures the various expressions of itself—the field that transcendentally structures each expression without determining that expression in advance and without being exhausted by any of them. In other words, the Text is not a thing; it is a "methodological field" (*WT*, 157). As a field or set of potentials, a text can cut across a work, or several works, and "*is experienced only in an activity of production*" (*WT*, 157). The work "closes on a signified," whereas the text must be "approached, experienced, in reaction to the sign" (*WT*, 158). This indicates that the Text is an "infinite deferment of the signified," forever "off-centered" and "without closure" (*WT*, 158–59). To recall the opening epigraph, the work can be deciphered, whereas the Text invites us to an endless task of *disentangling*.

Each text, then, is *intertextual* in the sense that it is created and gains meaning within the larger Text of textuality itself. Each Text is a *call to* and *function of* incessant citation and repetition. As such, the Text is plural in the manner of an interweaving network or fabric. That is, its plurality is not the coexistence of two or several meanings or interpretations held simultaneously, such as a "rich" or ambiguous "work." Rather, the plurality of a text is the plurality of rhizomatic thinking, and the Text thus is at once "difference" and "unique," "woven entirely with citations, references, echoes, cultural languages . . . which cut across it through and through in a vast stereophony" (*WT*, 159–60). Each Text, then, is "held" within the "intertextual," which is not the origin of the Text; rather, the "citations which go to make up a text are anonymous, untraceable, and yet *already read*: they are quotations without inverted commas" (*WT*, 160). Texts have no single author—they are multivoiced, though so subtly that the voices and allusions remain the invisible or the unheard, and erasing this multivocality in favor of the authority of an Author is the error of the classical interpretation of a work. For Barthes, the Text is not a filial relation with a Father, but a network (*WT*, 161). A work is meant to be consumed, whereas the Text is the site of play and production. Finally, the pleasure of the work is the pleasure of possession/consumption; the pleasure of the Text is the *jouissance* of production, a pleasure resulting from the distance between the reader and the writer collapsing in the reading/writing.

How does this distinction between work and Text enter into Silverman's philosophy? I believe that his longest discussion of the distinction occurs in a pivotal chapter in *Inscriptions*, titled: "Sartre/Barthes: writing differences." Silverman emphasizes the fact that a text cannot be experienced as a "static unity," but rather "only in an activity of production" (*I*, 249). For example, the "text" of love is held within a language generally, and the works that address "love" (such as Plato's *Symposium*) are what he calls "fragments" of the text of "love." Plato's *Symposium* as a work gives us a definition of love. Plato's *Symposium* as a text offers us an experience of love and yet an infinite deferral of a final definition. The Text appears across works, and it is meaningful because of this crossing. Silverman draws out Barthes's discussion of how each text exists intertextually and with an anachronistic *citationality*, because a text by Stendhal alludes forward to Proust, and the giddy love of Stendhal's Bishop of Lescars cites, anachronistically, Flaubert's description of apple trees. There is, in *intertextuality*, a "reversal of origins, the ease which brings the anterior text out of the subsequent one" (Silverman citing Barthes, *I*, 250). But Proust is only referenced by Stendhal through Barthes's reading. This intertwining is *produced*, but not by an act of will or explicit interpretation—as Silverman rewrites by citing Barthes:

> Proust is what comes to me, not what I summon up; not an "authority," simply a *circular memory*. Which is what the inter-text is: the impossibility of living outside the infinite text—whether this text be Proust or the daily newspaper or the television screen: the book creates the meaning, the meaning creates the life. (Silverman citing Barthes, *I*, 250)

So the reader is the site of this *circular memory*, the establishing of an inter-textuality between the work being read and all that has been read by this reader, and the meaning is what looms up in this event.

When introducing this discussion, Silverman reminds his reader that all cultural functions can operate as sign systems, and he mentions literary works, clothing, films, and so forth. In short, beyond the study of literary objects, the theory of textualities is generalizable to the fields of cultural production in relation to experience. The study of intertextuality in literary criticism thus reveals one part of an open story about the postmodern self, what Barthes calls the "paper-I" of the self of the intertextual reading. In the textuality of the works, there is an experience of the "readerly self," the self of the reading, which is produced in the reading and which is simultaneously the producing of the reading. This is a "paradoxical logic of expression" that finds nothing prior, or, as Silverman puts it, "nothing beneath" this strange movement of self-arrival.[5]

Now, if the possibility of "philosophy as intertextuality" looms up in *Inscriptions*, it becomes even more explicit in *Textualities*. Silverman produces an important parallel between the invisible (in the Heideggerian/late–Merleau-Pontian sense) and the "supplement" (as understood by Derrida). The parallel leads to a particularly fascinating moment in the early part of *Textualities* in which Silverman reflects upon the methodologies of phenomenological interrogation and deconstruction. For Silverman, phenomenological interrogation reveals that there is always something more to be found, that the process of exploring the invisible is one that always remains to be furthered—philosophy is the endless task of the interrogation of Visibility as the between of the visible and the invisible. This, he suggests, is also the meaning of "supplementarity" on the textual and intertextual plane as it is conceived by Derrida. Silverman writes: "For Derrida, this logic of supplementarity operates at the textual and intertextual plane. The something more lies at the edge of the text, at the borders of the painting, in the framing of the work of art" (*T*, 43). But it seems that Silverman understands deconstruction less as a parallel than as a necessary supplement for phenomenology, as a practice that produces a between in which we might catch sight of the decentered self. As he writes: "The supplement is a textual invisible that hovers at the limits of any particular text and that is brought into play through deconstructive practice" (*T*, 44). The practice of deconstruction, according to Silverman, is to *become writing*, that is, to produce *oneself* as "another text, a critical text which supplements and incorporates the one or ones in question" (*T*, 44). That is, deconstruction is a reading that *produces a between*, between texts, but also between the past and present, between modes of engagement, between all the sign-systems of the cultural field. The invisible provides the hinges, connections, and differences that will give the text meaning, and each self is the establishing (on no prior stable ground) of oneself as a Text, understood as a complex interwoven fabric that frays in all directions, at all edges, that has no permanently straight edge.

How does Silverman justify this expansion of the notion of Text in the context of *Textualities*? In the introductory remarks, he suggests that his account in his first book (*Inscriptions*) marked out the "places of difference" through his intertextual reading of the tradition. The project seems broader, somehow, in *Textualities*. Silverman writes: "*Textualities* reiterates the 'place between' as the locus of multiple textualities" (*T*, 2). This, of course, raises the question: *what is a textuality?* I have discussed the distinction between a work and a Text, but what is "a textuality"? Offering a pithy answer to this question, Silverman writes: "a textuality is one of various meaning-structures of a text. But such a translation is too simple, for a textuality is a differential notion and not a matter of identity" (*T*, 2). Each text comes with layers of textualities that structure its unique meaning network. For instance, Nietzsche's *Ecce Homo* exudes a certain "autobiographical textuality."

This is not to ask and answer the question about whether *Ecce Homo* offers a clear and accurate picture of Nietzsche's life or personality, but rather to recognize that something of the "autobiographical" is at work *texturing* this text itself. As Silverman writes: "autobiographical textuality operates throughout the text, along with many other textualities (such as philosophical textuality, religious textuality, literary textuality, etc.)" (*T*, 2). A part of this work, then, is the Text of autobiography, which is a rich potential of this text. But even more so, what this shows is the manner in which *textualities* are the meaning-systems that shape all texts and all expressions. A "philosophical method" as intertextuality would have to look for the intertwining of textualities as the support structure and product of a reading. The self is the between that allows for the production of *textualities*. And textualities permeate or flow from all human activities, from the production of written texts, to paintings, to photographs, to participating within relations and institutions.

If this is Silverman's understanding of textualities, how (we might ask) does this translate into something like a philosophical methodology? At several reprises he tests out and hones what he calls "hermeneutic semiology." Now, as Silverman is quick to admit, the "conjunction of semiotics and hermeneutics is a difficult space to occupy" (*T*, 22). Hermeneutics involves situating oneself within the hermeneutic circle in order to establish an interpretation; semiotics involves gearing into an endless chain of sign relations and sign production that takes place regardless of any interpretive activity at all. Yet for Silverman, following of course Heidegger, the "hermeneutic circle" is not meant to invoke a structure utterly closed in upon itself. That is, the hermeneutic circle is not necessarily *viciously* circular (*T*, 23). Rather, "to enter the hermeneutic circle is to hope for the disclosure of truth in the space of difference produced by an interpretive activity" (*T*, 23). As Silverman sees it, the art of interpretation is the practice of creating a reading in which difference(s) appear(s); it is the practice of establishing a between as a non-dogmatic or non-closed foothold upon the immense texture of the production of difference. This is possible because *Dasein*, as an interpretive activity, is the place of the ontic-ontological difference, and of course this relation is deepened as Heidegger discovers that Language speaks through the space of difference, suggesting that the hermeneutic circle is the place in which the meaning of Being itself is disclosed and is disclosedness itself. This structure allows Silverman (still following Heidegger) to deflate the activity of the interpreter in the traditional understanding of hermeneutics. Silverman writes: "Moving around the circle, across the spaces of difference, origination, and relationality, the interpreter lets the being or the work (depending on which is in question) speak for itself" (*T*, 24). There is no *Author* of the hermeneutic interpretation; something happens through the *writer*, an establishing of the truth of being and of the interweaving of textualities.

If this suggests the manner in which hermeneutics moves toward semiology through Silverman's semiotic reading of Heidegger, what of the other direction? The reverse movement indeed, as Silverman confirms in *Textualities*, is possible through semiology as understood by Barthes. In his early study *Writing Degree Zero* (1953), Barthes locates the event of writing as the zero-point between the vertical y-axis, which represents the writer's individual style, and the horizontal x-axis, which represents the language that makes the writing possible. Writing is the meeting point between individual style and language. This has the virtue, according to Silverman, of allowing for an account of writing that privileges neither. Neither the author nor the language is in control, and this is what makes *expression* possible in a new way, as well as what makes the theory of the Text possible. Returning to the ground mentioned already in Barthes between "The Death of the Author" and "From Work to Text," Silverman suggests that the Text is "located and operates at the intersection of semiotics and hermeneutics" (*T*, 28). If the Text leads hermeneutics toward semiology, it also draws semiology toward hermeneutics. But this is not because of a *nostalgia* for the Author. It is because *something happens* where the Text is located. The Text according to Silverman is "an open field participating in the proliferation of sign production" (*T*, 29). By pushing on this notion of the Text from Barthes, supplemented by Gadamer and Ricœur on the hermeneutic side and Peirce on the semiotic side, Silverman produces a *between* hermeneutics and semiology. As a result, "hermeneutic semiology would seek to offer a reading of the text in terms of its meaning structures as they relate to elements in the world and as they refer back not to a centered self but to the interpretive activity itself" (*T*, 30). This is what takes place in the between, what Silverman calls the "*milieu* as a *reading* of the textuality (or textualities) of the text" (*T*, 30).

In chapter 8 of *Textualities*, "The Language of Textuality," Silverman demonstrates how the promise of this hermeneutic is fulfilled in the mode of deconstruction. The first line is telling: "The text is an indecidable" (*T*, 80). The text is an indecidable because of its textuality, because textuality is inherently indecidable, and not because the reader cannot decide and not because the text has multiple references. As Silverman writes: "The text's indecidability lies in its textuality or textualities through which the text (or a text) establishes its identity as a text" (*T*, 80). A text is what it is through its layering of textuality, which are trajectories and relations, and thus the text is always more than itself. A text might have a layer of autobiography, for instance, but the autobiographical textuality of a text is not the essence or definition of the text; rather it is a single moment in a dynamic whole, and this textuality will be shaped and reshaped as other layered textualities emerge or change. The result is that the very thing that makes the text a text happens where the possibility of a definition or summary of it escapes. The text, insofar as it is text, is forever "off-center" (ex-centric) because of the specific and general decentering that happens through textualities.

Why is this the case? Silverman suggests that an answer lies in the necessity of *reading*. He writes that the "text is *what* is read, but its textuality or textualities is *how* it is read" (*T*, 81). The reader produces the meaning of the text not by *deciphering*, but by *disentangling* the textualities at work, and this involves drawing out the layers of textuality that give the *event of the reading* a meaning. The words on the page may have a certain formal self-reference built into the sign-system chosen, but the text only has an *autobiographical textuality* insofar as it is read as a meaningful expression of a life, and this only in concert with the various other textualities at work in the productive intertwining of the event. But if this is the case, why insist that a text is "indecidable"? Silverman writes:

> Through its textuality, the text makes itself mean, makes itself be, makes itself come about in a particular way. At the same time, through its textuality, the text makes itself other than what it is in a particular way or ways. Through its textuality and textualities, the text relinquishes its status as identity and affirms its condition as pure difference. (*T*, 81)

The text provides itself through its textuality with a certain meaning, and yet invokes other texts and alternate readings. Each work is a possibility of further events of reading, and the text is the trajectory of these readings, an open and endless defining/re-defining of itself in relation to all of language and to all of the past and future brought to bear by readers.

Intertextuality as philosophical method, then, leads to a hermeneutic semiology as the practice of deconstruction. The text is indecidable, and thus calls for a Derridean approach that will operate within the between of the neither/nor of binary pairs: visible/invisible, inside/outside, present/absent, unity/multiplicity, and so forth. The indecidability of the text is never resolved, but is navigated through a taking up of the threads of the layered textualities that are nowhere other than in the reading. If the "self" remains at issue for Silverman, we can see that the self of this philosophical practice is nothing less than the "between" of these binaries. In each event of reading, a sense is given to a text, and yet all other possible readings linger just beneath the surface, carried forward as the "roads not taken."

The text, and the between more generally, is indecidable, because the pathway we take is not marked by its own borders alone, but by its relation to all of the pathways that were possible. Robert Frost is certainly right, then, that the road taken will make all the difference, because the difference is produced as the meaning of the event of walking/reading. And Silverman reminds us that this is only because the roads not taken are never forgotten by the ongoing metastable trajectory. Even if they are left aside, they still shape the future through their *not-having-been-taken*. As it turns out, the roads not taken, as much as the one taken, are in the end what makes all the difference. And this is precisely Silverman's philosophical method, an *Ausflug* down the roads taken and not taken, a production of difference through the event of reading, and the cultivation of a unique "between" that sadly collapsed *too soon*.

Notes

1. Roland Barthes, "The Death of the Author," in *Image—Music—Text*, trans. Stephen Heath (New York: Hill & Wang, 1977), 147. Henceforth cited as *DA*.

2. The current essay is indeed no more than an "essay" in the formal sense, an attempt. Each time I began to write, it felt like I was writing "too

soon." Perhaps it is always too soon to have to say goodbye, and today is certainly too soon to have to write about Hugh, as if he were not Hugh, but rather "Silverman." This is perhaps what makes it as important as it is painful, because death is so often too soon, and so we often speak too late—a wrenching temporality. A memorial is a "too late" act in the face of the "too soon" event; it is an act of nostalgia for a time when the "too soon" seemed so far away as to never even register itself as looming. So, forgive me, Hugh, for in fact I am *too late* to speak *too soon* . . . and forgive me as well for addressing this for the most part not to you, Hugh, but to "Silverman," because it is both too soon and too late (at least for me) to address you by the name that renders you present as a friend.

3. Maurice Merleau-Ponty, *Texts and Dialogues: On Philosophy, Politics, and Culture*, ed. Hugh J. Silverman and James Barry Jr. (Amherst, NJ: Humanity Books, 1992).

4. Roland Barthes, "From Work to Text," in *Image—Music—Text*, trans. Stephen Heath (New York: Hill & Wang, 1977), 155–64. Henceforth *WT*.

5. Here I allude to the other road, the one I did travel with Hugh, into the work of Merleau-Ponty. I can see now, thanks to this essay, that my reading of Merleau-Ponty has been subtly shaped by the weight of Hugh's reading of Barthes. See Donald A. Landes, *Merleau-Ponty and the Paradoxes of Expression* (London: Bloomsbury, 2013), particularly the introduction.

4

Autobiographical Textualities

Hugh J. Silverman on Writing the Self

Galen A. Johnson

> An autobiography must situate itself at the place where metaphoricity meets literality, where the substitution of life is life itself, where the writing of a life is the life, where the activity of translating is living.
>
> —Hugh J. Silverman (*T*, 99)

Hugh J. Silverman's last book, *Textualities: Between Hermeneutics and Deconstruction*, contains both a theory of the text and textuality as well as demonstrations of that theory in practice. I would like briefly to take up some ideas in the theory of textuality, then turn in particular to autobiographical textualities and the project of writing the self.

Text and Textualities

In *Textualities*, Professor Silverman develops a first approximation of his theory of the text and textuality: a text is the site or locus for textualities. The text is a kind of focus for discourse; textualities are the framework—autobiographical, historical, psychological, scientific—that identifies a text as the kind of text it is (*T*, 56–57). Professor Silverman summarizes the situation in terms of textual space: "Epistemologically, *hermeneutic-phenomenological meaning and semiological-structuralist signification* are equivalent"; however, ontologically they do not occupy the same place (*T*, 75). Therefore, a deconstructive hermeneutics raises the question of textuality "without offering a general account of the text" (*T*, 70). The text is an indecidable meaning-site for the reading and deconstructive interpretation of multiple textualities. Professor Silverman says that a text is "a complex fabric of signs" and that "textuality is the condition according to which a text is a text" (*T*, 73). The text, we might say, is a deconstructive "neo-noema," bringing together phenomenology and deconstruction in this way, that is, the text is neo-noema for a reader who textualizes. The Subject-author who writes and the Subject-reader who interprets are both replaced in semiological space by the text itself, by the auto-text as neo-noema.

Professor Silverman's theory of the auto-text seems to me quite analogous to Derrida's notion of reading a text in a "nontranscendent fashion." A "transcendent" reading would be one that seeks to go beyond the text to some external meaning or referent. In contrast, an immanent or nontrascendent reading operates with the signs and their differences within the text, and such a way of reading is possible for literary, scientific, journalistic, and philosophic discourses, or textualities, to use Professor Silverman's preferred term. It is worth noting that Derrida has characterized this type of nontranscendent reading precisely by adopting the phenomenological language of the noema, which he insists is a necessary language even though it must finally be dislodged. In his 1989 interview titled "This Strange Institution Called Literature," Derrida stated that "the literary character of the text is inscribed on the side of the intentional object, in its noematic structure . . . There are 'in' the text features which call for the literary reading and recall the convention, institution, or history of literature."[1] Because the literary text is a noematic object in this nontranscendent sense that calls forth a literary "experience" rather than a literary essence, Derrida remarks that "the phenomenological conversion of the gaze, the 'transcendental reduction'" Husserl recommended, is "the very condition . . . of literature."[2] Thus, the "suspension of the natural attitude" is as much in play for literature as for the sciences, though this phenomenological language ends up being dislodged from its certainties regarding an absolute transcendental consciousness.

On Writing the Self

With this brief preamble, let us turn to the complex and complicated experience of "writing the self," which Professor Silverman offers as a specific form of textuality. *Textualities* includes a wonderfully interesting chapter titled "Autobiographical Textuality and Thoreau's *Walden*," and the first footnote to that chapter speaks of the inspiration Hugh[3] took from that text.[4] In autobiography, "I write myself." In French, the most approximate phrase would be "*je m'écris*," although native French speakers would likely find the expression odd and take it, at best, to mean "I write to myself," as when jotting down a reminder to oneself. Be that as it may, I do not want to say, "I write about myself" in the same sense as "I write about someone else." Rather, we mean to emphasize by this expression, "I write myself," that through writing, a self is formed; at least a certain image or aspect of the self is expressed. The discipline of writing actually and literally brings forth whom the self will become. Here I am really only following Hugh's own text: "Autobiography is writing and specifically writing one's own life" (*T*, 92). So who is this "I" who writes itself, and who is this "me" who is written?

Thoreau's *Walden* is seldom read as an autobiographical text and is not included among the standard lists of autobiographies (*T*, 91); rather, it is more often read as a naturalistic treatise, a utopian experiment, a Romantic literary text, an enactment of transcendentalism, a philosophy of voluntary simplicity, or, today, an early statement of ecological imperatives. Thus, Hugh's autobiographical reading is unusual. Nevertheless, it is justified. You may remember the famous opening lines of *Walden*:

> When I wrote the following pages, or rather the bulk of them, I lived alone, in the woods, a mile from any neighbor, in a house which I had built myself, on the shore of Walden Pond, in Concord, Massachusetts, and earned my living by the labor of my hands only. I lived there two years and two months. At present I am a sojourner in civilized life again.[5]

Hugh argues: "Writing his own life, Thoreau's text announces itself as autobiographical. The self is textualized . . . given in the first person singular as an 'I' describing the 'me'" (*T*, 91).

Stanley Cavell, renowned interpreter of both Thoreau and Emerson, published *A Pitch of Philosophy: Autobiographical Exercises* in 1994, the same year as *Textualities*. Like Hugh, Cavell includes *Walden* as an instance of autobiography, one that he calls "signing the world."[6] Merleau-Ponty called expressive speech "singing the world," but for writing, Cavell speaks of "signing the world," creating a world under one's own signature. Subsequently, Cavell would again take up the task of writing his own autobiography, somewhat so in a book titled *Philosophy the Day after Tomorrow* (2005) and even more fully in *Little Did I Know: Excerpts from Memory* (2010),[7] to which we shall return.

According to Hugh's analysis, autobiography institutes both a distinctive temporality and spatiality. Its temporality is most often chronological or diachronic, though involving a unique feature that Hugh names the "flash-forward" device. This contrasts with fictional narratives, which rely upon only a "flash-back" technique, thereby limiting the narrative to foreshadowing devices with respect to the future. In *Walden*, the work is structured according to the cycle of the seasons over the course of one full year from the time Thoreau took up residence at the Pond in mid-summer on July 4, 1845, through the fall, winter, and spring of the next year. We encounter both the chronological temporality and "flash forward" when Thoreau writes at the end of the penultimate chapter, titled "Spring": "Thus was my first year's life in the woods completed; and the second year was similar to it. I finally left Walden September 6th, 1847" (*W*, 308). With respect to this truncation, Hugh points out that Thoreau need not write the second year because the second, established according to the rhythms of the seasons, will be a repetition of the first, and both Thoreau and the reader already know the season's patterns. Something similar can be said of Sartre's autobiography, *Les Mots*, in which he narrates only the first eleven years of his childhood in two parts: *Lire* (Reading) and *Écrire* (Writing), for "[o]nce the young Sartre has entered into writing, the rest is just a postscript" (*T*, 129). There will be loves and friendships and betrayals and politics in the later adult life of Sartre, but these are background to what Sartre called the "fundamental project" that has originated: he is a writer of philosophy and literature. In both these autobiographies, that of Thoreau and that of Sartre, the "I" who writes acts upon the "me" who is written, interrogated, and dispersed throughout the texts.

Another literary writer of autobiography, José Saramago, is the Portuguese winner of the Nobel Prize for Literature in 1998, and his autobiography has recently appeared in English, posthumously titled *Small Memories: A Memoir*. The title, *Small Memories*, replaced the original title, *The Book of Temptations*, which was to have been a book on thorny subjects drawn up, Saramago says, from "the mind's most grotesque and most sublime thoughts, lusts and nightmares, every hidden desire and every manifest sin." Saramago came to realize that his "literary gifts fell far short of such a grandiose project," and *The Book of Temptations* became *Small Memories*, "the small memories of when I was small."[8] Indeed, like Sartre's *Les Mots*, Saramago's memoir offers an account only of his early and adolescent years. Here is the kind of flash-forward temporality Hugh is discussing from early in Saramago's memoir:

> The child I was did not see the landscape as the adult he became would be tempted to see it from the lofty height of manhood. The child, while he was a child, was simply *in* the landscape, formed part of it and never questioned it, never said or thought, in these or other words: "What a beautiful landscape, what a magnificent panorama, what a fabulous view!"[9]

Likewise, here is a complex series of temporal modalities with their layering of tenses that Saramago has written near the end of his memoir about his grandfather, Jerónimo:

> He bears on his back seventy years of a hard life full of privations and ignorance [Jerónimo was illiterate]. And yet he is a wise man, taciturn, one who opens his mouth to speak only when necessary . . . He doesn't yet know that a few days before his final day, he will have a presentiment that the end has come and will go from tree to tree in his garden, embracing their trunks and saying good-bye to them, to their friendly shade, to the fruits he will never eat again.[10]

As there are such zigzag temporalities available to autobiography, there are also distinctive textual spatialities. Hugh has described the space of textuality as a topological space, a *topos* that has features derived from geography together with features derived from rhetoric (*T*, 90). He adds that autobiographical space is a "pure spatiality" (*T*, 95), that is, a limit, an interface or intersection with other texts linked with the author, the author's philosophical, political, aesthetic, and other writings (*T*, 91). Certainly, as well, we should add that autobiography is a space of risk and of openness, as the author writes himself in plain view for readers; as the pages unfold, the author's life unfolds. The book itself is like a landscape in which the author and reader journey together, get lost together, suffer together, and are happy and sad together. Neither the "I" of the author nor the "I" of the reader predominate, but there is formed an anonymous self that blends the two "I's" and is not reducible the one to the other. The reader sees the landscape "according to" the author but also according to him- or herself, therefore according to a mixture or *mélange*. This anonymous *mélange* is based upon an intimacy that builds between autobiographer and reader, even an intimacy with someone we have never met or known. In a remarkable essay on the "Phenomenology of Reading," George Poulet has written that reading "is the act in which the subjective principle which I call *I*, is modified in such a way that I no longer have the right, strictly speaking, to consider it as my *I*. I am on loan to another, and this other thinks, feels, suffers, and acts within me."[11]

Nevertheless, there is also a different spatial textuality as well, instead of unity, proximity, and intimacy, one of distance, taking a step back, for the reader is evaluating not only the life of the author as it is unfolded, but also the author's account over against other accounts we may have received. The reader thus forms a critical awareness and distance from this coeval, anonymous "I." Poulet has written of this as a "gap, disclosing a feeling of identity, but of identity within difference."[12] In this way, criticism oscillates between "a union without comprehension, and a comprehension without union."[13] This "gap" or "step back" complicates the question of the "I" who writes in relation to the "me" who is written, and both the "I" and "me" of the author in relation to the reader.

Today, autobiographies proliferate in many forms: collections of letters written and edited, logs, blogs, journals, diaries, memoirs—Saramago calls *Small Memories* a memoir—and I take it the memoir is indeed smaller and more fragmentary than autobiography, bringing into focus small but salient and poignant memories. Yet of all these, perhaps above all, autobiography "participate[s] in a discourse of truth" and "proposes to tell the truth about a life" (*T*, 96), according to Hugh's text. Thus, he raises the question of literary genre: "Is autobiography fiction or nonfiction?" (*T*, 96) As a unique literary genre, autobiography falls on the side of nonfiction rather than fiction. Indeed, Hugh writes, "the project of *Walden* is one of non-deception and nonfictionalization" (*T*, 93). In fact, Hugh characterizes fictionalization as "a discourse of lies" (*T*, 96) and writes, "Thoreau engages in autobiographizing that produces both a fictional lie and a nonfictional truth" (*T*, 97). Hugh's analysis goes this way:

> *Walden* is a work of letters . . . Above all, it is read, studied, and treated as literature. Its delicate sensibility, its careful attention to detail, and its expressive flourish all indicate its orientation toward the fictional, toward literature. The work cannot be true: Thoreau's remarks are not available for scientific verification . . . *Walden* is a lie . . . Yet the lie is not with an intent to deceive. On the contrary, it is to offer perceptions that inform, delight, and provoke. (*T*, 98)

If *Walden* does not intend to deceive, as Hugh agrees, if fiction in general seeks not to deceive but to reveal truths and disclose worlds, then the language of lies falls to the side and is beside the point. So what is the point behind this strong and provocative language? I think the provocative language is meant to point us to something else about the very nature of autobiography and writing the self.

The genre question of nonfiction/fiction points to a deeper juxtaposition, namely literality/metaphoricity. As we cited Hugh in our opening epigraph: "autobiography is metaphoricity itself—the whole text is metaphorical" (*T*, 99). *Walden* as autobiographical textuality is Thoreau's life: for those years while at Walden Pond, he is those trees, he is that bean field, he is that pond, and most of all he is that writer. "Be a pond!" *Walden* says. The pond is a metaphor for character with its surprising, sometimes hidden, coves and inlets, its incredible clarity, its remarkable depth, and its beautiful blue ice, through which "the pure Walden water is mingled with the sacred water of the Ganges"

(*W*, 288), as Thoreau describes the winter ice cutting and shipping to faraway destinations. And there is another metaphor, equally odd, equally instructive: "Be a bean field!" Hoeing beans is cultivation of a garden, all the while it is a metaphor for self-cultivation, the cultivation of reading, thinking, and writing. And the beans themselves: "I was determined to know beans,"Thoreau wrote (*W*, 156), playfully reversing the old expression "He doesn't know beans." He claims that a simple bean is sincerity, truth, simplicity, faith, and innocence, and these are the virtues to be planted and grown (*W*, 158). Thoreau's last and posthumous book is titled *Faith in a Seed*.[14] Autobiography searches out those metaphors that translate the author's life, which remain faithful to the past, present, and imagined future of that life, but express that past, present, and future in moments and metaphors that grip the mind and capture the heart: he is a pond, he is a tree, he is a writer. Metaphoricity is human being itself. We are wrapped in metaphors and stories, which are transformative and, indeed, transfigurative.[15]

Therefore, to write the self is to write the body and the body's being-in-the-world. It is to create an encounter with the living body in the pages of the text. Hugh has said this not about Thoreau but about one of his very favorite authors in his maturity, Roland Barthes, who playfully titled his own autobiography simply *Roland Barthes*, so it is known sometimes as *Barthes by Barthes*. His autobiography gives us the "language of the body" (*T*, 128). The written text of Barthes's autobiography—and there is much more than writing, which we will come to in a moment—the text begins from a poem by Heinrich Heine titled "A Palm Tree": "A hemlock tree stands lonely / Far north on a barren height. / He drowses: ice and snowflake / Wrap him in sheets of white / He dreams about a palm tree / That far in an eastern land / Languishes lonely and silent / Upon the parching sand." Barthes comments: "According to the Greeks, trees are alphabets. Of all the tree letters, the palm is loveliest. And of writing, profuse and distinct as the burst of its fronds, it possesses the major effect: falling back."[16] So trees are at the beginning, and at the end of Barthes's autobiography comes the body: "To write the body. Neither the skin, nor the muscles, nor the bones, nor the nerves, but the rest: an awkward, fibrous, shaggy, raveled thing, a clown's coat."[17] Alongside this odd but endearing fragment appears a drawing of the human body from Diderot's *Encyclopédie* titled "*Anatomie*." Barthes's note designates the drawing as the "stems of the vena cava with their branches dissected in an adult body."[18] This would have been an illustration of the veins of the circulatory system as understood in 1750s France.

In writing our life, we write the body, and above all we write our voice. Certainly we write the events of our life and we write our signature, but the autobiography gives us the author's voice, its rhythm, cadence, and tone. The tone of philosophy has often been tone-deaf to the nuances and complexities of poetic meaning, formalistic and strident, a tone of authority rather than the personal "I" of authorship. I do not find such stridency in Hugh's voice and way of doing philosophy, which I think is evident in one of Hugh's unpublished partly autobiographical texts. The occasion was the celebration of the centennial of Merleau-Ponty's birth in 2008 at the fall conference of the Merleau-Ponty Circle held at Ryerson University in Toronto, Canada, and Hugh presented a paper on the history of the Merleau-Ponty Circle from its founding in 1976 through its thirty-three years at that time, now grown to forty years in 2015. That is a longer time span, as Hugh's talk pointed out, for the continuation of Merleau-Pontean thought than the time Merleau-Ponty himself had to work out his philosophy. Hugh titled his talk "Co-Memorating Merleau-Ponty through and with those who keep him alive and well . . ." This will be a rather long citation from Hugh's text.

> How does one remember or even commemorate the birth or life of a philosopher? One can commemorate an event that happened long ago with those who wish to share in the success or continuity of that event—not just remembering it (since most of "us" were not there) but keeping it alive through our own lives, interactions, sharing, community . . . As we know, Merleau-Ponty was only 53 when he died in the Spring of 1961 (and I was a teenager at the time). Reading Sartre and Camus in those years brought me in proximity to Merleau-Ponty's world but I first began to read *Phenomenology of Perception* in 1967—soon after the publication of some posthumous writings. And it wasn't until 1971–1972 that I had the opportunity to first meet Claude Lefort and then Madame Merleau-Ponty at her apartment on the Boulevard St. Michel . . .
>
> And then there are those Merleau-Ponty Circle moments—such as the session where we were all asked to

> stand around a "clearing" (a *Lichtung* of sorts) and to sway like trees, or rather to be the trees withstanding wind and rain (something like the trees in the *Lord of the Rings*). And in Oregon, we watched films of chimpanzees and were asked to think of ourselves as like those apes, behaving in similar ways . . . Cocktails on Mark Johnson's porch in the Oregon woods will remain vivid in my memories. Galen and I remember the Hurricane coming across to London, Ontario from the US and wondering how many of our houses were still standing . . . Kym [Maclaren], Ernie [Sherman], and Bernhard Waldenfels will probably not forget walking on the beach outside Salisbury State in 1998 with Ernie looking like Derrida's silhouette followed by the long drive in Michael Sanders' car to the Newark Airport. I think we all went to Beale Street to listen to music the first time the Circle was in Memphis . . .

I will break it off here; there are many more pages like this, but in all of them we experience the predominance of the personal and singular in Hugh's way of doing philosophy.[19]

Stanley Cavell's autobiographical exercises, called *A Pitch of Philosophy*, arrive at six conditions for finding a language for writing the self, the most interesting and difficult being "perfect pitch."[20] This is a musical metaphor, and Cavell tells the story of the testing of perfect pitch among himself and the other students in Ernst Bloch's music theory class at Berkeley. Bloch played a four-part Bach chorale at the piano with one note altered by a half step from Bach's rendering; then he would play the Bach unaltered. With the drama mounting, Bloch demanded: "You hear that? You hear the difference?" . . . "My version is perfectly correct; but the Bach is perfect; late sunlight burning the edges of a cloud."[21] The challenge, the condition—and I have no doubt impossibility—of autobiography is finding that almost perfect pitch for hearing one's own voice and tone. In these terms, perfect pitch is a regulative ideal, and the difficulty becomes modulating the voice as auto-affection, that is, as one's own voice is heard on the inside, so to speak, with the way in which our voice is heard on the outside by others, which is the voice spatialized. In *Speech and Phenomenon*, Derrida argues that " 'hearing oneself speak' is an auto-affection of a unique kind," for it occurs without passing through the detour of the world, the sphere of what is not our own. "Every other form of auto-affection must either pass through what is outside the sphere of 'ownness' or forego any claim of universality."[22]

Therefore, perfect pitch is the hardest condition to achieve and must somehow or other go beyond being only privately ratified; that is, somehow it must be confirmed by others: sharp tone, abrupt tone, welcoming tone, soothing tone, and more. Cavell argues it is not about hearing and writing perfectly; rather he means it "as the title of experiences ranging from ones amounting to conversions down to small but lucid attestations that the world holds a blessing in store . . . in recognizing the autonomy or splendid separateness of another, the sheer wonder in recognizing the reality of the presence of someone whose existence you perhaps thought you had already granted."[23] In other words, it is the simple, humble, but exceptionally difficult task of writing the self while listening to the outside, thereby expecting lucid testimony and blessings. Perfect pitch is the search for blessings amid memories. The paucity of pitch is cynicism; the excess is nostalgia, twin dangers of writing the self, both forms of being tone-deaf.

This voice of autobiography is, then, the middle voice, the voice in between the active and passive, which in fact is both active and passive at one and the same time. The middle voice is modeled on the Greek aorist tense, a tense missing in English and French. We must say: "I write myself," "*Je m'écris*," as we have previously expressed it. In Greek, the middle voice of the aorist tense expresses this activity/passivity, that is, the "I" who acts on "me," without needing the reflexive personal pronoun. The middle basically signals that the subject of the action both generates the action and in some way acts upon himself. "I write myself" reflects the sentiment that when we write and what we write forms a perception/image of who we are or want to be read as being.

Referring once again to *Speech and Phenomenon* and its culminating chapter on "Differance," Derrida argues that *differance* recalls the middle voice because "it speaks of an operation which is not an operation, which cannot be thought of either as a passion or as an action of a subject upon an object, as starting from an agent or from a patient."[24] Moreover, it is precisely this middle voice, Derrida argues, that has been repressed in Western philosophy, which has forced philosophical thinking to be distributed either as active voice or passive voice.[25] The truth is it is neither, or equally both, a voice that is truly middle, in-between, and so neither transitive or intransitive and yet both transitive and intransitive. In that sense, it is a perfect state of being and the perfect state of writing.[26] Therefore, one is led very close to the conclusion that autobiography, which is the voice of the middle, is also the voice of philosophy: philosophy as autobiography. This conclusion of great risk, if it be true, is testimony to the claim that what is most singular is also plural, perhaps universal. With this, I think Hugh would have found considerable agreement. We recall that it was Nietzsche who wrote in *Beyond Good and Evil*: "Gradually it has become clear to me what every great philosophy so far has been: namely, the personal confession of its author and a kind of involuntary and unconscious memoir."[27]

A supplementarity of middle voice in writing myself is showing myself in portraits, in images: text/image. Saramago's *Small Memories* concludes with a series of family photographs of himself as he grew from infancy to adulthood, of his little brother who died at age two, of his parents, his aunt, and the grandparents who raised him until age twelve. Likewise, Roland Barthes's autobiography begins, rather than concludes, with forty-two pages of photographs: Barthes as a young man lying on a beach; scenes of a child sitting on a wall; Barthes standing among friends; looking thoroughly bored on a conference panel; at work in his office surrounded by papers. Saramago's self-portraits and family portraits are arranged chronologically, but Barthes's are not. For example, a 1942 picture is placed above one from 1970. Indeed, *Barthes by Barthes* has been referred to as anti-autobiography for the absence of chronology until the last two pages provide a chronological list of dates and events. Rather, inspired by the Greek insight that trees are alphabets, which we cited earlier, Barthes's autobiography consists of a series of fragments with titles arranged alphabetically from A through T—"*Actif/réactif*" through "*Le monstre de la Totalité.*" Here the work breaks off with no fragments given for U through Z, then appear the dates of August 6, 1973, through September 3, 1974, which one presumes give the time frame for the writing of the book.

We know of Hugh's fascination with photographs, self-portraits, and indeed his own capacious picture taking. *Textualities* includes what is, for me, one of his greatest pieces of philosophical writing, titled "The Visibility of Self-Portraiture: Merleau-Ponty/Cézanne," published elsewhere as "Cézanne's Mirror Stage."[28] It gives a highly original interpretation of Merleau-Ponty's *Eye and Mind* that begins like this: "Self-portraiture is the hidden agenda of Merleau-Ponty's last essay: *Eye and Mind* (1961). Although he does not mention any particular self-portraits nor does he cite the activity that produces them, the question of self-portraiture serves as the organizing feature of the whole essay" (*T*, 162). In an illustrated presentation on self-portraiture and *Eye and Mind*,[29] Hugh juxtaposed the self-portraits of Cézanne displaying his robust, bearded face, often wearing various hats to create various poses, with self-portraits by Egon Schiele, who lived only twenty-eight years (1890–1918), showing himself as an emaciated body with prominent hands and bony fingers, bearing resonances of crucifixion scenes.

Hugh himself engaged in writing his own autobiography, which he titled "Philosophical Passages: An Essay in Self-Presentation," when he was still quite a young man at age forty-four.[30] It is a valuable account of his early philosophical itinerary and his first encounters with Stanford University and numerous luminaries in France, such as Barthes and Derrida. In fact, as Hugh says in the closing paragraph, his essay veers off from the focus on self "to disperse the attention, the reading, and perhaps even the understanding into the places of those whom one reads, those from whom one has learned, those whom one teaches . . ."[31] One of the more remarkable aspects of the essay is this use of the third person; the "I" does appear, but more often he explicitly writes "me." Hugh's 1989 "self-presentation" is dedicated to his father, who brought him up into an academic way of life, and who also was a professor, "a distinguished member of the Harvard faculty," Hugh records: "to the memory of my father, Professor Leslie Silverman, Sc.D., 1915–1966."[32] He also, as we see, died far too young.

Sometimes autobiographies also arise out of the need to answer certain questions and explore certain mysteries about one's past, to talk them through and give them voice. This latter is the desire of repetition, to live life over again, perhaps to live it better, maybe only to savor its joys and sorrows again.[33] When we read Thoreau today, and Sartre and Barthes and Saramago and Cavell and Silverman and all the other writers of autobiography, they are absent, as is now Hugh. But, in fact, the absence of the living author is always a requisite condition of autobiographical writing, for the author lives in his text for the reader, with whom there is formed this anonymous, intimate, but also distant, bond. Derrida goes further with this thought and argues that this absence, even the ultimate absence that is death itself, is a requisite condition of all writing: the possibility of the sign is the possibility of my disappearance.[34] Thus, to say "I am" is already to say "I am mortal." Another way to say this is that the possibility of textualities rests upon non-textualities.

Saramago tells another story about his grandparents, and with this I wish to conclude. In addition to raising him, Jerónimo and Josefa also raised pigs, and here is Saramago's story about birth and death and heaven on earth:

> Among the newborn piglets there would be the occasional weakling that would inevitably suffer with the night cold, especially in winter, which could prove fatal. However, as far as I know, no such piglet ever died. Every night, my grandfather and grandmother would go to the sty to find the weakest of the piglets, wash their feet and legs and lay them down in their own bed. They would sleep there together, beneath the blankets and the same sheets, with my grandmother on one side of the bed and my grandfather on the other, and between them, three or four piglets who must have thought they were in heaven.[35]

Notes

1. Jacques Derrida, "This Strange Institution Called Literature," in *Acts of Literature*, ed. Derick Attridge, trans. Geoffrey Bennington and Rachel Bowlby (New York: Routledge, 1992), 44.

2. Ibid., 46.

3. And here we will now begin to adopt a personal form of address for the remainder of the chapter, because Hugh the professor and erudite scholar was also a very long-term personal friend.

4. The first footnote to Silverman's chapter on *Walden* reads, in part: "Since I had a penchant for both philosophy and literature, Thoreau's *Walden* suited my fancy most appropriately. During my adolescence, I read the book eagerly. . . . I read *Walden* as, for me, the paradigm of American letters." (*T*, 247, n. 1). Once, before *Textualities* appeared, Hugh told me that when he was young, Thoreau's *Walden* was his Bible. Hugh grew up in Dover, Massachusetts, and Walden Pond is only twenty miles to the north of Dover. Hugh also attended middle school and high school at Noble and Greenough School in Dedham, Massachusetts, seven miles to the east of Dover and only

twenty-four miles from Walden. So Hugh had the opportunity to experience Walden Pond many times over in all the different seasons of the year, just as Thoreau lived them for two years, two months, and two days from 1845 to 1847.

5. Among the many editions of *Walden* by Henry David Thoreau, I cite the fully annotated edition edited by Jeffrey S. Cramer (New Haven: Yale University Press, 2004), 1. Henceforth cited as *W.*

6. Stanley Cavell, *A Pitch of Philosophy: Autobiographical Exercises* (Cambridge: Harvard University Press, 1994), 35. Also cf. 41.

7. Stanley Cavell, *Philosophy the Day after Tomorrow* (Cambridge: Belknap Press of Harvard University Press, 2005) and *Little Did I Know: Excerpts from Memory* (Stanford: Stanford University Press, 2010).

8. José Saramago, *Small Memories: A Memoir*, trans. Margaret Jull Costa (Boston: Mariner Books, 2012), 26, 28. The English translation of the Portuguese original, *As Pequenas Memórias*, is posthumous, though the original appeared in 2006.

9. Ibid., 5.

10. Ibid., 118–20.

11. George Poulet, "Phenomenology of Reading," *New Literary History* 1, no. 1 (October 1969): 57.

12. Ibid., 60.

13. Ibid., 63.

14. Henry David Thoreau, *Faith in a Seed: The Dispersion of Seeds and Other Late Natural History Writings*, ed. Bradley P. Dean (Washington, DC: Shearwater Books, 1993).

15. On the centrality of metaphor in human life and the transformation and transfiguration available in symbolic expression, cf. Vincent Colapietro, "Striving to Speak in a Human Voice: A Peircean Contribution to Metaphysical Discourse," *The Review of Metaphysics* 58, no. 2 (December 2004): 367–98, esp. 395.

16. Roland Barthes, *Roland Barthes*, trans. Richard Howard (New York: Hill and Wang, 1977), 41.

17. Ibid., 180.

18. Ibid., 186.

19. Hugh sent me his text following the 2008 Merleau-Ponty Circle conference, and I hope to incorporate parts of it into a future brief work on the history of the Circle.

20. Cavell, *A Pitch of Philosophy*, 39, 47.

21. Ibid., 49.

22. Jacques Derrida, *Speech and Phenomena: And Other Essays on Husserl's Theory of Signs*, trans. David B. Allison (Evanston, IL: Northwestern University Press, 1973), 78.

23. Cavell, *A Pitch of Philosophy*, 47.

24. Derrida, *Speech and Phenomena*, 137.

25. Ibid., 137.

26. I thank classics professor and scholar Timothy S. Johnson for these explanations and elaborations of the meaning of middle voice and aorist tense in classical Greek. Tim is professor and chair of classics at the College of Charleston, South Carolina, and is my brother, with whom it is a privilege to share many scholarly conversations.

27. Friedrich Nietzsche, *Beyond Good and Evil: Prelude to a Philosophy of the Future*, trans. Walter Kaufmann (New York: Vintage, 1966), §6, 13.

28. The essay is published under the title "Cézanne's Mirror Stage," in *The Merleau-Ponty Aesthetics Reader: Philosophy and Painting*, ed. Galen A. Johnson (Evanston, IL: Northwestern University Press, 1993), 262–77.

29. The occasion was Hugh's visit as guest professor at my seminar at the University of Rhode Island in 2005 to discuss *Eye and Mind* with my students and the possibilities and limits of self-portraiture. I have fond memories of our collaboration in preparing the PowerPoint slides for that event, he the creative director, I the technical assistant.

30. Hugh J. Silverman, "Philosophical Passages: An Essay in Self-Presentation," in *American Phenomenology: Origins and Developments*, ed. Eugene F. Kaelin and Calvin O. Schrag, Analecta Husserliana (Dordrecht: Kluwer, 1989), 374–83. I express my gratitude to Peter Gratton, Memorial University of Newfoundland, for telling me about this essay and sharing a copy with me.

31. Ibid., 382.

32. Ibid., 378, 374.

33. On autobiography as repetition, see Joseph G. Kronick, "Philosophy as Autobiography: The Confessions of Jacques Derrida," *MLN* 115, no. 5 (December 2000): 997–1018.

34. Cf. Jacques Derrida, "Meaning and Representation," in *Speech and Phenomena*, 53–54.

35. Saramago, *Small Memories*, 120–21.

PART 2

Silverman and Derrida

Justice/Hospitality/Writing

5

In Memoriam—an Indecidable

For HJS

Michael Naas

Incapable, incompetent, and more than a bit intimidated—that is how I feel before the task of trying to respond to the work of Hugh Silverman, a work to which so many of us in this volume are so deeply indebted. Incapable, inadequate, and incommensurate with the task—that is how I feel before a work that, in ways both big and small, at once obvious and inconspicuous, has been such an influence on so many of us. It is because of this inescapable feeling of incompetence and inability that I have thus chosen as my way in to this rather incredible corpus not a book or article, not even a single theme or word, but a mere syllable, more than a dash or a slash, it is true, but just a syllable nonetheless, a Silvermanian syllable—a prefix, really—that I would like to argue Hugh signed, marked, or, better, inscribed in a unique and inimitable way, a syllable he would have made his own, like an insignia or an initial, like those initials HJS with which he had taken to signing and inscribing himself, as we say, *in propria persona*.

You have probably guessed it: the syllable I am speaking of is the simple prefix *in-*, as in the words initial and inscription, though also, and especially, indecidable. Though I long hesitated about how to approach Hugh's work for this memorial volume, wondering whether I should go back to some of those magnificent early essays on Heidegger, Sartre, Merleau-Ponty, Foucault, or Derrida, or whether to follow Hugh's work on autobiography from Thoreau to Nietzsche to Levi-Strauss, or whether to try to trace the incredible itinerary Hugh had taken over the course of his thinking, from earlier works on German and French philosophy, on Husserl and Gadamer in addition to Heidegger, on Barthes, Lyotard, Ricœur, and Kristeva in addition to Sartre, Merleau-Ponty, and Derrida, though also on Hjelmslev and Ingarden—essays on semiology, structuralism, aesthetics, phenomenology, hermeneutics, and deconstruction—right up through groundbreaking essays on Agamben, Eco, and Italian philosophy in general, once I remembered the question of the *in-* in *indecidable*, all my indecision vanished.

Incapable, then, of responding as fully as I should to Hugh's work, I would like to recall my enormous debt by focusing almost exclusively on the syllable *in-* in *indecidable*, a Derridean word that will have been given a Silvermanian twist, which is as it should be because I first started reading Derrida seriously only as a graduate student in Hugh's seminars back at Stony Brook in the early to mid-1980s. In recognition of and in gratitude for those seminars, for their inventiveness and playfulness—for if they were not always, one has to be honest, overly structured or obsessively organized, they were always inventive, innovative, and inspiring—I should probably begin my reading of Hugh's work, like I might have begun a protocol for one of his seminars, by saying "I shall speak therefore of a syllable," an echo, of course, of the opening line of Derrida's "Différance" essay, an allusion that Hugh would have been the first to hear and the first to smile at. Inventive, innovative, and inspiring, those seminars left me anything but indifferent, and if I find myself still interested in and still working on Derrida some three decades later, it is no doubt in large part because of those early seminars.

I will speak, therefore, of the syllable *in-*, because, as far as I know, Hugh was just about the only person who used this syllable to translate Derrida's word *indécidable*. That word, *indécidable*, is almost always, indeed pretty much systematically, translated into English as *undecidable* rather than *indecidable*, and yet Hugh insisted on the *in-* of indecidable for reasons that I would like to explore. For if, as I far as I know, Hugh gave no sustained justification for this translation, at least not in print, it is indisputably much more than a Gallicism or mere idiosyncrasy; indeed, it was an intentional and well-reasoned choice that just might tell us much about what Hugh considered deconstruction to be and much about Hugh's own work in general.

Now to understand just what an indecidable or undecidable is in Derrida's work, one can find no better guide than Hugh. Though it is difficult to pinpoint exactly when Hugh began taking an interest in this aspect of Derrida's thought, the theme is most prominent in Hugh's work of the early 1980s, right around the time I arrived at Stony Brook. In terms of Hugh's published work, it seems to fall chronologically somewhere between the final essays gathered in *Inscriptions* and the first ones collected in *Textualities*. It is thus evoked in the introduction to *Inscriptions* but really only gets treated in latter chapters. It is thus not inaccurate, and indeed perfectly appropriate, to say that the indecidable is most insistent in Hugh's work *in between* these two major texts, in the place of their chiasm or their slash. In the introduction to *Inscriptions*, titled—and I return to this later—"*continental philosophy in America*," Hugh writes:

> The present study . . . is inscribed in the place between phenomenology and structuralism. This space of difference is the place which Merleau-Ponty and the later Heidegger on the one hand, and the later Barthes and Foucault on the other, entertain as the place where their own philosophizing can occur. This place—and the language of place is significant—is where a hermeneutic semiology opens onto a deconstruction, a reading of texts in terms of their differential, marginal, *indecidable* features. (*I*, 7–8; my emphasis)

Notice, first, that it is under the name of deconstruction that the indecidable, or at least the phrase "indecidable features," first emerges in Hugh's text. But perhaps more important here is Hugh's own emphasis on the importance of place, the significance of the language of place, and thus the significance, no doubt already, of the *in-*. One can perhaps already foresee the stakes, then, of maintaining that *in-* in a translation of the Derridean *indécidable*, the desire or need, perhaps, to identify the in-between or more simply the *in-* within a certain deconstruction, or, better, to identify the *in-* as itself a deconstructive indecidable. Just a couple of lines later, still in the introduction, Hugh makes it clear that the between or the *in-* is not some locatable place within or outside a text but the very place that locates without itself being located.

> [T]he place between is not just a between—slash theory as it might be called. The place between is also beyond either phenomenology and structuralism. The place between must be at least a post-phenomenology and a post-structuralism. But the beyond is not a Hegelian *Aufhebung*. The beyond is inscribed entirely within the frameworks of a continental tradition and set of reference texts which it can go beyond only by operating within its contexts. The place of difference is where philosophy can find its place at the margins of its own traditions. (*I*, 8)

Hence the *in-* is itself, as it were, a place-between that itself situates rather than being itself situated, a beyond that is neither outside nor squarely inside. By saying that the "place between is not just a between," Hugh is clearly suggesting that we rethink the very nature of place or space. Let me note in passing here that if one wanted to think space or place in the 1980s, Stony Brook was most definitely the in-place to be, because Patrick Heelan, Don Ihde, and, of course, Ed Casey, among others, were all working on this question. While one might not immediately think of Hugh as a thinker of place or of space, this passage from *Inscriptions* should suggest that he certainly was; indeed, that he was perhaps first and foremost a thinker of space.

The notion of the indecidable—or at least the adjective "indecidable"—thus emerges in the introduction to *Inscriptions*, but it is not really developed until much later in the book, that is, in part 4, which bears the title "The Difference Between (And Beyond)," the parentheses signaling here, it seems, that "the difference between" is not something different from "beyond" but a different inscription of it, not some transcendental signifier but a beyond that is inscribed—without being located—*within*. In the first chapter of this part of *Inscriptions*, "The Limits of Logocentrism," the noun "indecidable" appears first in relation to Heidegger or, rather, in relation to something that seems to emerge at the limit or in the margins of Heidegger's work, the place, it seems, where Derrida will ultimately come to be situated.

> With Heidegger, I show that we are situated alongside Logos in the ontological difference. In the process, it becomes clear that Logos *qua* language is both the house and the name of the Being of beings. On this basis, Logos is taken to its limits where language itself occupies the place of the indecidable or hinge at the edge of the discourse of metaphysics. (*I*, 281)

Once again, *indecidable* is related to place, to the question of the *in-*, to this strange place at the end of the discourse of metaphysics; not wholly within it and not outside it but at its edge, at the *hinge*—a word that also pivots around an *in* at its center (*I*, 281; see also 285).

Whereas the word was used as an adjective in the introduction, it is now used as a noun, "the indecidable," a term that will soon develop into a full-blown *indecidability*, one that Hugh will identify not, in the end, with Heidegger but with Derrida. Listen to how Hugh, still in this chapter on Heidegger from *Inscriptions*, locates deconstruction at the place of the edge or hinge that Heidegger's text will have opened up or indicated, all the while withdrawing from it so as to become, in the end, more fully inscribed within metaphysics, that is, "within the metaphysical texture which calls for origins and announces ends." For if Heidegger's philosophy "announces the end of philosophy" and "moves quite close to the deconstructive machinery," it nonetheless "falls decidedly *on this side* of the history of metaphysics" (*I*, 285–86). It is, among other things, this notion of teleology, the idea of a project within or along which something unfolds, a history with an origin and an end, that seems to characterize this metaphysics. And it is deconstruction, the deconstructive machinery, as Hugh puts it, that breaks most definitively with that teleological project. Hugh thus writes, still in this chapter on Heidegger, which looks more and more like a hinge chapter between Heidegger and Derrida:

> Deconstruction . . . can inscribe neither teleology nor archaeology. It can only work with (and play at) the traces, supplements, and edges of discourses which presuppose and incorporate metaphysical features. In short, deconstruction looks for the crack, the hinge, and the tear in the manifold of a metaphysical texture. Deconstruction situates itself there at the place where placement spills over. (*I*, 284–85)

Place is thus an essential topic and trope *within* the metaphysics that Hugh is reading alongside Heidegger, Derrida, and others. But it is also—in the guise of the *in-* or the in-between—an essential operative term for determining, precisely, what is inside, what is outside, and what is at or on the edge of metaphysics. *In-*, unlike *un-*, carries place, and inscribes a certain fate of place, to cite Ed Casey's phrase, within it. No wonder Hugh would insist, as we will see, on the importance of maintaining the in- of *indécidable* in the English translation of that word.

According to Hugh, Heidegger would thus be close to the edge of metaphysics but still within it, while Derridean deconstruction would come to be inscribed right at that edge, where neither teleology as the projection of ends nor archaeology as the retrieval of origins is possible. It is thus Derrida, and not Heidegger, who will come to be most closely identified with the indecidable and everything that goes along with it. This is already evident in the chapter of *Inscriptions* devoted essentially to Derrida, a chapter where the notion of place, not coincidentally, is once again prominent, as another *in* word makes itself heard—and already from the title: "Self-Decentering: Derrida Incorporated." It is particularly poignant for us today that in what I take to be one of Hugh's earliest texts on Derrida, a text first published in 1978, it is the theme of the crypt, of place and of mourning, that already attracts his attention. Though the indecidable is mentioned only once in this early text, its placement could not be more significant. After reading "Fors," one of Derrida's most important texts on mourning, and after repeatedly reposing the question that Derrida poses throughout that essay, "What is a crypt?," Hugh writes: "In this case the self is a crypt—but no doubt one on the way to its own decentering. The crypt," he continues, "occupies the position of the '*un*decidable.' Is it the self which is inside or is it the self which is outside?" (*I*, 308; my emphasis).

A couple of remarks on this remarkable passage. First, you will notice that it is Hugh himself who speaks here of the *un*decidable, not the *in*decidable, as if he himself were uncertain or undecided about which it should be, as if, in 1978, he had not settled on *in*decidable rather than the standard undecidable as a way to speak of the Derridean *indécidable.* Second, this question of the decentered and undecidable nature of the self would need to be thought in relation to all of Hugh's work on self and autobiography, from an early text co-written with his colleague David Dilworth on differing senses of self in East and West right up to Hugh's wonderfully insightful and discretely autobiographical essay on Thoreau's *Walden*. As for this latter, it would be essential, for what I am trying to argue here, to pay particular attention to the edges or borders of Hugh's text on *Walden*, to camp out for a time on its shores. One would want to look, for example, at its opening line, which suggests that "the intersections of phenomenology and semiotics are typically marked by a borderline—the one ends where the other begins,"[1] and then at its first footnote, where Hugh begins writing—*even as he suggests he is not*—in a poignantly autobiographical mode:

> Henry David Thoreau's *Walden: or Life in the Woods* is a text which would play an important role in my own autobiography—were I to write one. Thoreau was born in Concord, Massachusetts, in 1817—I was born not far from there about a century and a quarter later. Like Thoreau I grew up in the countryside within the environs of Boston. Since I had a penchant for both philosophy and literature, Thoreau's *Walden* suited my fancy most appropriately. (*T*, 247, n. 1)

Hence the IAPL, we might say, owes its genesis in part to Hugh's fellow Bostonian Thoreau, not the first figure one usually associates with the IAPL, but the one whom Hugh, it seems, might have placed at its center alongside Shakespeare, Montaigne, and Goethe. Hugh's footnote continues:

> I read the book eagerly, and just as an Englishman might return on occasion to Shakespeare, a Frenchman to Montaigne, and a German to Goethe, I read *Walden* as, for me, the paradigm of American [USA] letters. Since then my reading has taken me far from the New England terrain where I grew up and was educated. I now return to this textual homeland in order to develop the space and limits of its autobiographical textuality. (*T*, 247, n. 1)

Space, place, self, autobiography, textuality: all these notions are part of a single textual configuration or economy. If Hugh's work was from the very beginning about space or place, it was also already about the self and the textual practices that make writing about the self possible.

But to return to the question of the indecidable, which, as we have seen, makes an appearance in *Inscriptions* but is not treated in any detail—indeed, it even appears once in the guise of the undecidable—the indecidable is an essential operative term in *Textualities*. Whereas in *Inscriptions* the word seemed poised between the late Heidegger and Derrida, in *Textualities* it is identified almost uniquely with Derrida before then getting reinscribed in a idiom that is Hugh's own, as indecidability becomes a central feature of what Hugh—following Derrida to some extent but also leading him in new directions—would call *textuality*.

In his "Introductory Remarks" to *Textualities*, Hugh himself develops and documents the transition or itinerary from *Inscriptions* to this later book, emphasizing, for example, the centrality of autobiography for this latter, the place of those autobiographical texts I just recalled. But another way to think or to trace the transition between these two works is to follow the fate of the indecidable within them.

The indecidable first appears in *Textualities*—and again this is not insignificant—in a chapter of and about transition, that is, a first chapter titled "Phenomenology: From Hermeneutics to Deconstruction." This chapter in effect compares various ways of reading—the semiotic, the hermeneutic, and the deconstructive—by putting them all to the test of another classic American literary work, Robert Frost's poem "The Road Not Taken." Hugh writes, for example, contrasting deconstruction with hermeneutic semiology: "Deconstruction . . . offers a way of reading texts such that the zero degree and point of departure for a hermeneutic semiology can itself be decentered and disseminated in a field of writing, differance, and indecidables" (*T*, 20). Whereas Hugh spoke in *Inscriptions* of what happens at the edges, borders, or margins of a text, the deconstructive text or a deconstructive reading of a text here seems to perform this operation on itself, as it were, a bit like the autobiographical text that at once locates and decenters the self, that both reconciles and forever separates the self that writes and the self that is written about. Hugh continues: "The text is self-circumscribing, its outside (pre-texts, con-texts, inter-texts) implies its inside. At the hinge or borderline between the two, at the meeting place of the oppositional relation, the reading of writing and the writing of a reading take place" (*T*, 20). Once again, notice, emphasis is placed on the hinge between inside and outside and then, importantly, on the relationship between reading and writing. It is right at this point that we get a first example of an indecidable, namely, writing, the *pharmakon*, from Derrida's "Plato's Pharmacy."

> Writing is that originary space in which a text is communicated, disseminated, displayed, incorporated, limited, contexted, and so forth. As Derrida has demonstrated in "Plato's Pharmacy," writing is neither a remedy nor a poison, yet as *pharmakon* it has features of both. It supplements in that it adds on to what has been written elsewhere, yet it also supplements in that it repeats and takes the place of what it recounts. Writing is an indecidable. (*T*, 20–21)

Writing as "originary space," writing as *pharmakon*, is thus an indecidable, and it is this notion of the indecidable, taken explicitly from Derrida, that provides Hugh with the most powerful reading of the Robert Frost poem. To understand, for example, "two roads diverged in a wood," one must understand, as Hugh demonstrates, that indecidable called writing or, better, *différance*: "*Différance* is the indecidable which does not choose one road or the other"; it is what "requires the divergence, the opposition, the meeting of two distinct ways" (*T*, 21).

Just a few pages later in *Textualities*, in an essay titled "Interrogation and Deconstruction"—this word "interrogation," as in the interrogation of a work of art, being yet another one of Hugh's many important *in-* words—Hugh clarifies and expands on the indecidable:

> Just as writing and the *pharmakon* are indecidables (either speech or writing, remedy or poison) so too "truth in painting" is an indecidable (either truth in the act of painting or painting what is true). To deconstruct "truth in painting" is to bring out not only its indecidability but also its supplementarity. That the supplement itself is also an indecidable (either addition or replacement) is only an additional feature of the deconstructive strategy. (*T*, 44)

The problem or the promise of the *indecidable* is not just that it means or can mean two different things depending on the context, but also that it "means" both at the same time—and because one cannot parse or translate or even understand *both at the same time*, one is forced to reduce this both/and to an either/or. The indecidable is thus not a regulated polysemy but more like what Freud, following Karl Abel, called the antithetical (or ambivalent) meaning of primal words. It is as if *pharmakon* meant *both* remedy *and* poison in the unconscious or in the unconscious of language but then came to mean *either* remedy *or* poison as soon as it entered the time of decision, that is, as soon as any light whatsoever was shone upon it and it rose up to consciousness.

Hugh goes on—in the passage from *Textualities* that I am still reading—to give an even more programmatic statement regarding the indecidable that is of enormous utility in helping us understand Derrida and that already gestures beyond Derrida to Hugh's own theory of texuality:

> Deconstruction goes to the place of indecidables such as communication (oral presentation/transmission of messages), *écriture* (speaking/writing), difference (distinction/deferral), *pharmakon* (poison/remedy), trace (footprint/imprint), correspondence (exchange of letters/matching of similarities), supplement (addition/replacement), and so forth. In addition to the horizontal proliferation and displacement of one text into another, and in addition to the vertical reexamination of traditional binary oppositions, the deconstruction of texts requires the elucidation and elaboration of indecidables and their indecidability. The indecidability of texts is a feature of their textuality. (*T*, 46)

The indecidable thus makes an appearance in the opening chapter of *Textualities*, and the term indecidability appears in the subsequent chapter on "Interrogation and Deconstruction." But it is really in the chapter of *Textualities* titled "Writing (on Deconstruction) at the Edge of Metaphysics" that we find the most developed and explicit treatment of the indecidable. This is a wonderful chapter on deconstruction—intelligent, sober, precise, and, while not unplayful, clear that deconstruction cannot simply be reduced to linguistic play. As Hugh nicely puts it, "To imitate Derrida's style—employing the puns, play, *double entendre*, etc.—does not as such make for a deconstructive practice" (*T*, 61–62). What deconstruction does do, as we might have predicted from earlier claims made by Hugh, is offer "a reading of the frames, boundaries, and limits of writing whether they be contemporary or imbedded in the history of writing" (*T*, 65). Hugh thus goes on in this chapter to consider the various problematics treated by deconstruction, the strategies employed in deconstruction, and the "indicators" that identify the practice and the elements of deconstruction. It is under the rubric of deconstructive strategies, then, that Hugh speaks of "the inscription of one's own writing at the place of 'indecidables' by demonstrating their differential function" (*T*, 66). Hugh then writes, in a fairly long passage that I would like to cite in its entirety because it is, as far as I know, Hugh's most complete account of the Derridean indecidable:

> In *Positions*, Derrida offers something like a definition of indecidables. He describes them as [and Hugh now quotes Derrida's *Positions*,] "unities of simulacrum, 'false' verbal properties (nominal or semantic) that can no longer be included within philosophical (binary) opposition, but which, however, inhabit philosophical opposition, resisting and disorganizing it, *without ever* constituting a third term, without leaving room for a solution in the form of speculative dialectics." (*T*, 66)[2]

Let me interrupt this quote for a moment to note here that Hugh has just cited verbatim Alan Bass's English translation of Derrida's definition of *indécidable* in the book *Positions*. Hugh cites Bass's translation verbatim, except that whereas Bass translates *indécidable* as *undecidable* throughout this passage (e.g., "certain marks, shall we say . . . that *by analogy* (I underline) I have called undecidables . . ."[3]), Hugh instead speaks of *indecidables*. Hugh thus substitutes *indecidables* for *undecidables* and, even more interestingly, he does so in silence, that is, without signaling this change in either the text or a note.

Given Hugh's impeccable French, and the fact that Hugh always read Derrida first in French and then went looking for the English to cite in his works, one might hypothesize that Hugh—influenced by Derrida's *indécidable*—actually "saw" or "heard" the Gallicism *indecidable* there where the Bass translation had *undecidable*. That kind of thing can easily happen. But, as we will see in a moment, Hugh himself excludes this hypothesis when he explicitly opposes the *un-* to the *in-*, leading us to conclude that he consciously decided, for what he believed to be good philosophical and/or linguistic reasons, to impose the *in-* over the *un-* in an unspoken or undeclared way, undoing the *un-*, as it were, through the *-in*, thereby remarking, signing, and silently inscribing himself in the place of this Derridean idiom. Whatever his reason or his motive, *indecidable* would remain from here on in the favored if not unique translation in Hugh's work for *indécidable*. Hugh continues:

> Indecidables operate where philosophical oppositions arise. They are not elements of the opposition, yet they mark the oppositions and relate different oppositions to one another. Indecidables have a double character. They seem to raise the possibility of turning in either direction within a whole variety of philosophical oppositions, yet they do not assume the position of either side of such oppositions. . . . They [also] avoid becoming a third term: an *Aufhebung*, a synthesis of two dialectically related terms. They do not carry the possibility of resolve that a Hegelian third term permits. The indecidable is precisely "the limit, interruption, destruction of Hegelian *Aufhebung*. (*P*, 40)
>
> Examples of indecidables include: sign, structure, writing, communication, genre, difference, and so on. (*T*, 66)

Now a couple of pages later, Hugh returns to this theme of the indecidable, and while he does not explicitly justify his translation of *indécidable* by *indecidable* rather than *undecidable*, he gives us, in a passing comment, a way to contrast the two terms. Having spoken of how "the neither-nor/either-or placement situates the indecidables at the horizontally proliferated dissemination of the sign structure throughout Western metaphysics," Hugh adds that "the indecidable itself is not undecidable—not passively incapable of resolution nor fully active in not working out resolution" (*T*, 67). Unlike *undecidable*, then, where the *un-* could suggest, it seems, a passive incapacity for resolution or else an active undoing, *indecidable*, on Hugh's understanding, does not fall prey to this binary pair of passivity and activity. Insofar as undecidable would be the opposite of decidable, and so would be one pole in a binary opposition, it would seem to be less appropriate than *indecidable* for translating what Derrida appears to have meant by *indécidable*.[4]

Unable to pursue here this intriguing but difficult connection between indecidability, textuality, and philosophy, I would like to begin inching toward a conclusion by suggesting that *indecidable* was Hugh's word, Hugh's signature, the word *indecidable*, but also, by contagion, and even more expansively, as the signature, perhaps, of what Gail Weiss aptly calls "The Silverman Network," the prefix *-in*, with all its ambiguity, indeed, all its indecidability. For the *in-* is not only, like the *un-*, a trace of the Greek alpha privative, a prefix that deprives the stem of a word of its positive meaning. It also intensifies or locates, as in, precisely, intensity, inherent, inhabit, and inhere. When the two valences are thus combined, *in-* can itself be heard as an indecidable, that is, not only as a privative *or* an intensive but as *both* at once, thereby undoing or displacing its own placing or localizing, destabilizing or decentering the very self or meaning that is inscribed by, in, or within it, de-ontologizing or in-ontologizing, as it were, that which has been ontologically affirmed. At once negation and affirmation, privative and intensive, this incredible, indecidable *in-* might then be heard creeping into other of Hugh's *in-* words, like inscription, for example, where it would suggest both a scription, a writing or scribing *in* or *on*, and a *de-* or *un*-scription, a negation of or withdrawal from inscription, an inscription *as* or *of* what withdraws from inscription.

If the indecidable was one of Hugh's words, then the *in-* will have been one of his signatures, one of his marks, one of his insignias—though also, it has to be noted, one of his own scholarly interests. In an early chapter of *Textualities* Hugh cites Heidegger's *Poetry, Language, and Thought*, where what is at issue is the intimacy of world and thing and the relationship between the Latin *inter*, the German *unter*, and the English *inter-*, and all of this in an attempt to find not some intermediary term that binds but a difference that keeps things apart in their intimacy: "The middle of the two is intimacy," writes Heidegger and cites Hugh, "in Latin, *inter*. The corresponding German word is *unter*, the English *inter-*. The intimacy of world and thing is not a fusion. . . . In the midst of the two, in the between of world and thing, in their *inter*, division prevails: a *dif-ference*" (*T*, 35).

Hugh will have thus taught us that deconstruction is from the very beginning the deconstruction of a certain conception of space, a certain understanding of the *-in*, of any opposition or any space of opposition that thinks it can isolate its inside, the inside of a concept, for example, from its outside or its opposite. Hugh's emphasis on the slash, on what is neither inside nor outside, makes it clear that what was always at issue for him was a deconstruction of the supposed purity of the inside, every inside. Indecidable, then, rather than undecidable, would have been his way of recalling the permeability and lack of indemnity of the "inside itself."

If indecidable, which differs from undecidable only by this *in-*, will have been in the end Hugh's word, then *in-* will have been, as I have said, his syllable, his prefix. And it is, of course, everywhere, from *Inscriptions* and all the other *in-* words I have recalled here to the institutions that Hugh not only inspired but initiated and inaugurated, starting with the institution of Cont*in*ental Philosophy itself, a term that Hugh will not have been for nothing in fashioning and disseminating. By interacting with and inviting over the years so many scholars from around the world to Stony Brook and to the United States, Hugh did as much as anyone in the United States to make Continental Philosophy a truly international enterprise. And the same goes, of course, for everything that has taken place thanks to Hugh's ingenuity and initiative in the works of the International Association of Philosophy and Literature and the International Philosophical Seminar, institutions for which we all owe him an inordinate debt.

The *in-* will thus have been Hugh's signature, his flourish, his initialing, the sign of the Silverman Network, mission, congregation, or order. Indeed at the risk of exposing what will no doubt appear to be a rather idiosyncratic set of associations, I have always seen in those initials with which he had come to sign things—HJS—something slightly clerical, if not Jesuitical, something in the order of an order or at least an initiation. I am not thinking of Leopold Bloom in *Ulysses*, who sees the letters or the initials INRI inscribed at the top of the cross and thinks that they must stand for "Iron Nails Run In." No, as a graduate of Holy Cross College in Massachusetts—for, yes, I too am from Massachusetts—I am thinking of the SJ that followed the name of many of my professors there, and then even more of the IHS on their vestments, IHS for *in hoc signo*, that is, in or by this sign. *In hoc signo*, then, because *-in* itself will have been, I think, HIS sign, Hugh's sign, the sign of HS, the sign or initialing of HJS, where the J is perhaps there to recall a Jewish heritage and a joyous spirit behind all these very serious Christian signs.

My claim here is ultimately that Hugh would have seen himself, discovered or invented himself, in this *in-*, and that he would have then bequeathed us this *in-* as a sort of inheritance, our inheritance. Under the sign of this *in-* we are thus invited to recall so many characteristics, his incredible intelligence, his ingenuity, the inspiration he has provided so many of us, though also, for we owe it to the truth to recall other not inappropriate *in-* attributions, his insistence, his incredible memory and inability to forget, and, thus, his incorrigibility—just try to wiggle out of hosting an IAPL and you would know just how insistent and incorrigible Hugh could be. Insistent, incorrigible, and thus also, if I could coin this term in his honor, as a term of endearment, *inpossible*. Hugh was, sometimes, it simply has to be said, simply *inpossible*, and however seemingly incongruous and incompatible this may seem, it was this *inpossibility* that in-deared him to so many of us and made us want to share in that intimacy of difference and of distance that I recalled just a moment ago.

My sole regret today is that I was never able, that I was incapable of telling him all this much earlier in writing, or else, even though I suspect that this too would have been in Hugh's eyes another indecidable, *in person*—leaving me condemned to offer it all today only *in memoriam*. And yet I remain consoled by the fact that *in memoriam* is, as it were, for every thinker of the indecidable, the very inspiration for everything that goes by the names of writing, inscription, and textuality, though also intimacy, integrity, and friendship—in short, everything Hugh Silverman believed in.[5]

Notes

1. "Autobiographical Textuality: The Case of Thoreau's *Walden*," *Semiotica* 41, nos. 1–4 (1982): 257–75. Chapter 9 of *Textualities* is a revised version of this essay (*T*, 89–102).

2. See Jacques Derrida, *Positions*, trans. Alan Bass (Chicago: University of Chicago Press, 1981), 43.

3. Ibid., 42–43.

4. At the conference at Stony Brook University on September 13–14, 2013, where this paper was first read, Peter Gratton recalled Hugh making precisely this argument *against* the translation of *indécidable* as *undecidable*. Hugh noted that university students are said to be *undecided* before they have declared a major. Hence *undecidable* would suggest that there is some time in which one can remain *undecided*, whereas the point of the *indécidable* is that a decision is always required even if there can never be no real justification for it.

5. One final note: I have spoken of Hugh Silverman throughout this essay as if he were the disembodied author of so many texts on the prefix *in-*. But *in my memory* he is and will always remain located in some space or attached to some place. In other words, he will always remain *in-*, whether it be in a classroom at Stony Brook, in his office at Harriman Hall, in a green Volvo on the Long Island Expressway, in the house in Port Jefferson that he shared with Gerda, in Wrigley Field in Chicago, in Italy and in France, in Brétigny and in Montléry, and in Septeuil in July 1990, with his daughter, Claire, late at night, at the end of a long wedding celebration, in a field beneath a still stormy but clearing sky.

6

Of Philosophy, Friendship, and Justice

Debra Bergoffen

Every new project begins with a blank page—a where/how to begin? But writing to remember Hugh, a friend—that blank page was filled with memories. That where to begin was emotionally charged. Perhaps as a way of putting off the reality of Hugh's absence, or perhaps listening without knowing that I was listening to what my bones already knew, I found myself pulling Derrida's *Politics of Friendship* from the shelf. Reading Derrida's words, I discovered familiar names scribbled in the margins. Reading these names, I found myself reliving the conversations provoked by this text at one of the International Philosophy Seminars (IPS) that Hugh and Wilhelm Wurzer organized in the Südtirol.

In the announcement for these seminars, Hugh and Wilhelm wrote: "The seminar provides a framework for thought in an unconstrained environment with a view toward an intensely rigorous exchange of ideas, philosophical views and theories." This formal language barely captures the spirit of these events. It gives no hint of the ways that they epitomized the idea and pursuit of philosophy at its intellectual and democratic best. There would be twelve to fifteen of us gathered around a table brought together by a text. Whether you were a graduate student, a new professor, or the occupant of a named chair, at the IPS you presented your paper and engaged in discussions as an equal. No hierarchies here. The seminars thrived on intellectual differences, challenges, probes. They also thrived on the mountain air, the meals together, the walks, the evening drinks (where I developed a taste for Orzo) and the talk, always the talk. To break up the intensity of the week, we would take a day off to explore the mountains—hiking among the local walkers in their knickers, the goats and cows with their bells, and the flowers . . . everywhere glorious flowers.

As I think of these seminars, I think of them as epitomizing Hugh's legacy to us as philosophers. They also capture what he meant to me as a friend, for these seminars cultivated the friendship(s) of philosophy. They created the space for the intertwining of the personal and the philosophical. I think of the friends I met at these seminars, Ewa and Krzysztof Ziarek and Robin Schott, to name a few, and the friendships that were memorably deepened, and realize that this was Hugh's signature. The other organizations he created were larger and more flamboyant, but they were made of the same mold—bring people together, to keep the life of the mind embedded in the joys of the flesh. Surround provocative thinking with good food, good drink, and beautiful spaces, so that ideas remained alive and attached to persons, so that intellectual disagreements would not degenerate into polemical diatribes. Well, that at least was the idea. Some of the seminars were more successful than others. We are, after all, human all too human.

More than the occasion for remembering the Hugh Silverman of the IPS seminars, I found Derrida's *The Politics of Friendship* speaking of Hugh, of his thinking, of the way he created unique philosophical places, and of what he expected of himself and of us as philosophers. In writing about philosophy, friendship, and justice, I hear Derrida asking the questions that Hugh asked. I hear him asking whether we are up to the task of being a friend to Hugh.

Quoting Nietzsche, who in *Human All Too Human* writes, "Perhaps to each of us there will come the more joyful hour when we exclaim: 'Friends there are no friends!' thus said the dying sage; 'Foes there are no foes!' say I, the living fool," Derrida speaks of a friendship to come where "it is not enough to know how to bear the other in mourning; one must love the future," the possibilities for/of the future opened up by friendship.[1] Derrida speaks of this future as the yet to be determined that is created by the questioning we call philosophy.[2] He tells us that the question of friendship and the friend is nothing but the question of philosophy.[3] Friendship as philosophy, Derrida goes on to say, is love and respect and response to/for the other.[4] Noting that it is one thing to do justice to an argument and quite another to do justice to a friend, he asks whether it is possible to do justice to both—to justice and friendship, which, as I read it, is the question of whether it is possible to do justice to philosophy.

I write this in the hope of doing justice to my friendship for Hugh, the philosopher who was my friend, and in the belief that Hugh practiced philosophy in the pursuit of the possibility of friendship and justice. As a possibility, justice and friendship concerns the future. As the practice of philosophy, it concerns the present. So the question seems to come to this: How does the practice of philosophy today open the future to the promise of justice and friendship?; and to this: What is philosophy? Who is the philosopher? What sort of subject practices philosophy? Who/What is the subject of philosophy? As I read it, these questions lie at the heart of Hugh's 1994 work *Textualities*.

The What of Philosophy

Leaning on Merleau-Ponty to decipher the what of philosophy, Hugh charges the philosopher with the task of saying what is still to be said. By interrogating the silence that pervades the what is still to be said, the philosopher produces a discourse that gives voice to this silence and gives it a name (*T*, 205–6). A most puzzling definition of philosophy. More a conundrum than a description of a discipline. If the task of philosophy is to speak what is still to be said, how can it speak at all? How can philosophy speak without self-destructing? How can it break the silence of the yet to be said while preserving its undecidability?

Philosophy as it is often practiced may not like the answer. If Merleau-Ponty and Hugh are right, then in claiming to be the queen of the sciences entitled to speak of absolute, universal, and immutable truths, philosophy betrays itself. It evades the paradox of philosophy embedded in the task of philosophy: the charge to say what is still to be said. It risks becoming dogma. Eschewing the comfort of the discourse of absolutes, a discourse that claims to say everything there is to say, philosophy, remembering there is always more to be said, must embrace the speech that in speaking remains open to names of the yet to be spoken silence(s). In preserving this openness to the yet to be said, philosophy must also preserve the contingency of this yet to be said. It cannot sneak in ideas of universal and immutable truths through the back door of the temporality of progress. No absolute spirit can be invoked to guide the philosophical way to/through the silences of the future. As the more of the unsaid, philosophy disrupts the very idea of a teleological directive or direction.

It is no accident that the Merleau-Ponty who spoke of philosophy as speaking of the yet to be said was a philosopher of the epoché, for this more to be said is the more of the epoché. Like the epoché, it interrupts the assumptions that hold the givens of established truths in place and exposes these givens as obstacles to the work of philosophy. This epoché opens the future by probing the unsaid of the past. Thus Husserl retrieved Descartes to write his *Cartesian Meditations*, and Irigaray returned to Nietzsche as a lover.[5] Listening for the unsaid of its past, philosophy hears the yet to be said of its present. Doing this, it opens itself to the contingencies of a future that, lying on the horizon, has yet to speak. Being open in this way is what I think Aristotle meant when he described philosophy as being born in wonder. Today, living in the wake of the death of God, we are more apt to speak of this contingency in terms of anxiety. Part of the task of philosophy in our times, as I see it, is to preserve the Aristotelian and phenomenological sense of wonder in the face of these existential anxieties—to acknowledge these anxieties without allowing them to fuel a flight from the temporality of a discourse that lives on the border of the present and future.

The Who and Where of Philosophy

If disrupting the present in the name of the wonder of the future is the "what" of philosophy, who is the philosopher? What sort of person can speak in this way? Where can this speaker find a home? We, Hugh, I and his many philosopher friends, are housed in colleges and universities. We are employed by these institutions of higher learning to teach, to research, to write. Whether we are at home in there, however, is another question—a question that entails a series of questions. Is the practice of philosophy, the discipline that interrupts the given of the status quo, compatible with the culture of the established powers that contextualize the university and fund it, the state and private corporations? Is philosophy valued by the university and the institutions that support it because it teaches techniques of analysis and logical thinking, or because it cultivates the wonder that speaks of the "wildness of brute Being" (*T*, 207)? Can philosophy, given its task of opening the present to the critique of the future, a critique that includes an assessment of the values of the university, be retained as an employee in good standing?

These were Hugh's questions. Asking them, he turned to Nietzsche, who also found them a matter of/for concern. Today, the job of university assessment is given to technocrats. Nietzsche gave the job to philosophers. Echoing many of today's university's critics, he held that this assessment required an external tribunal. Following this logic to its conclusion, he found that, to do its work, philosophy would have to withdraw from the university. Given Nietzsche's logic, we ought to welcome today's defunding of the humanities and the threat it poses to their continued presence within the university. We do not. Though we—Hugh, many of our philosopher friends, and I—accept the idea that philosophy is in a unique position to remind the university of its mission, we do not follow Nietzsche in claiming that to do this work, philosophy must expel itself from campus. Faced with philosophy's precarious position within the university, we see its marginalization as a sign of the fact that the university is already losing its way. We fear that by finding philosophy in particular and the humanities in general peripheral to its mission, the university is on its way to becoming little more than a training ground for technocrats and entrepreneurs.

I suspect that there are many of you who, like me, have found yourselves sitting on committees charged with writing "mission of the university" statements—a pretty time-consuming and ultimately unsatisfying task that inevitably produces a "mother and apple pie" document that in saying many things says nothing close to Nietzsche's idea of the mission of the university as that of cultivating the person of culture and creating the genius. Surely this elitist version of the university has no place in a democratic society—or does it? It all depends on our concept of the genius. Without claiming that associating the ideas of genius and innate brilliance are totally ill founded, Simone de Beauvoir directs us to a concept of the genius that speaks to Nietzsche's idea of genius as a thing to be cultivated and allows us to see the ways that the questions of philosophy, the university, and genius were pieces of the same puzzle.

Responding to Stendhal's statement: "All the geniuses who are born *women* are lost for the public good," Beauvoir writes: "If truth be told, one is not born, but becomes a genius; and the feminine condition has, until now, rendered this becoming impossible."[6] Beauvoir, against common sense, insists that the appearance of a genius cannot be attributed to genes or DNA, but must be considered in terms of the possibilities of individuation offered by the infant's situation. As seen by Beauvoir, the genius is the one who is recognized by all as absolutely unique. The genius is the excellence of singularity. The difference, according to Beauvoir, between the situations of girl and boy children seen in terms of this possibility comes down to the fact that though neither the boy nor the girl is born a genius, the boy's situation, by inviting him to cultivate his singularity, makes it possible for him to become one. The girl's situation, by directing her to clothe herself in the myth of the eternal feminine, makes the becoming singular that is essential to becoming a genius impossible. Understood in terms of the famous line from *The Second Sex*, "One is not born (a) woman but becomes one," the scarcity of women geniuses reflects the fact that the becoming of a woman is a process whereby the singularity of the subject is erased as the myth of femininity takes hold. Directed to embody the idea of the eternal feminine, the girl, whatever her IQ and DNA, cannot become a genius. The boy, subjected to the process of becoming a man, on the other hand, is invited to individuate himself and with this invitation in hand can become a genius (which does not necessarily mean that he will).

Taking this idea of the genius to the genius-university-philosophy puzzle, the question is this: can the cultivation of the genius, the one who according to Beauvoir embodies singularity, and who according to Nietzsche has learned to think, where learning to think means identifying the limits of one's culture and its values and seeing what needs to be done (*T*, 197), be the goal of the university, an institution intended to serve the state and its economic structures? It depends of course on what sort of state we are talking about. It seems to me that linking the idea of genius to the independent thinker whose singularity is cultivated by the conditions of his or her life, rather than thinking of the genius who by virtue of genes or DNA stands above us, allows us as philosophers to perform the task of critiquing the university while remaining on campus. As members of the university, we are in a position to see whether or not it provides the conditions for the becoming of the genius. We are also in a position to protest those university prejudices that thwart students in their quest for singularity. Advocating the fostering of genius in this sense is also a matter of justice, for by acknowledging that the singularity of the subject is a matter of nurturing the conditions of its life, not a matter of social privilege or birth, the university, as charged with creating, supporting, and sustaining these conditions, opens the social contract of the democratic tradition to the future of its unfinished business.

In traveling with Nietzsche in seeing the philosopher as the person of culture who can see what needs to be done but departing from the idea that cultivating the sort of thinking that characterizes the genius exiles philosophy from the university, Hugh rejects this inside-outside model of thinking. He advocates a thinking that speaks of porous margins, permeable boundaries, and open bridges to invoke the idea of a marginal philosophy. (Re)envisioning philosophy in this way, Hugh speaks of/to the ways that we, as teachers, readers, writers, and critics who are living within the culture of the state and the university, are responsible for making sense of these cultures, for identifying their complimentary and competing values, and for creating dialogues between them (*T*, 203).

Hugh's description of the philosopher as the one who works on the margins is what we would now call a "selfie," a self-portrait, a description of how he saw himself. It allows us to understand why he devoted so much time and energy to creating organizations, conferences, workshops, and seminars both inside and outside the university where marginal philosophy was welcomed, where marginal philosophers were supported, and where paths between philosophy and the university were cleared.

For the Love of Language and Justice

As Hugh turned to Merleau-Ponty to pose the question "What is philosophy?" and to Nietzsche to confront the danger of the university co-opting the values of philosophy, he looked to Kristeva to address the problematic relationship between philosophy and language and to fill out the portrait of the philosopher. Hugh opens chapter 16 of *Textualities*, "The Text of the Speaking Subject Merleau-Ponty/ Kristeva," with the following words: "[T]he speaking subject is embedded in a difference between the semiotic and the symbolic or between indirect language and a pure language" (*T*, 175). As Hugh walks the bridges and moves through the margins of the very different philosophical approaches of Julia Kristeva and Maurice Merleau-Ponty, we find that more is at stake than a matter of discerning the ways that Kristeva's account of the semiotic-symbolic relationship speaks to and of Merleau-Ponty's discussions of *le langage parlé* and *le langage parlant*. In turning to Kristeva, Hugh looks to the analyst to assuage the anxieties aroused by Merleau-Ponty's fear that in the end established language will dominate our discourse (*T*, 180).

According to Hugh, though both Kristeva and Merleau-Ponty spoke of language in terms of its function of expressing the established meanings of things and its role in creating new meanings of the world, they saw this duality of language differently. For Merleau-Ponty, *le langage parlant*, the language that interrupts establishment language—that breaks the boundaries of its conventions—is at war with *le langage parlé* (*T*, 179). Fearing that the linguistic forces of creativity were not up to the fight, Merleau-Ponty turned to other modes of expression—painting in particular—to bring the unsaid into our lives. Hugh loved language—the language of philosophy—the language of literature. He believed in its creative powers. And this, I think, is why he put Merleau-Ponty on Kristeva's couch. Where Merleau-Ponty turned to painting to contest the sedimentations of language, Kristeva looks to poetic language, the voice of the semiotic, to disrupt the assertive, definitive symbolic voice of language. Because she frames the relationship between the semiotic and the symbolic in terms of a relationship between an energy source and its structured effects, Kristeva sees this semiotic source as inseparable from the desire that propels the symbolic's speech. She does not give the symbolic the power either to absorb the semiotic into itself or to destroy it, for in doing this the symbolic would self-destruct. As the source of the symbolic, the interruptions of the semiotic keep it alive.

Whether Kristeva's assurances can calm Merleau-Ponty's and Hugh's worries, whether the structures of the symbolic will remain margins through which the semiotic will pass or whether they will become barriers to *le langage parlant*, I cannot say. What I can say, however, is that it is not just the issue of language that is at stake. Given that we live in language, what is at stake is the matter of the subject. Given that philosophy is charged with saying the unsaid and the yet to be said, it is the matter of philosophy. The matter of justice is also in play, for unless our political culture endorses the cultivation of the singularity called genius, unless it can hear the interruptions of the given that challenge vested interests, its democratic values will be undermined. Thus the philosophic and analytic matter of keeping the margins of the symbolic open to the semiotic is also, and perhaps essentially, a matter of cultivating those on the political margins so that they can establish themselves as singularities entitled to speak and to interrupt the politics of exclusion that infects today's democracies.

If Hugh needs Kristeva to quell his and Merleau-Ponty's fears regarding the life of *le langage parlant*, we also need her, I think, to save the idea of singularity from coagulating into the idea of the self-same autonomous insulated subject. We need her to remind us that the subject can be open to the otherness of the yet to be said only if it is open to the otherness it harbors within itself. For Kristeva, the subject is embedded in the difference between the semiotic and the symbolic. It exists in their margins. As the symbolic is interrupted by the semiotic, the subject is destabilized by its otherness. The movement of language puts the subject in motion. The singularity of the subject is a process, not a substance. It is charged with accepting its other within and in this sense is also and necessarily a subject on trial—a political subject, not a solipsistic one.

This trial became public, according to Kristeva, in the events of May 1968. Speaking of May 1968, she writes:

> It expresses a fundamental version of freedom . . . freedom to revolt, to call things into question . . . liberty-as-revolt isn't just an available option, it's fundamental . . . The telling moment in an individual's psychic life, as in the life of societies at large, is when you call into question laws, norms and values . . . Because it's precisely by putting things into question that "values" stop being frozen dividends and acquire a sense of mobility, polyvalence and life . . . May

> 1968 [. . . was] a desire to come up with new, perpetually contestable configurations.[7]

I read this politics of the freedom to revolt as the politics of the semiotic interruption. The protests of May 1968 are the street scene of the poetic. Here the disruptive energies of poetic language take the form of revolutionary questioning. Calling this questioning a political right that is essential to freedom and seeing this right as expressed in the phrase "I revolt therefore we are . . . still to come" (*RSS*, 44), Kristeva puts the philosopher (or at least Hugh's philosopher of the margins) who is charged with saying what is yet to be said at the center of this politics of justice.

What is especially significant, I think, in Kristeva's translation of her logic of language into the politics of revolt is the way the symbolic's tendency to ossify, its threat to the justice of revolt, is also essential to this justice, for the symbolic as the representation of the law is an essential reference point for the person and the polis (*RSS*, 32). In Kristeva's words:

> There is no revolt without prohibition of some sort . . . the intra-psychic limit and prohibition are the indispensable conditions for living and for the life of language and thought; the codes of modern democracies can only seek out the optimal social variants of these so they can protect us from aggressive drives and yet ensure their creative exercise all the same. (*RSS*, 31)

The contestation is there, but necessary "to achieve private jouissance, not 'in private' nor even away from the world . . . but in the public domain, extended from the family, to society, to the nation, while demanding that it make itself receptive to the right to singular and absolute jouissance" (*RSS*, 35).

That May 1968 began with students suggests that the university, or at least a French university at that time, succeeded in the way that Hugh wanted it to. As subjects in process and on trial, these students insisted on their singularity, their genius, their right to activate the yet to be said of a we whose law rejects the homogeneity of the second-person plural for the plurality of the first-person differences that make the we of philosophy, friendship, and justice possible.

Notes

1. Jacques Derrida, *The Politics of Friendship*, trans. George Collins (London: Verso, 1997), 28–29.

2. Ibid., 38.

3. Ibid., 240.

4. Ibid., 252.

5. Luce Irigaray, *Marine Lover of Friedrich Nietzsche*, trans. Gillian C. Gill (New York: Columbia University Press, 1991).

6. Simone de Beauvoir, *The Second* Sex, trans. Constance Borde and Sheila Malovany-Chevallier (New York: Alfred A. Knopf, 2010), 152.

7. Julia Kristeva, *Revolt She Said*, trans. Brian O'Keeffe (New York: Semiotext(e), 2002), 12. Henceforth cited as *RSS*.

7

Return to Sender

The Atopia and Non-Synchronicity of Autobiographizing

Eduardo Mendieta

> *Moi, je* ~ Myself, I
>
> Here is a series of outdated propositions (if they were not contradictory): *I would be nothing if I didn't write. Yet I am elsewhere than where I am when I write. I am worth more than what I write.*
>
> —Roland Barthes[1]

Introduction

Hugh J. Silverman was a great reader of Jacques Derrida as well as an indefatigable promoter of deconstruction, that Derridean undisciplined and undisciplining practice. More than a postmodern, Silverman was a deconstructivist, if by deconstruction we understand the practice of rereading the writing that makes up metaphysics. Metaphysics is a sediment of writing and deconstruction sifts through all the detritus left behind by all genres of writing. Writing is never one, but plural, and so are its sedimentations, its cinders, to use one of Derrida's favorite words. Still, as Silverman noted in several places, metaphysics is written in and through the practice of writing the self. The self is implicated in metaphysics, and thus the task of deconstruction is to also—or perhaps most primordially—dismantle the metaphysics of the self. It could be asked: which is the shadow of the other: metaphysics or the self? The so-called "death of the author" does not announce the death of the writer, but the death of a certain notion that the authorial self preexists the text, or a text, that purportedly becomes an alibi to some sovereign subject that, as it were, stands before, behind, in front of its text. The text exists, therefore the author is. Or, more accurately: the author exists and therefore texts can be. This seems to invert a deconstructionist version of the Cartesian motto of modern metaphysics: *cogito ergo sum* had become "I write, therefore I am." Before there is cogitation, there is writing. The arché of all self-hood is this practice of writing. For Silverman, however, the arché of writing that writes the self is what he calls "auto-bio-graphizing," that is, the autographing of the self, the writing of one's life. Part 3 of Silverman's *Textualities: Between Hermeneutics and Deconstruction* is titled "Autobiographical Textualities." This section is made up of five short, incisive, suggestive, but also poignant readings of some classical biographical texts, predominantly by philosophers. Silverman discusses Henry David Thoreau's *Walden*, Friedrich Nietzsche's *Ecce Homo*, Sartre's *The Words*, Roland Barthes's *Barthes by Barthes*, and most interestingly, the exchange between Martin Heidegger and Mayer Shapiro via a reading of Derrida's own reading of the exchange. For Silverman, the genre of the autobiography offers the exemplar par excellence of the primacy of textuality. "Auto-bio-graphizing is the writing of the self as text" (*T*, 90). The self thus is a text, full of textualities. As such, it is always already decentered. Or, to put it more precisely, as he does in his earlier work, *Inscriptions: Between Phenomenology and Structuralism*, "Self-decentering is the elaboration of identity throughout a play of *differances*. The self is dispersed and disseminated in writing, specifically what Derrida calls 'arché-writing'" (*I*, 294). Thus, precisely because the self is written as a text, the self is the trace of an autobiography that we either tell ourselves, when we give an account of ourselves, or write ourselves so as to remember how it is that we have become whom we have become. This very writerly constitution of the self entails that it is always a self-decentering. In writing ourselves, we self-decenter. The textual weaving of the self is at the same time its unweaving. Writing oneself through and in a biographical text, however, is part of a genre that remains without borders, sovereignty, or particular generic shape. Silverman makes a series of observations, which merits extensive citation:

> Autobiographical textuality is a *topos* in that it describes a unique topic and a place in the scheme of things. More specifically, autobiography involves a *topos* because it forms a type of discourse with an apparent space all of its own. Writing the self as text has its own features just like other *topoi*, such as architecture, metaphysics, the body, political economy, etc. Yet under closer scrutiny, it becomes evident that autobiography as a genre is situated at the limits of discursive spaces and that it does not have a distinctive space of its own. This should not imply that autobiography is a counter-*topos*, an anti-discursive space, for a counter-*topos* or an anti-discursive-space would already be a sort of *topos*. (*T*, 90)

Here we find some generative provocations. The autobiographical text is a *topos*, the locus of the inscription of a self. The self, as it were, is held together, if tenuously, between the covers of the text. And, perhaps, the mirage of the consistency of the self is the very materiality of that textuality. The authorial and putatively sovereign self finds itself held together by narrative that has a discrete spatiality. But Silverman immediately notes that this *topos* is situated at the "limits of discursive spaces." Autobiographizing inscribes a *topos* at the very edge of discursive space, and, one should add, the limits of textuality as such. Then a second qualification is added: but as a *topos* at the limits of discursive space, autobiographizing is neither a counter-*topos* nor an anti-discursive space. If, however, the *topos* of the autobiographical textuality is at the limits, at the edge, at the very border of all and any discursive space, then it can operate as if from without to disrupt and rupture the very borders and limits of discursive space. An autobiography can also disrupt and rupture these very borders from within by overflowing the established discursive limits. In other words, as a *topos* at the limits of discursitivity and textuality, auto-biographizing is both the generation of counter-*topoi* and anti-discursive spaces. This is in fact what is already entailed in the formulation we find in Silverman's earlier book, *Inscriptions*, namely that the "self is dispersed and disseminated in writing" (*I*, 294). Auto-bio-graphizing is this very self-decentering. Here we are neither contradicting nor refuting Silverman. We are uncoiling what is coiled in his very analysis. Thus far, then, the question of the *topos* of the self, the place of the self, the darkness at the base of the lighthouse of the self is projected by the textuality of the autobiographical text.

Silverman, like Derrida, was mesmerized by the heterogeneity of autobiographical texts, and by this is not meant that there are as many types of autobiographies as there are different types of selves. The autobiographical text is anarchic, not simply because each iteration is sui generis, but also because the self can decide to write its autobiography in different ways. This way, or ways, is part of the exercise of writing the self. The autobiographical text is a *topos* made of many *topoi*, or rather, each one of its iterations generates a differential *topoi*. This is another way to read the claim that the autobiographical genre is a *topos* at the limit and of the limit. Silverman, however, takes up, beyond space, the *topos* of the self. He also takes us past space to time, the *chronos* of the self. The self is a temporal textuality. As a textuality, it has its own time, it generates times. Silverman approaches the temporal textuality of autobiographizing by way of a meditation on Claude Levi-Strauss's *Tristes tropiques*, a quasi-autobiographical text, a memoir cum autobiography of the anthropologist who unlearns his profession. Like Thoreau's *Walden* and Nietzsche's *Ecce Homo*, Levi-Strauss's memoir/travelogue/diary/autobiography is anarchical. It is the writing of the self through disruptive acts of self-ironizing. Read against Nietzsche's pseudo-autobiography with its future perfect, Levi-Strauss's text allows Silverman to thematize the question of the time of the self, the will have already become, the going to become what we will have become. Silverman writes:

> Instead of simply marking time in the autobiographical text, autobiographical temporality re-marks or re-formulates lived time in one of many possible ways. The time as actually lived by the autobiographer is written as remembered/imagined. The remembering/imagining is a re-formulating as text . . . There are many ways to narrate one's own lived time. (*T*, 121)

Auto-bio-graphizing, then, is a chronotopological practice. It is the writing of a topos, but also the generation of a certain temporality. Indeed, to write one's life is a way to give time, to hold the self in time, to mold the self by shaping a narrative within a certain temporal matrix. Writing the self takes time and gives time. The autobiography as a temporalizing practice is also a practice of temporalizing as such. If we follow Heidegger, we can say that *Dasein* is the extending out into the nothing of time. *Dasein* is its freedom because it is thrown-projection, but this is saying nothing else than *Dasein* is distended between its past and its future. Being a self, then, is this making time, marking time, giving time. Insofar, however, as writing the self is the practice of marking time, then becoming who one has become, is nothing but marking time in a sui generis way. How we temporalize our autobiography is the sine qua non of auto-bio-graphizing. Silverman puts it thusly: "As a feature of autobiographical textuality, autobiographical temporality sets the particular way in which the positions of markings of time are ordered or structured. It provides the manner and design in which the various temporal marks are related to each other" (*T*, 124). Here, one must ask, to parallel the qualification concerning the *topos* of autobiographical textualities, whether in the autobiographical genre there is not something like a counter-temporality, an achronology, that disrupts all attempts at providing docile and legible temporal markings? Indeed, such a qualification, or specification, is inchoate in Silverman's analysis of both Thoreau's and Levi-Strauss's autobiographizing texts. In fact, Barthes's *Roland Barthes* exemplifies one way to disrupt the linear temporality that is generally associated with the autobiographical narrative, with its predictable temporal vector. Hitherto, then, the counter-temporality and achronology of the written self. By this, however, I mean to foreground that the practice of auto-bio-graphizing is at its core a non-synchronizing practice. The self writes itself, and in so doing, it is always either already ahead of itself or always catching up to itself. To write one's auto-bio-graphy is to render oneself non-synchronous with oneself. Autobiographizing is a practice of *untimeliness* (*Unzeitgemässelichkeit*). What this reveals is that the self is aporetic, always already in the process of self-decentering, as Silverman made clear, because it is always already *untimely*.

In this essay I would like to weave some of what Silverman wrote on autobiographizing with some of what Derrida wrote on *envois*, on letters, on postcards, on posts, on sending and the hope that it will be delivered, on the threat that everything that is a sending does not ever have a guarantee of delivery. I want to bring together Silverman's *Textualities* with Derrida's *The Post Card: From Socrates to Freud and Beyond*, in order to invite us to reflect on the inter-textuality of the biographical genre and the epistolary genre.[2] These two genres are quite close, so close as to be incestuous. An autobiography is a type of letter, and letters are forms of autobiographizing. Many autobiographies in fact quote from letters that were written by the author, and letters may be used as alibis, as witnesses, in verifying the authenticity and accuracy of an autobiography. Letters are gifts of friendship, but they are also ways in which a self both gives an account of itself and renders itself vulnerable to a future court of appeal. They are moments of exposure and vulnerability; so is autobiographizing. I am interested in the in-between textuality of the autobiography that is a letter and the letter that becomes integral to auto-bio-graphizing.

Lost Mail: Derrida's Envois

It could be said that all of Derrida's texts are *envois*, sendings that he hoped would find their appropriate addressee. He wrote sanguinely without the alibi of secured delivery. All his texts traveled haunted by the postal threat of "return to sender." Derrida wrote for all and no one, for readers who do not yet exist and for those who read him faithfully and yet still found themselves challenged to have to learn to read him anew. He created new readers and remade those who had settled in their reading and writing habits. Silverman was one of those readers and writers. While Silverman cites Derrida's *The Post Card* at least twice in *Textualities*, it is interesting that he does not do so in the section on "Autobiographical Textualities." We may think of this as a missed opportunity, but one that we can still take up on his behalf, with him in his absence. I thus want to briefly reflect on "Envois," which makes up half of *The Post Card*, before I turn to some important letters, about which Derrida writes extensively in this text.

The Post Card is made up of four sections: "Envois: To Speculate—on 'Freud'"; "Le facteur de la vérité"; and "Du tout." The longest section of the "book" is made up of "Envois." Alan Bass's "translator's introduction," which carries the playful but evidently intertextual subtitle of "L before K," has a section titled "glossary." There we find a richness of references, cross-references, allusions, connotations, echoes, etymologies, homonyms, and homologies. Thus, we read: "*envois, envoyer: envoyer*, to send, is derived from the Latin *inviare*, to send on the way . . . Every possible play on *envoi* and *envoyer* is exploited throughout. For example, the English 'invoice,' meaning bill of sale, is actually derived from *envoi* (and *inviare*), thus linking the senses of sending, message, and debt" (*PC*, xx–xxi). Envois, however, occupies a very peculiar place in this book that allegedly Derrida has "not written" (*PC*, 3). The "Envois" part of the *Post Card*, we are told, might be read as the "preface" of a book that was not written. This is what "Jacques Derrida" writes in the "preface" to "Envois," which is indeed signed by him. Every letter, every postcard is putatively signed by its author. Its very existence as a sending, as a text sent to someone by someone, is itself an avowal. To send a letter is to step onto an authorial pedestal, the witness stand, the place before those who would call us to give an account of what we sent: "Did you not write this on such and such date, and mailed it to so and so?" For all of us who write, we hear in these words an interrogation we too may one day be forced to undergo. Are we not all some Kafkian despondent juridical subject?

Note, however, that pages 3 to 6, the unnamed preface to "Envois," end with a footnote in which "Jacques Derrida" addresses the suspicion that his very signature invites:

> I regret that you [*tu*] do not very much trust my signature, on the pretext that we might be several. This is true, but I am not saying so in order to make myself more important by means of some supplementary authority. And even less in order to disquiet, I know what this costs. You are right, doubtless we are several, and I am not as alone as I sometimes say I am when the complaint escapes from me, or when I still put everything into seducing you. (*PC*, 6, n. 1)

Doubtless, Silverman would interject and note that this "we might be several," and "we are several" is a reference to the self-decentering subject/agent. Note also that the back cover of the book carries a text, signed "J. D.," which is not inside the text. This is the kind of text an author writes for the editor, which generally asks for a "description of the book." In this text, which is not part of the book, but which describes it, and which allegedly was written by J. D., we find two interesting statements. The first one reads:

> You were reading a somewhat retro loveletter, the last in history. But you have not yet received it. Yes, its lack or excess of address prepares it to fall into all hands: a post card, an open letter in which the secret appears, but indecipherably. You can take it or pass it off, for example, as a message from Socrates to Freud. (*PC*, back cover)

This claim is interesting because now "Envois" seems to have engulfed the entire book. The whole book is itself a "retro loveletter." But can we be sure what a "retro loveletter" is? Are not in fact all books retro loveletters, gifts of friendship that we hope will be delivered and received, if not with gratitude, at least not with scorn and neglect? Still, here "J. D." does not simply tell us that we "may" read this text this or that way. We are in fact told what it is that we are reading. We are reading a "retro loveletter."

The second interesting statement we find in the "blurb" by "J. D." on the back cover of the American edition of the *Post Card* reads:

> You situate the subject of the book: between the posts and the analytic movement, the pleasure principle and the history of telecommunications, the post card and the purloined letter, in a word the transference from Socrates to Freud, and beyond. This satire of epistolary literature had to be farci, stuffed with addresses, postal codes, crypted missives, anonymous letters, all of it confided to so many modes, genres, and tones. In it I also abuse dates, signatures, titles or references, language itself. (*PC*, back cover)

Here it is declared that, indeed, we are reading a book, one that is written, held together between two covers, made up of 4 parts, 521 pages in the University of Chicago Press English edition. Is this the book that that Derrida claims he did not write, in the preface to Envois, or is this a different book, the product of a different authorial plan? Note also that in this back cover blurb it is claimed that "[t]his [is a] satire of epistolary literature . . ." "Envois" seems to have become the metonym for the entirety of *The Post Card*. For "Envois" is indeed more like a parody than a satire, as I try to illustrate briefly. The word "farci" here is also noteworthy, as we are also invited to think of farce, or the farcical, as something that borders on the absurd and preposterous. In fact, we are in the thicket of a Borgesian textuality: a book that was not written, but that we are holding, that has a preface, that is itself prefaced, that has a blurb that tells us how to read the book, that was not written, in which we are also told that the whole thing is a satire and perhaps even a farce.

If we turn now to the "Envois" themselves, we discover that this section of the book is made up of letters that are dated, beginning with June 3, 1977, and ending with August 30, 1979. The signed, untitled "preface" is dated September 7, 1979, while the back cover blurb is dated November 17, 1979. A minimally judicious reading of "Envois" is beyond the reaches of the present text. But aren't all texts insufficient to their task?—we can almost hear Silverman echoing Derrida. Here I can only refer the reader to Gregory L. Ulmer's extremely useful and insightful review essay in *Diacritics:* "The Post-Age."[3] Still, I want to foreground some themes, or unique characteristic of the text, as a way to underscore the theme of the inter-textuality of letters and autobiographies. First, these "fictitious" or "farcical" letters, which are in fact not signed, nonetheless are from "Derrida." Derrida is inscribed in them not simply because of what he reveals about himself, as the author of the letters, but also because throughout them there are references to Derrida's friends, his travels, his readings, his seminars. These letters could have been written by Derrida to a "real" addressee. They are marked by verisimilitude. In fact, one could engage in an exercise in which one tries to match Derrida's real-life itinerary between the years 1977 and 1979 and the events, travels, conversations, readings, and so forth that are described in the letters. The real question, however, beyond whether we can actually corroborate their biographical accuracy, is: To what extent are we not always fictionalizing ourselves when we write a letter to a friend or lover? A second theme that is related to this "fictionalizing" of ourselves in one of the most intimate of texts we can write is that "Derrida" is not only continuously writing these "letters," these "posts," but that they are either preceded or followed by a phone call. The "live voice" is not enough to communicate: speech is either insufficient or not detailed enough for the purposes of communication. The "posts" expand on phone conversations or anticipate a theme to be discussed on the "phone." Between the postcard and the phone call, which one is more the theater of the self, the stage for the performance of some affective work: love, honesty, friendship, gratitude, contrition, or forgiveness? In fact, these "satirical" letters are relentlessly returning to the theme of love: of declaring one's love, of affirming it, of being held hostage by it, of suffering it, or of never been sure that it has been acknowledged. All love is always deferred. It is the work of *différance*. Love is also predicated on holding back something, or at least on not being able to reveal all. All love has a secret—it is a secret. The theme of the secret in love appears in "Envois" in the figure of a letter that gets temporally lost because its address was truncated. The letter, which revealed a secret, and which carried a confession, was not delivered. It was temporally lost, until it got returned to "J. D.," who did not open the envelope. This "lost in the mail" letter in fact becomes the synecdoche for all secrets that became a liability, as grounds for an extortion or exposure. In fact, we are told in the unnamed "preface" that there are "passages" that are missing from these "envois," perhaps because they were burned, that nonetheless are marked by a "blank of 52 signs"—which, incidentally, only is marked right between the "preface" and the first letter of June 3, 1977.

The two other themes on which I want to briefly focus are related. Many of the letters deal with a postcard that Derrida discovers, allegedly at the Bodleian Library (which is the famous main research library at Oxford). The postcard is on the cover of the University of Chicago Press edition of the translation. My edition of the book, in fact, has two additional reproductions of the postcard. On page 251, there is small reproduction of the postcard in color. We can see that it used to be colored: the green tint or shadow of the edges has faded slightly, but one can see that the names "Socrates" and "plato" were written with red ink. The second reproduction appears as a flyleaf in the very back of the book. There it is reproduced in black and white. I hazard to postulate that this additional reproduction is made to size. It is approximately twice as big as the one on page 251 and occupies three-quarters of a page. It is unfortunate that the image on the cover of the book could not have been done in color. In any event, the image is the front piece to a fortune-telling book from the thirteenth century by Matthew Paris, which was titled *Prognostica Socratis basilei*. The image portrays a bearded man, wearing a pointed hat, seated at a desk, ambidextrously writing; or, at least, one hand seems to be writing, while another is dipping a writing tool in an inkwell. Over this image is written "Socrates." The first letter is capitalized. Behind this man, another one, wearing a cap rather than a hat, is stepping up on the back edge of the desk. With one hand, this smaller man is either scratching or trying to catch the attention of the man labeled "Socrates." With the other hand, the man is pointing at something, or in a direction. The index finger is raised in an upward direction. This man with his raised index finger is labeled "plato." The "p" is lowercase. "Envois" repeatedly returns to this haunting image: Socrates writing, Plato gesticulating from behind, as if to indicate to him what to write, or about what to write. This inverts the chronology of the canon: first Socrates, then Plato, but we know the first because the second wrote what the other allegedly said. Who wrote whom, this picture seems to be asking. Who came first? In a nontrivial sense Plato came first, in writing and in history, although temporally, he came second. But Socrates came first because he sent Plato on the task of writing. Who is greater, or has greater stature? This image seems to suggest that Socrates is the taller, and thus more important, and Plato a smaller and thus lesser figure. But would Socrates have become the father of "Western" philosophy without Plato's paternity? Or is Plato the lesser figure because his philosophical system betrayed Socrates's teaching? In many ways, "Envois" is an extended epistolary engagement with this arresting image.

Incidentally, there is a picture that replicates the interaction in Paris's image in Geoffrey Bennington and Derrida's book *Jacques Derrida.*[4] On page 11 there is a picture of Derrida, seated, with his hands over a keyboard typing. He is looking at a computer screen—what appears to be an old Mac. Bennington is standing behind him, one hand resting over the back of the chair on which Derrida is sitting. His left hand is pointing at something on the computer screen. The caption under the picture reads: "Post Card or *tableau vivant*: with Geoffrey Bennington at Ris Orangis, during the preparation of these pictures—and of this book, 'a hidden pretext for writing in my own signature behind his back'" (*Derridabase*, 316).[5] *Derridabase* is the title of Bennington's text, which makes up the upper part of the pages of *Jacques Derrida*, while the lower part of the pages of the book are taken up by Derrida's *Circumfession*. If we turn to page 316 of *Derridabase*, there we find a section titled "Envoi." Here Bennington provides us with an explanation of what method he has followed to present the "essential features of Derrida's thought."[6] In any event, the sentence that is quoted in the caption of the picture on page 11 reads fully: "This is why this book will be of no use to you others, or to you, other, and will have been only a hidden pretext for writing in my own signature behind his back."[7] Bennington, at the end of his book, tells us that what we have just read has been of no use to us, the reader, the other, who would have read this book, hoping to understand Derrida. This book in fact turns out to have been but the indulgence of Bennington to write in his own name, behind Derrida's back, which here can only mean following behind Derrida, standing behind his back, signaling at a screen that is now a page in Bennington/Derrida's book. If this reading is not persuasive enough, let me then turn again to the picture on page 11. Upon closer inspection of the picture, we can see in the foreground of the picture a stock of books, and leaning against it facing the viewer is the arresting image from Paris's book of Socratic divination. The photograph quotes the image that is at the center of "Envois" in *The Post Card*. The photograph, evidently, was posed and orchestrated. Socrates/plato; Bennington/derrida. Who is the author? Who writes whom? Who is the disciple, and who is the teacher? Is Derrida's relation to Bennington analogous to the relation between Socrates and Plato? One last question before we move on to the second related theme: who wrote the caption on page 11? Does it belong to Bennington's *Derridabase* or to Derrida's *Circumfession*? What comes after the colon may give us a clue: "with Geoffrey Bennington at Ris Orangis . . ."

The second theme that I now want to foreground is closely related. "Envois" also gravitates around the question/problem of Plato's letters. One of the longest "posts" in "Envois" is made up of an extended discussion, circumlocution, meditation, and reflection on Plato's epistolary corpus. Derrida discusses the French and German reception of the letters and the scholarship that over centuries has debated their authenticity and usefulness. The entry for September 9, 1977, runs from page 78 to page 91. In this post we find the following statement:

> These letters of "Plato," that Socrates, of course, would have neither read nor written, I now find them greater than the works. I would like to call you to read you out loud several extracts from the "stands" they have mandated, commanded, programmed for centuries (as I would like to use them for my *legs*. I am typing them, or rather one day you will return this letter to me). (*PC*, 85)

Did Derrida ever think that Plato's letters, of which he knew two or three at most, were judged authentic, were greater than the Platonic works? As the "Envois" elaborates: letters are the *topos* for both the presentation, the writing of oneself, and the dissimulation, the concealment, of that very self. Derrida, however, focuses on the famous, longest, and most provocative, seventh letter, in which we find Plato giving us both an (auto)biography and a key to why he wrote and took up the vocation of the philosopher. Derrida, however, foregrounds how these Platonic letters belong to the genre of *principum specula* or "mirror for princes," which arguably goes back to Isocrates (436–338 BC), and which found its most paradigmatic exemplars in Machiavelli's and Eramus's texts. But what I want us to take from Derrida's extended reflection on Plato's letters is that he is urging us to read them intertextually with Plato's other works. These letters, whether penned by Plato or not, occupy a unique atopic or heterotopic place in the Platonic corpus: they were meant for a certain public, and they aim to give an apologia for Plato's travels to Syracuse and his eventual disenchantment with his attempts at being a king's philosopher. Like Derrida's posts in "Envois," Plato's letters help us weave an auto-biographical textuality that exceeds the boundaries of autobiography and the epistolary craft.

I write (to) You, You write (to) Me

In this text I have wanted to weave a textuality that reads Silverman with Derrida on the question of letters, autobiographies, and friendship. I sought to throw some light on the in-between textuality that emerges between letters that contribute to the writing of the self and the auto-bio-graphizing that can be read as a type of letter—a letter to a future self, to other future others. In problematizing the in-between textuality of letters/autobiographizing, I have also problematized what calls for philosophy and can be called philosophy. To close, but without concluding, I want to return to Hugh J. Silverman's text. Toward the end of the wonderful chapter on Sartre and Barthes, in the section titled "Autobiographical Textualities," Silverman writes:

> Autobiographizing is an interface activity whose condition as pure limit is situated between the non-space of atopia and the ideal space of utopia. This autobiographical *topos*

> is the inscription of a self at the juncture between reading and writing—in Barthes as well as Sartre. (*T*, 132)

To expand on this point, Silverman then quotes Barthes from *Roland Barthes*, the entry titled "*L'atopie* ~ Atopia":

> Pigeonholed: I am pigeonholed, assigned to an (intellectual) site, to residence in a caste (if not in a class). Against which there is only one internal doctrine: that *atopia* (of a drifting habitation). Atopia is superior to utopia (utopia is reactive, tactical, literary, it proceeds from meaning and governs it). (*T*, 132–33)[8]

Let me linger over the parenthetical remark "of a drifting habitation"—against being sequestered and pigeonholed within a doctrine or a caste or a class, there is the doctrine of atopia, which here is described as a "habitation"—a habitat. Habitats, which we inhabit, are results of habits. Thus utopia is a habit, a habituation, a way of inhabiting ourselves while drifting, while resisting the reactive, meaning, and literary rule of the stable and legible—law of the sovereign. Silverman closes his chapter this way: "Autobiographizing is writing a space which cannot be a space: it must remain active as it moves close to its self-defining limits at the self-inscription of Sartre and Barthes" (*T*, 133). This space that cannot be a space is in fact an inter-textual space that is negotiated among friends through the gift of their letters and their posts to future friends. Philosophy is the practice of making friends who are yet to be born, and we draw them into the circle of the intimacy of our thought through our (love) letters and our auto-bio-graphizing.

Notes

1. Roland Barthes, *Roland Barthes*, trans. Richard Howard (New York: Hill and Wang, 1977), 168, 169.

2. Jacques Derrida, *The Post Card: From Socrates to Freud and Beyond*, trans. Alan Bass (Chicago: University of Chicago Press, 1987). Henceforth cited as *PC*.

3. Gregory L. Ulmer, "The Post-Age," *Diacritics* 11, no. 3 (Autumn 1981): 39–56.

4. Jacques Derrida and Geoffrey Bennington, *Jacques Derrida*, trans. Geoffrey Bennington (Chicago: University of Chicago Press, 1993).

5. Ibid., 11.

6. Ibid., 316.

7. Ibid.

8. Barthes, *Roland Barthes*, 49.

Part 3

Postmodern Heroes, Subjects, and Responsibilities

8

The Space-in-Between

The Frame and Excess in the Thought of Hugh J. Silverman

Leonard Lawlor

I would like to begin with a quotation from Professor Silverman from his 1994 book, *Textualities*:

> Dying makes remembering possible. Remembering another is retrieving the other from obscurity, making the other live again—in memory. Marking that memory not only with a memorial, a tombstone, an epitaph, an obituary, a biography, a testimonial, a recollection, or a prayer but also with a reinscription of the line of difference between living and dying as the line of difference between dying and remembering. (*T*, 220)

I had forgotten so much. I had forgotten that so many of Hugh Silverman's essays consist of carefully and precisely constructed comparisons of so many diverse *philosophical* figures: Nietzsche, Husserl, Heidegger, Gadamer, Saussure, Sartre, Merleau-Ponty, Barthes, Lacan, Lévi-Strauss, Foucault, Derrida, Lyotard, Kristeva, and Nancy. And, among these diverse philosophical figures, we find in his essays just as many references to and descriptions of works of *non-philosophy*: novels, poems, paintings, and especially films. Even though I heard Professor Silverman speak countless times, I had forgotten the style of his writing. The essays always start with questions: "What time is it in New York" (*T*, 210) or "What is writing on writing" (*T*, 183)? Or the essays begin with definitions such as "the philosophical text presents itself as a monument" (*T*, 151) or "autobiographical textuality elaborates the autobiographical features . . . of a text" (*T*, 89)—but these definitions, not being self-explanatory, amount to disguised questions. The same for the essays' endings: making assertions that seem to answer the questions posed at the beginning, the endings pose as classical conclusions. However, calling for more explanation, these answers are, once again, disguised questions. It is these explicit or implicit questions that keep the text open. Then there is the striking rhythm of Silverman's writing—always a variation of short sentences set off and completed with a long sentence composed of several subordinate clauses that include conjunctions, disjunctions, or reversals. It is this rhythm of the short and the long sentences—which are arranged almost poetically—that draws one's attention to the spaces between the words, the spaces between the sentences, between the essays and chapters, and especially the spaces between the ideas. Yes, I am embarrassed to admit that I had forgotten a lot about Hugh's work. But what I always remember (and will always remember) either quite consciously (I am his student) or at least semiconsciously (my student days were a long time ago) and most often unconsciously (this idea defines me as a philosopher) is Silverman's constant stress of the "the space-in-between."

As one ages as a philosopher, one finds oneself at times wondering how one's philosophical persona was formed. Why do I have this set of questions? Why this idea and not another? What criticism from which teacher stopped me from pursuing this idea? What comment by what teacher steered me in the direction of this question? One is never certain how to answer these questions. However, I can say with confidence that were it not for Silverman's lectures and writings, I myself would *not* have been drawn to the question of the "between." Strangely, I do not think that it was his lectures on French thought, on Sartre or Merleau-Ponty, on Barthes or Derrida, that most influenced me. It was the times that he spoke of Heidegger. I knew that when Silverman spoke of the "frame" (the *Gestell*), this word alluded to Heidegger's essay "The Question Concerning Technology." Yet only now do I realize that he was opposing this idea of a frame to that of a "between," to a difference between. The opposition Professor Silverman was conceiving seems to go like this.

Like the one around a picture, the frame determines what is inside it as a recognizable identity; the framed identity then allows one to compare it to other things also framed; consequently, one is able to mediate the framed identities with a general concept, making them all the same. With the frame, there is no excess beyond sameness. In contrast to this restrictive frame, we have the "difference between," which is like the margin around a page.[1] While the frame is a determinate space, with clear edges that begin and end and that thereby separate one thing from another, the margin is indeterminate. It is not clear that the margin has edges because the white of the margin blends into the background of the printed words laid out on the page. The blankness of the margin suggests an impenetrable depth. Because it is impenetrable, we have to wonder whether the margin begins at the edge of words, and does it then end with the fold of the page? Does the margin make what is written inside it or on top of it extend to other pages in the book, to other books by the same author, to other books on similar topics, to other books in general? Does the margin extend to all the traces that are possible? Simply, we do not know where a margin begins and ends. Remaining indeterminate like the margin, "the space-in-between" does not present a general concept that mediates different identities; it does not produce sameness. Consequently, the "between" *de-limits* in the double sense of making a limit and going beyond it. It does not restrict; it opens that which it delimits to that which *exceeds* it. I have already mentioned my title—"The Space-in-Between"—but now you see my subtitle: "The Frame and Excess in the Thought of Hugh J. Silverman."

Here I would like to examine two essays in Silverman's large and formidable corpus to illustrate this relation of the frame and excess. The two essays I have chosen are "The Mark of Postmodernism: Reading *Roger Rabbit*" (1995)[2] and "Excessive Responsibility and the Sense of the World (Merleau-Ponty and Nancy)" (2008).[3] I have selected these two essays because we find in them together—linked, as we shall see, through the word "hero"—something like an ethical or political outlook that Silverman calls in the second essay "excessive responsibility." Although it only became apparent in his later work, this idea of excessive responsibility, I suspect, animated Hugh's work from the start. Because of this suspicion, here I want to remind us—indeed, I want to remind *myself*—of this excessive responsibility. In fact, I think we cannot forget this excessive responsibility because it leaves us with a pressing question. As we shall see, it is perhaps this question and the path of thinking it opens that might be Hugh Silverman's most enduring philosophical legacy.

The Postmodern Hero: Silverman's Reading of Who Framed Roger Rabbit

You recall that *Who Framed Roger Rabbit* is a 1988 Robert Zemeckis film in which animated figures (called "toons," as in "car-toons") interact with real humans. The plot of the film consists of the title character, "Roger Rabbit," being "framed" for the murder of a Hollywood producer named "Maroon." As Silverman says, "the question is: who did kill Maroon?" (*RR*, 154). Yet this is not the real question Silverman is asking. He is asking, "[W]hat are we to do—conceptually—with a film in which the cartoon characters mingle with the human world and vice versa?" (*RR*, 152–53).

The answer to this question lies in the fact that although, throughout the film, it seems that Roger Rabbit is kept in the *film* frame—and Silverman explicitly mentions Heidegger's *Gestell*, alluding to the ordering principles of technology (*RR*, 155)—"Roger Rabbit does not stay on the set—as it is clear from the outset, the frame for cartoon is a cartoon frame . . . Roger transgresses the frame. The frame does not keep cartoons in and the humans out" (*RR*, 155). In other words, humans and cartoons interact in the same space; improprieties abound; category mistakes happen everywhere. "Indeed," Silverman says, "the frame is interrupted" (*RR*, 155). How? Simply, Roger Rabbit messes everything up. More precisely, he messes everything up *not* just like any other cartoon character. When the anvil falls on Wile E. Coyote's head, Wile E. Coyote sees stars. However, when Roger Rabbit is hit on the head, he sees Tweety Birds (RR, 158). However, the Tweety Birds appearing over his head (instead of stars) are not the only thing that Roger Rabbit messes up. Stars, not Tweety Birds, are *supposed* to appear over his head because Roger Rabbit is an actor acting in an animated film (*RR*, 158). So, paradoxically, we have a cartoon character actor playing a cartoon character. And, even more, there is a sort of filmic *mise en abyme* because the animated film in which Roger Rabbit is acting takes place within the Zemeckis film *Who Framed Roger Rabbit.* Thus, as Silverman concludes, Roger Rabbit is an "impossible construction" (*RR*, 163). As far as I know, Silverman even coins a philosophically interesting phrase to describe this impossible construction; he calls it "counter-anachronism" (*RR*, 157). The idea of counter-anachronism is that in 1988 Roger Rabbit is a kind of throwback to an earlier age of animation and storylines, to the 1930s and 1940s; to those of us who are watching *Who Framed Roger Rabbit* now, Roger Rabbit looks to be an anachronism. However, because he messes everything up in ways we've not seen before (the Tweety Birds instead of stars), he is something other than anachronistic, something against anachronism: counter to anachronism. But this counter-anachronism, according to Silverman, is not merely something like "the shock of the new." That shock is still part of modernism (*RR*, 163). What Roger does is interrupt the modern categories; he interrupts the modern "large narratives of history" (to use Lyotard's phrase) by being "older than the new." Thus, as postmodern, Roger Rabbit, as Silverman says, "operates difference" (*RR*, 164). He does not operate *differences.* He is the existence of the very process of differentiation that, while not being separate from the things differentiated, is not located in any of them. The process of differentiation (what Derrida would have called "differance") is what takes place *between* differences, *and*, as exceeding all of them, cannot be presented. As Silverman says (borrowing explicitly a formula from Lyotard), Roger Rabbit "presents the unpresentable" (*RR*, 164).

It is this presentation of the unpresentable that transforms Roger Rabbit into a "postmodern hero" (*RR*, 157). As always for Silverman (but all great philosophers proceed in this manner), we begin with negative definitions (*RR*, 157). The postmodern hero is *not* an anti-hero like, for example, Beckett's Lucky and Pozzo. Roger Rabbit offers no insights into human consciousness; he does not shift into some sort of alienated consciousness or absurdity; he is not plagued with the feeling of despair or anguish before existential choices. Again, these figures are like the shock of the new, still a part of the modernist narrative. So, to answer the question of what is a postmodern hero, we must ask: what does it mean to operate difference, what does it mean to transgress the frame? As far as I can tell, Professor Silverman's answer to this question lies in a way of speaking. In particular, Silverman stresses that Roger Rabbit has "a sense of humor" (*RR*, 157). We should note immediately that humor is frequently, and perhaps always, a form of criticism of commonly accepted behaviors, attitudes, and beliefs. If we recognize that humor is always a form of criticism, then we also have to recognize that humor is dangerous and risky. Silverman extends this idea by saying that Roger Rabbit's sense of humor is "the operation of irony" (*RR*, 159). To ironize, of course, is to say one thing and mean another, something almost the opposite of what is said. Irony, Silverman seems to be suggesting, may be the only possible use of speech in which one is able to refer with something present to what is unpresentable. We have to realize, however, that this sort of reference to the unpresentable remains necessarily insufficient because it is only ever *indirect*. To operate difference through humor and irony therefore is at once, always and necessarily, risky and insufficient. Taking the risk to criticize the present through humor and irony and remaining aware of the insufficiency of the speech act defines perhaps the postmodern *hero*.

Excessive Responsibility: Silverman's Appropriation of Nancy

"Excessive Responsibility and the Sense of the World" (*ER*) mentions the word "hero" *once*. It appears only in the first epigraph, which is from Saint-Exupéry: "Only the hero lives his relation to humans and the world to the limit." The Saint-Exupéry quotation that Silverman reproduces is quite long and entirely in French except for this one sentence that contains the word "hero." The other two epigraphs, which are equally long, also appear in French. However, if one looks carefully in each, one sees one sentence rendered in English. In the second epigraph, Silverman quotes Merleau-Ponty, but within the French one finds in English the sentence that "language is destined to play a crucial role in the perception of other people." Finally, in the third epigraph from Nancy, within the French one finds in English the phrase "a praxis of thinking, its writing in the sense of a responsibility for this excess" (*ER*, 307). Therefore, thanks to the word "hero" in the first epigraph, we see clearly that here in this later (by thirteen years) essay, Professor Silverman is continuing his reflections on the postmodern hero that we saw in the "Roger Rabbit" essay. And while the word "postmodern" does not appear in the later essay, the Lyotard formula of "presenting the unpresentable" appears (*ER*, 313–14). In fact, the opening three epigraphs lay out a line of thought that goes from hero (from the postmodern hero) to language and then to excessive responsibility. The line of thought indicates that now (in 2008) the postmodern hero is someone who takes up the responsibility for the excess (that is, for the unpresentable) in a praxis of writing or, more generally, in a work of language (that is, in a presentation). This definition of the postmodern hero raises a question. As we have already suggested with the insufficiency of Roger Rabbit's operation of humor and irony, the question we must ask is the following: what sort of *praxis* or even what sort of *speech act* is required by excessive responsibility? I return to this question at the end.

There is one other similarity between this essay and the earlier "Roger Rabbit" essay. In the "Excessive Responsibility" essay, Professor Silverman also presents a reading of a film, in this case, Paul Haggis's 2004 *Crash*. Although the reading of *Crash* plays only a minor role in the "Excessive Responsibility" essay (it appears in the last section and occupies only about one page of text [*ER*, 314–15]), it brings our attention to something that I find somewhat surprising. Through the reading of the film *Crash*, Silverman draws our attention to the "violence, aggression, fear, or oppression" that arises with crashes or through crashes. Crash itself is a violent image, and the film of course is quite difficult to watch because of the conflicts presented in it. In the essay, the film *Crash* reinforces what Silverman is generally interested in: the crashing together of, and therefore the violence between, cultures. It is these cultural crashes that make up the world (*ER*, 307–08). Thus, to be responsible for the sense of the world is to be responsible for the conflicts that constitute the world. Compared with what we saw in the "Roger Rabbit" essay, the responsibility for conflicts and even violence seems to be a new element in Silverman's thinking—or at least in the earlier essay this element of responsibility for conflict remained unstressed.

Despite this new stress on conflict in the "Excessive Responsibility" essay, the same logic that we saw in the "Roger Rabbit" essay seems to be operating here. Once again, the frame as a determinate and restrictive enclosure is criticized. For instance, Silverman says, "The ex-orbitant responsibility exceeds the limits, borders, *frames* of any singularity" (*ER*, 312, my emphasis). And the world from which this responsibility evolves does not refer to any object in the world. Nor does it refer to the collection or set of objects in the world. The world is not a totality of objects. Instead, the world is, of course, that space between things in the world; it is the background for all the things in the world. Being nothing determinate *in* the world, the world is the unpresentable, and therefore it is excessive: it exceeds or transcends any determinate thing in the world. Therefore, responsibility for the world is also necessarily excessive: it goes beyond being responsible for oneself, for any particular thing in the world; it goes beyond being responsible for any determinate thing in the world.

Yet in the "Excessive Responsibility" essay there seems to be a *second sense* to this excessiveness. Here the engagement with Nancy seems to bring forth something else that is new. Following Nancy, Silverman uses the term "singularity" to designate the things in the world. The idea of a singularity—an idea so important in French thought since the 1960s—has its own paradoxical logic. One has to be clear about the idea of a singularity: strictly, for a singularity to be a singularity, it must be absolutely unique, unlike any other singularity. This uniqueness, I think, is why Nancy revives Descartes's phrase (and this revival is strange if one thinks of Merleau-Ponty) "*partes extra partes.*" For a singularity to be a singularity, it must be "extra," exterior, outside of, away from, really different from anything other. If it is not exterior in this strict way, it is no longer a singularity. But this exteriority of the singular is only half of the logic. *Also*, for Nancy, whom Silverman follows, a singularity is always "with" other singularities; a singularity is always "shared" or "distributed." When Nancy speaks of this togetherness of the singularities, he makes use of the Latin preposition "cum" to stress this "with," and he always uses the French verb "*partager*," which means "to share" or "to distribute." The paradox of the logic becomes apparent when one realizes that the sharing of a singularity with other singularities has to imply that the singularity is *pluralized* through the sharing and thereby it is no longer unique. In short, the pluralization of the singularity destroys it. With the fact of this violent distribution of singularities, we have to hold onto the strict definition of singularities. *Strictly*, a singularity cannot be pluralized; as such, a singularity remains exterior and outside. It remains unattainable for the pluralization. Thus, to be responsible for the world is not only to be responsible for the whole background that is the world—itself unpresentable and thus unattainable—but also to be responsible for the violent pluralization of the singularities in which they nevertheless, they too, remain (like the world) unpresentable and unattainable. It is this violent distribution and unattainability of the singular that leads Silverman to appropriate the word "vestige" from Merleau-Ponty (*ER*, 308). These vestiges of the singular, for Silverman, are reflected within general meanings or significations, within, for example, cultural meanings; however, the vestiges exceed these general significations because they are "traces" (Silverman's word) of what has been destroyed and lost, of what is singular, and of what therefore remains unpresentable and unattainable (*ER*, 311–12).

The problem of the vestiges being reflected within the general meanings of a culture brings us to the last aspect of Silverman's "Excessive Responsibility." To be responsible for the world is to be responsible for the *sense* of the world. Like so many philosophers before him, Silverman plays on the double sense of the French word "*sens*," which, like its German counterpart, means both "meaning" and "direction." *Not only* is being responsible for the sense of the world being responsible for how the unpresentable background space of the world pluralizes singularities, how it puts singularities "with" other singularities, how it makes them crash violently into one another, *but also* to be responsible for the sense of the world is to be responsible for the vestiges of the unpresentable singularities who remain "extra." To be responsible for the sense of the world consists in being responsible not only for the crashes but also for the vestiges of the singularities involved in the crashes: both at once, *cum* and *partes extra partes*, with and outside of one another. However, there is a twist in being responsible for the sense of the world (*le sens du monde*). Being responsible is not only being responsible for *this sense of the world* (*ce sens du monde*). It also consists of being responsive. And thereby, responsibility consists of changing the *direction* of the world (*un autre sens du monde*). This responsibility is *truly* excessive. *Not only* is it a responsibility for what lies beyond and behind every particular thing in the world, for what lies beyond and behind every present being—the sense of the world lies somewhere beyond and behind all of them—*but also* this responsibility—in its attempt to change the direction of the world—moves toward what lies beyond and ahead of every particular thing and beyond and ahead of every present being. It is a responsibility at once for a beyond *behind* and to a beyond *ahead*. We have to conclude therefore that the beyond of the sense of the world is so excessive that the *praxis* of responsibility remains always and necessarily *insufficient.* No matter how responsible and responsive one is, one is always called beyond, always called toward more action, more speaking, and more thinking. Near the end of the "Excessive Responsibility" essay, Hugh refers to Derrida's idea of justice as the undeconstructible (*ER*, 316). But he could have referred to Derrida's frequent (late in his career) criticisms of good conscience, that is, the criticism of the belief that somehow one has responded to injustice and violence and that somehow that response is good enough.[4] In contrast to this smug attitude, the responsibility Silverman envisions is so excessive that no response is ever good enough.

Conclusion: The Line of Difference between Dying and Remembering

Earlier I said that Hugh Silverman formed my philosophical persona by stressing, in his lectures and writings, the "between." Now I want to say that I will never forget this idea—*Hugh's idea*—of excessive responsibility. From this moment forward, I will make it be part of my philosophical makeup. I am going to internalize his excessive responsibility by formulating a question that I think Hugh bequeathed to us. I think this question might be Hugh's most enduring philosophical legacy. I will not leave the question in disguise.

Through Hugh's idea of excessive responsibility, you can see, I hope, that the question of the *praxis* of excessive responsibility remains unanswered. Clearly, what we find in the interpretation of *Who Framed Roger Rabbit* is not satisfactory. Irony and humor are really not enough, I think, when one confronts injustice and violence. In the "Excessive Responsibility" essay, Hugh himself gives us only a few hints about how we might think of this *praxis* of excessive responsibility in a more sufficient way. From the Nancy epigraph we quoted earlier, we know that it is a *praxis* of thinking and writing (*ER*, 312), but also in the body of the essay Hugh speaks of a "*prise de parole*," and he speaks of "indirect language" (*ER*, 316–17). It looks therefore as though the *praxis* of excessive responsibility consists of a, so to speak, "taking of speech." In other words, when one is called upon to take the podium and speak, and especially when the call comes from violence and injustice, one must not be complacent. The call makes one feel obligated to speak. But obligated to say what? With the phrase "indirect language," Hugh is probably referring to Merleau-Ponty. If he is alluding to Merleau-Ponty, then the *praxis* of excessive responsibility must be a speaking that refers *back* to silence, in this case, to the silence of the world and to the silence of the singularities, to this beyond and this other of any particular voice. Yet, and this claim I think is consistent with Merleau-Ponty's thinking, the speaking of silence would also have to refer *ahead* to what is beyond and other. If we think of this "ahead" (and not merely back), then perhaps we are able to open a way toward the answer to the question of the *praxis* of excessive responsibility. The way seems to go in two directions. With the "ahead" and *futurity* of the speaking in mind, perhaps we can think that the *praxis* of excessive responsibility is a kind of *promising*, a promising whose fulfillment is impossible, so impossible that we always feel obligated to keep trying to keep the promise. *Or*, again with the *futurity* in mind, we might think that this *praxis* of excessive responsibility consists of *speaking frankly*, without fear, with speaking courageously despite the consequences that might come when one speaks out and speaks one's mind. Two ways to speak, two possible ways to answer the question of excessive responsibility's heroic speaking. Maybe the two ways diverge, or maybe the promise and *parrēsia* converge. I do not know. One thing, however, is clear. We must continue to ask *this question*: what sort of thinking, what sort of writing is required by excessive responsibility? More precisely, what sort of speech *act* (it must be an act, it must have an effect) is required to reduce, as much as possible, injustice and violence? By raising this question, I hope I have opened a path of thinking that Hugh would have been proud to have inspired. I hope this question is faithful to the vestige of the singularity that was Hugh J. Silverman. Indeed, I hope that I have somehow managed, for Hugh, to reinscribe "the line of difference between living and dying *as* the line of difference between dying and remembering."

Notes

1. See Jacques Derrida, *Marges de la philosophie* (Paris: Minuit, 1972), xix–xxi; English translation by Alan Bass as *Margins of Philosophy* (Chicago: University of Chicago Press, 1982), xxiii–xxv.

2. Hugh J. Silverman, "The Mark of Postmodernism: Reading *Roger Rabbit*," *Cinémas: Revue d'études cinématographiques/ Cinémas: Journal of Film Studies* 5, no. 3 (printemps 1995): 151–64. Henceforth cited as *RR*.

3. Hugh J. Silverman, "Excessive Responsibility and the Sense of the World (Merleau-Ponty and Nancy)," *Chiasmi International* 10 (2008): 307–17. Henceforth cited as *ER*.

4. Jacques Derrida, *L'autre cap* (Paris: Minuit, 1991), 71, 79; English translation by Pascale-Anne Brault and Michael B. Naas as *The Other Heading: Reflections on Today's Europe* (Bloomington: Indiana University Press, 1992), 72, 81.

9

From the Death of the Subject to Stories of Natality

Foucault, Arendt, and Silverman

Ewa Płonowska Ziarek

For Hugh Silverman

In his posthumously published essay "The Postmodern Subject: Truth and Fiction in Lacoue-Labarthe's Nietzsche," Hugh Silverman disagrees with Foucault's pronouncement of the disappearance of the modern subject erased from human sciences by the epistemic shift of knowledge. Silverman writes:

> In 1966, Foucault announces . . . that the human subject is dead, and that it will soon vanish from the terrain of human discourse. What this implies is that with the death of the subject, the subject will no longer participate in the contemporary *epistemē*, the *epistemē* which we have come to understand as postmodern.[1]

The actual "death announcement" Silverman refers to, expressed in the last sentence of Foucault's *The Order of Things*, is more hypothetical, a bit more open to chance, more like a philosophical wager: "If those arrangements were to disappear as they appeared . . . then one can certainly wager that man would be erased, like a face drawn in sand at the edge of the sea."[2] If I were reading these quotations from Silverman and Foucault several years ago, I would have approached them with an intellectual curiosity about the reasons why Silverman would wish to revisit and contest this well-known hypothesis of the death of the subject—which by now has become an oft-cited cliché, but a cliché endowed with a strange staying power—in order to offer an alternative theory of the postmodern subject as a fable. I would have also probably discussed in greater detail Foucault's specific metaphor of the face on the sand—"un visage de sable," rendered in the English translation as a kind of drawing—a metaphor, which evokes Foucault's equally famous opening of *The Order of Things* with his stylistically superb discussion of Velázquez's painting *Las Meninas*, focused on the incompatible visibilities of the painter standing back from his canvas and looking at his model, on the one hand, and the position of the spectator, on the other. I would have wondered about the unremarked position of the spectator looking at "un visage de sable," drawn so close to the water; about the person who made the drawing; about the reasons for this liminal location, so close, perhaps too close, to the edge of the sea; about the play of visibility and invisibility announced in the figurative language of Foucault's last sentence. What could be lost or gained in this philosophical anonymous wager? Why had Foucault chosen this particular image, this border, to use Silverman's favorite term, between the land and the water, evocative of the intertwining of the human/inhuman landscapes, both of which are (in our intellectual/political horizon) threatened by environmental destruction, oil spills, global warming, and so forth?

And this possible speculation implies already an intrusion of a story, of a certain kind of literature, into philosophical discussion, as if narrative could constitute a possible unfolding and continuation of a philosophical inquiry by other means. This narrative supplement raises several questions: First, are these kernels of possible stories in the philosophical texts enabled by unexpected twists and "turns"—to use another of Silverman's important tropes—of figurative language (for instance, in the last sentence in Foucault's *The Order of Things*), as poststructuralist critics have argued, J. H. Miller and Paul de Man, among others?[3] The second question pertains to the implicit, but nonetheless well entrenched in the history of philosophy and narrative theory, relation between death and storytelling. Is storytelling always solicited as a kind of memory beyond death, as a story of loss and survival?[4] How can this narrative *topos* of death be displaced? And finally, and most importantly, if the subject survives as a fable, what makes her narratable? Throughout my entire academic career I had only one academic forum where I could try out, discuss, and get comments on these types of inquiries: that was, of course, the annual IAPL conference. The creation of IAPL and co-organization of its annual meetings was one of the greatest of Silverman's academic, intellectual, and institutional achievements.

[However, I'm reading Hugh's brief commentary on Foucault in December 2014, when the author, who had been my close colleague for almost twenty years, is dead, and his biographical note at the back of the book's cover, *Subjects and Simulations*, of which he is one of the editors, is written in the past tense. I am stopped in my tracks . . . As I read Hugh's essay again, I am struck by the persistent and precise dating of both the publications of philosophical texts and the death of their authors. It is an uncanny, almost contradictory gesture in an essay devoted after all to the untimely, premature emergence of the postmodern subject, prior to the disappearance of the modern subject. Consider, for example, the following fragment, which is characteristic of Hugh's writing: "What Lacoue-Labarthe offers—almost a decade after the death of Merleau-Ponty and half a decade after Foucault's 1966 pronouncement concerning the death of the subject . . ." (*SS*, 50). Merleau-Ponty's death, Silverman's death, and the death of the subject do not belong to the same modality of temporality. It is as if dates stopped working as external, abstract markers of the important moments in the history of philosophy and all of a sudden began sounding like the ticking of a clock, like the looming deadline, which Hugh, perpetually late (and driving us, who were working with him on IAPL programs or book collections, insane), were sure to miss. . . .]

To be sure, Silverman refers to Foucault's death of the subject in order to articulate the disappearance of a certain structure of the philosophical subject of modernity, the famous transcendental-empirical doublet, imbalanced and suspended between the two orders of intellectual inquiry. Indeed, it is the epistemic function of the modern subject, and not the existential (non)significance of death that Silverman critiques; he too contests and wants to find alternatives to "the idea that the subject itself was the source of its own thinking processes," while remaining outside representations and appearances he (and, no doubt, this philosophical subject's gendered "he" despite his presumption of universality) produces (*SS*, 48).

[Yet I cannot read this discussion without thinking about Hugh's death, how shocking and unbelievable it still is . . . This unexpected irruption of "heterochronic" time,[5] which, according to Foucault, breaks ordinary time, including the academic calendar of deadlines, classes, and conferences, changes my usual mode of reading. It is still hard to imagine that Hugh, with his hat, will no longer participate in person in the arguments about phenomenology, postmodernism, aesthetics, "intervals," "chiasma," "borders," and "crossings" at the annual meetings of SPEP or IAPL conferences, not to mention the philosophical seminars in Northern Italy he also organized for so many years. I still expect him to catch me at the IAPL registration desk or the SPEP book exhibit and to remind me about submitting another panel for IAPL. The philosophical debate about the death of the modern philosophical subject at this particular moment seems . . . irrelevant.]

As I am thinking about Silverman's response to Foucault's wager about the disappearance of the subject, I am astonished for the first time by the double and highly improper use of prosopopeia in the expression "the death of the subject." This prosopopeia, first of all, aims to do the impossible, to personify death, which precisely marks the impossibility of all personification. Yet, as J. Hillis Miller reminds us, prosopopeia is always at work in the creation of possible characters of the story and thus is one of the conditions of storytelling. Consequently, the use of prosopopeia to mark the shift in the history of philosophical knowledge and the notion of the philosophical subject [abstract, universal, nonsexed but male, not racialized but white] creates a deliberate confusion between the transcendental and existential. What is the aim of this confusion beyond its dubious shock value? To add at bit of existential gravitas to our philosophical discussions? To inscribe obliquely the ubiquitous work of mourning into abstract philosophical language? As if we ever really mourned the disappearance of our ideas, performed a burial, went to the heterotopic places,[6] to use another of Foucault's phrases, called cemeteries, and returned to the land of the living?

Reading Silverman's disagreement with Foucault in the name of Nietzsche reminds me of another of Foucault's essays, not his famous

"Nietzsche, Genealogy, History," but "Of Other Spaces, Heterotopias," written in 1967, only a year after the publication of *The Order of Things*. As I am thinking of these works together, I am struck by their stylistic and methodological differences. Foucault's detailed description of the historical removal of the cemetery from the center to the outskirts of the city, where it marks as a liminal heterotopic space, an outside vis-à-vis ordinary spaces and times of culture, a border between the land of the living and the dead, has phenomenological and historical density.[7] By contrast, the announcement of the disappearance of the subject seems like a clever intellectual provocation, still in use to be sure, but lacking the same evocative power of the condensed cultural, historical memories and imaginings. And perhaps most surprising, Foucault in this essay, like Silverman in his numerous writings on Merleau-Ponty, acknowledges the importance of phenomenology, which he otherwise consistently criticizes for the complicity of the perceiving subject with the transcendental consciousness.[8] By contrast, in "Of Other Spaces" Foucault acknowledges that phenomenology has taught him that we do not live and think in abstract, empty spaces (and, I would add, in abstract empty time), "but on the contrary in a space thoroughly imbued with qualities and perhaps [haunted by fantasms] as well."[9] These spaces are also demarcated by power.

Do we need stories to convey these intensities, fantasies, dreams, and dangers? This might be one of the implications of Silverman's claim that postmodern subjectivity persists in the aftermath of its philosophical "death" as a fable. Silverman locates this premature appearance of the fictional subject, prior to its philosophical demise, in the work of Nietzsche, Lacoue-Labarthe's Nietzsche, as well as his own. As he writes, "What remains would be only remains . . . In the postmodern world, the modern subject will also have become a fable, a fiction" (*SS*, 48). Again I am tempted to interject that Foucault also noticed this opening in Nietzsche's philosophy, that he likewise argued that the death of God and man is not a "deficiency" but a possibility of thinking otherwise.[10] And yet I have to admit that Foucault, despite his turn to the aesthetics of existence in his later writings, and despite his work on Blanchot at the earlier stages of his career, did not examine rigorously enough the intersections between philosophy and literature—the intersections that were so important to Silverman's thinking and institutional organizing throughout his intellectual career. That is why Silverman abandons Foucault at this juncture and finds a more promising chiasmus between philosophy and literature in Lacoue-Labarthe's interpretation of Nietzsche:

> For Lacoue-Labarthe the subject is a fiction, a fable which is told not in opposition to some reality, nor as just some appearance, but as *outside* both reality and appearance, as a view of both reality and appearance . . . When the modern subject becomes a fable, it is a story that can be told again and again—often in different versions but never as some originary condition of reality. (*SS*, 50)

By transforming the disappearance of the philosophical subject into a fable, or perhaps multiple fables, Silverman reopens the debate between philosophy and literature by locating fiction within philosophy, and perhaps quite a bit of a philosophical wisdom in literature. Silverman's attempt to fictionalize philosophy is precisely at stake in his acknowledgment that literature in truncated or full-blown forms has always already inhabited philosophy from within: "Like philosophy itself, the subject is narrativized, textualized, contextualized. Like philosophy itself, the modern subject has become a fiction. The modern subject has become one story or another" (*SS*, 54). The stakes of literature for Silverman, in this particular essay and throughout his career, are high. First of all, the turn to fiction opens a possibility of thinking and reading outside the opposition of truth and appearance, outside the fiction of truth behind appearances, a truth that the philosophical function of the modern subject guarantees: "If fiction is somehow outside truth, then it is also outside appearance. Hence, the question of literature is a question of the thematizing of the subject without reference or appeal to its truth or appearance. Fiction is indeed the operative term for the postmodern discourses of the contemporary age" (*SS*, 49). But there is another, more subtle and more difficult task in Silverman's numerous turns to fiction in his thinking about postmodernism: what is at stake here is a therapeutic, if not cathartic, attempt to cure philosophy of its "profound fear of literature, of what might be nothing more than a story, of what is confirmed only through interpretation and critical readings" (*SS*, 50). Perhaps one of the undercurrents of Silverman's philosophical thinking, writing, and creating new institutional spaces for the intellectual exchanges between philosophy and literature is not just an attempt to intervene in philosophical discussions or to foster interdisciplinary exchanges, but to transform, if such a thing were possible, philosophical passions. Not just to diagnose this fearful affective tonality of philosophy, but to change its fear into admiration of literature, to return us to the state of wonder as the beginning of thinking. And one of the possible places of such transformation, of moving through and beyond fear, Silverman found in the notion of admiration articulated in Irigaray's *Ethics of Sexual Difference*.[11]

As I read Silverman's argument about the postmortem persistence of the postmodern subject as a story, a story beyond the Platonic opposition of reality and appearance, I could not agree more. And yet I am left with questions; I would like to hear more from Hugh about the way stories of the subject and philosophy can take us beyond the being/appearance binary. What makes subjects narratable in the first place? How is this narratability linked to the ontology beyond the being/appearance binary? As it happens, I read Silverman's essay while working on Hannah Arendt and her formulations of narration and action. Turning to Arendt's own thinking about subjects as fiction, we encounter, however, quite different configurations of narratability, stories, appearances, and subjectivities, a configuration that supplements the philosophy/literature debate with a political thinking of action. It is a shift from the fictionalization of philosophy to the meditation on the role of stories and narratives in political ontology—or what Arendt calls the "human condition." In the first volume of the feminine genius devoted to Arendt, with the subtitle of *Life as Narrative*, Kristeva underscores this dimension of political ontology framing Arendt's thinking about stories: "The narrative is the first dimension in which man lives, through *bios* and not through *zoē*, a political life . . . recounted to other people."[12] In this reframing of narrative in terms of political ontology [and I wonder whether Hugh would have called such reframing a postmodern turn or whether he would reject this reference to ontology], fictions open a possibility of negotiating among the vexed and conflicting relations among literature, philosophy, and politics.

Perhaps the most important intervention of Arendt's political and ontological displacement of narrative is a shift from the reflection on the death of the philosophical subject of modernity, or death as a condition of narrative, toward thinking about the human condition of natality. Despite more and more work devoted to this aspect of Arendt's thought, natality as the condition of action, human plurality, and narratability still remains undertheorized in the philosophical, cultural, literary, and political debates at large. As Arendt writes, though we are mortal, we "are not born in order to die but in order to begin."[13] Arendt's complex analysis of *natality* carries multiple interrelated meanings.[14] First and foremost, in a radical reformulation of Heideggerian "throwness,"[15] natality refers to the human condition of having been born, of entering the world through the event of birth. Never simply biological, this status of birth as a unique event means that human birth is an originary and obscure beginning of a subjectivity without a subject, the beginning of his/her constitutive exposure to others. This originary exposure to others is utterly unavailable to one's own recollections, except perhaps as stories told or withheld by others. By stressing the primacy of appearance understood as exposure, Arendt's meditation on the condition of natality dispels right away any philosophical notion of the isolated subject, whose presence to him- or herself is the source of knowledge. Yet although our birth is never our own, it is not, however, an occurrence of dispossession or loss. On the contrary, for Arendt it constitutes a possibility of *initium*: of ourselves, of living and acting with others, of sharing and transforming the world through our actions and stories. The possibility of *initium* brings us to the second meaning of natality, namely, to the possibility of a political transformation through action and language. Because it is an ontological condition of action, natality is the central category of the political. As Arendt famously writes in a frequently quoted passage, "since action is the political activity par excellence, natality, and not mortality, may be the central category of political, as distinguished from metaphysical, thought" (*HC*, 9). Never possible in isolation, action is the only human activity that has to be performed with others; it occurs always in the midst of what Arendt calls metaphorically "a web" of preexisting interrelations, institutions, and stories (*HC*, 184). And finally, the third meaning of natality is intertwined with the disclosure of the subject's uniqueness through acting and speaking with others. As we can see, such a natal, relational beginner can no longer posit itself, to quote Silverman again, as "the source of its own thinking processes" (*SS*, 48).

This radical reformulation of natality as the ontological condition of all kinds of beginnings and political transformations postulates a correlation between the act of *initium*, the capacity to begin, and the status of the subject as perennial beginner, always in relation to others. As Arendt puts it: "Because they are *initium*, newcomers and beginners by virtue of birth, men take initiative, are prompted into action. . . . With the creation of man, the principle of beginning came into the world itself" (*HC*, 177). The "impulse to begin something new" is never merely subjective but emerges from being and acting with others, with strangers and newcomers, whether these are immigrants, citizens, colleagues, friends, strangers, or new members of families. In a very suggestive formulation, Arendt argues that natality reveals a political capacity to enact with others the "birth" of a new world.[16] Usually ignored or associated with the politics of reproduction and compulsory heterosexuality, this reformulation of natality as the political birth of a new world not only implicitly inscribes the feminine inflection of agency into the political, but also connects it with the most creative aspect of collective action.

What is unique in Arendt's political thinking is the emphasis on multiple beginnings enacted by stories, newcomers, and actions—despite all the political dangers, ranging from biopolitics to totalitarianism to planetary destruction, that threaten to suppress them. These multiple beginnings are inseparable from the affirmation of human plurality, which entails a shift from the enduring fiction of the isolated philosophical subject to being and acting with others. I think a similar change of perspective is also implicitly performed in Silverman through an emphasis on multiple tales and multiple ways of being. It is as if the question of the story compels him to substitute the plural stories of multiple subjects for the fable of the postmodern subject with which he begins. That is why he writes:

> The postmodern subject is many fables—each juxtaposed alongside the others. The postmodern subject is indeed already many subjects, many stories, many different narratives, many ways to be. The styles are perhaps different, the contexts are perhaps different, the traditions are perhaps different, the engenderings are perhaps different, but the differences are not different. (*SS*, 55)

Consequently, even the fable of the postmodern subject is a philosophical misnomer because in fact it is impossible to tell any story of a single subject without her interactions, fictional or otherwise, with others. Like actions, stories cannot be told in isolation because they presuppose our relation to others with whom we share and inhabit the world.

Arendt's conception of natality provides another departure from the Platonic inheritance of Being and appearance, a departure also at stake in Silverman's analysis of postmodern subjectivities as fables. Silverman's argument allows us to see the radicalism of Arendt's thinking; and, vice versa, Arendt's ontology of natality explains why storytelling "deconstructs" the being/appearance binary. By turning the philosophical tradition upside down, Arendt's ontology of natality redefines appearance as the originary exposure of subjectivity to others, which precedes the subject's relation to self. The event of birth is the paradigmatic instance of appearing to others without being yet a subject, an appearing that precedes the emergence of a subject and its relation to self. No longer belonging to the Platonic opposition of Being and appearance, such a disclosure to others is an originary mode of sharing, acting, and inhabiting the world in common. If we destroy this modality of appearing by which we are interconnected with and disclosed to others, we do not reveal the truth of the subject or posit the subject as the foundation of knowledge but, on the contrary, cause her isolation and death.[17] As Arendt never ceases to repeat, such isolation is akin to death: a life without appearance to others: "A life without speech and action . . . is literally dead to the world; it has ceased to be a human life because it is no longer lived among men" (*HC*, 176).[18] Consequently the opposite of appearing to others is not the true Being of the subject, but isolation, political death, powerlessness, and exclusion from the world.

Beginning with birth, the manner of this appearing and exposing oneself to others precedes our identities, our knowledge of ourselves and others, intentionality, the distinction between truth or falsehood, or our plans for action. The redefinition of appearance-as-exposure is intertwined with the most common and the most political activities of all, namely, inhabiting the world with others (human plurality) and transforming it through political action. We appear, or more precisely co-appear, with others every time we act and engage in linguistic exchanges together. Arendt argues that this originary manner of interrelations in the political requires courage and gives us hope. Courage because appearing to others is intertwined with vulnerability and, I would add, with the risk and exposure to violence, which is still unequally distributed across the political spectrum even in so-called democracies. As the shocking killings of unarmed African-American teenagers and men—Trayvon Martin, Michael Brown, Eric

Garner, to name only a few—in the United States show again and again, appearing to others in public can be deadly. But as the protests, demonstrations, and "die-ins" in the wake of these murders suggest, appearing with others for the sake of action and the contestation of state-sponsored brutal violence is the only chance we have to fight racism, white supremacy, homophobia, and endless forms of discrimination that destroy human plurality.

[By establishing IAPL, Hugh created not only an institutional platform for the exchange of ideas for scholars working on the intersections of philosophy, literature, and literary theory, but also a safe space of appearance for the most vulnerable members of our profession, those who were at the very beginning of their careers, that is, graduate students. IAPL conferences have always been graduate student friendly and encouraging, demanding, and supportive, without being patronizing. I cannot imagine my own career without IAPL and without the numerous supportive and inspiring thinkers I met there who later became my friends and colleagues: Dalia Judovitz, Stephen Barker, Andrew Benjamin, Tina Chanter, Kelly Oliver, Dorota Glowacka, Ros Diprose, Robyn Ferrell, and so many others. My own intellectual life would have been very different, much poorer, without this rich web of relations and stories we share.]

In another crucial departure from the Platonic heritage, Arendt argues that although action and storytelling depend on human plurality, they at the same time disclose the singularity of each and every agent for others. However, the manner of such political disclosure, which reveals at once the singularity and plurality of political agents, remains utterly paradoxical. Perhaps Silverman would call this paradox the most postmodern aspect of Arendtian thinking. Certainly he would have been sympathetic with Arendt's claim that a disclosure of uniqueness/singularity through action reverses the usual relation between agency and act. According to Arendt, it is not the agent who is the author of the action, but, on the contrary, it is the action with others that reveals the uniqueness of the agent for the first time. Because there is no doer without the deed, no speaker without the speech act, no agent without the act, their uniqueness can be glimpsed only retrospectively, in the aftermath of acting. Consequently, Arendtian thinking contests not only the epistemic function of the subject as the source of knowledge but also the autonomy of the political subject as the basis of politics.

The disclosure of singularity through action and language to others also inverts the usual oppositions between inner and outer, public and private, clear and obscure. Once we depart from the premise of the autonomous political subject as the basis of politics, we have to accept that actors not only do not know others with whom they act, but, as Arendt insists, they do not know themselves. Because the disclosure of uniqueness happens only through action/linguistic act and occurs first to others, it is accompanied by the obscurity of political motivations and the obscurity of agents to themselves. That is why Arendt writes that political motivations are like "demons" or "dark oracles," more visible to others than to the actors themselves: uniqueness "which appears so clearly and unmistakably to others, remains hidden from the person himself, like the *daimōn* in Greek religion" (*HC*, 179). Therefore uniqueness remains a mystery to ourselves: "nobody knows whom he reveals when he discloses himself in deed or word, he must be willing to risk the disclosure" (*HC*, 180).

Arendt famously associates this paradoxical disclosure of singularity through the act with the notion of a "who" as opposed to "what." The *whatness* corresponds to a more conventional notion of identity, to the attributes and qualities, or to the set of differences, which in my interpretation (though not in Arendt's) include race, gender, class, profession, ethnicity, age, nationality, occupation, religion, as well as all kinds of affiliations and contributions we make, and so forth. Only the *whatness* of the subject can be defined, but, I would add, this definition always occurs in the context of the differential relations of power/knowledge and therefore is intertwined with objectification, discipline, normalization, abnormality, or exclusion. As feminists, critical race theorists, and postmodern political theorists have shown, the attributes defining subjectivities are relational, imbricated in the relations of power and knowledge, caught in hierarchies and exclusions. Consequently, the contestation and redefinition of "what" is also at stake in the political struggles against marginalization and exclusions.[19] However, what Arendt's work adds to the political analysis of the contestation of the power relations of race, gender, and class is the claim that such struggles, in addition to changing power relations, also disclose the uniqueness of a "who" of every participant.

Because the uniqueness of a "who" exceeds any political category of classification and normalization as well as the philosophical or cultural attributes of identity, it cannot be defined but only posed in the form of a question, "Who are you?," addressed to every newcomer to the political. Clearly such a question cannot be answered in the form of a description or a definition, which is necessarily general, shareable, and repeatable and therefore slides into "what." Any attempt to answer the question "Who are you?" seems to run against the generality that language itself presupposes as a condition of communicability. As Arendt puts it, "The moment we want to say *who* somebody is, our very vocabulary leads us astray into saying *what* he is; we get entangled in a description of qualities he necessarily shares with others" (*HC*, 181). Is, therefore, a question about somebody's uniqueness answerable at all? Does it push subjects and language to the limits of expression? Arendt seems to suggest so by saying that we are invariably confounded, perplexed, as if unable to speak: "The manifestation of who the speaker and doer unexchangeably is, though it is plainly visible, retains a curious intangibility that confounds all efforts toward unequivocal verbal expression" (*HC*, 181). The question about "who" seems like a riddle, perhaps like a notorious Sphinx's riddle, which, however, can no longer be answered in terms of the Oedipal presumption of the philosophical universality of "man."[20] Already straying afield of political philosophy, Arendt evokes ancient oracles to stress the enigma of the uniqueness of the agent disclosed through action: "The manifestation of the 'who' comes to pass in the same manner as the notoriously unreliable manifestations of ancient oracles, which . . . 'neither reveal nor hide in words, but give manifest signs'" (*HC*, 182).

All these perplexities of uniqueness do not silence us but, on the contrary, call for storytelling. The final disclosure of a who in the web of human relations, the only possible answer to "Who are you?," occurs in the form of a life story. According to Arendt, action " 'produces' stories" the way other activities, such as work, produce objects (*HC*, 184). Action makes lives narratable regardless of agents' intentions or desires. Why is this the case? Although Arendt does not discuss the relation between action and narration in great depth, narratability is enabled by the performative effects of action. First of all, the exposure of agents to others through speech and action prior to their relation to themselves positions those others, whether they are actors or spectators, as potential narrators. That is why Cavarero links being exposable to being narratable.[21] Because life is narratable thanks to others in their roles as potential narrators, the crucial implication of this indebtedness of narration to alterity lies in the reframing of any autobiography as always already a biography. The reason why the primary genre of any life story is biography rather than autobiography is because every auto/biography takes place within the parameters of stories told or withheld by others: "*Who* somebody is or was we can know only by knowing . . . his biography" (*HC*, 186).

The second reason why action makes life narratable is precisely because it discloses the uniqueness of a who in the midst of often conflicting relations and interactions. The emergence of the uniqueness of an agent in the multiplicity of appearances creates the possibility of a distinct character of a life story. That is why Arendt suggests that the disclosure of uniqueness through action in the web of the already existing and conflicting relationships "eventually emerges as the unique life story of the newcomer, affecting uniquely the life stories of all those with whom he comes into contact" (*HC*, 184). Thus, thanks to the disclosure of uniqueness to others we have a possibility of both narrators and characters of life stories. However, to be a character in one's own life story, or to be a narrator of somebody else's story, is different from authorship. Neither character nor narrator occupies the classical position of an author. As Arendt argues—and it is perhaps her most "postmodern" argument in Silverman's sense of the term—life stories do not have an author: "[N]obody is the author or producer of his own life story" (*HC*, 184). The absence of an author is precisely what makes autobiography impossible, or more precisely, what makes every autobiography always already a biography. If there is an "author" of a life story at all, then perhaps it is action itself, because action fabricates stories the way other activities produce objects.

However, for lives to be narratable something else is needed, something like the possibility of a plot, which for Aristotle constitutes the primary feature of narratives imitating, or more precisely, reenacting, action. Indeed, for Aristotle as for Arendt, action enables stories because it creates the possibility of a plot (*mythos*).[22] Despite this similarity, Arendt's and Aristotle's understandings of the relationship between plot/mythos and action are different. In contrast with the Aristotelian definition of the mythos, the Arendtian notions of action and narration do not have a clear sense of an ending. Less concerned with the completion of action and plot, Arendt focuses primarily on the way action creates a new beginning, which in turn calls for a new story. Without a new beginning, there is neither need nor desire for a new story. Paradoxically, it is this open-endedness of action, its lack of a predictable *telos*, that generates storytelling, which reveals the meaning of action retrospectively through the act of recollection. Still, such a retrospective disclosure of the meaning of action through the narrative act is itself incomplete; it engenders further, often conflicting narratives and the interpretations of these narratives.

Action produces living stories, or narratable lives, understood, as Kristeva reminds us, as *bios* rather than *zoē*. This interpretation of *bios* in terms of narratability is already implied, let us recall, in Arendt's own claim that life without action and speech is dead to the world, that is, it stops being *bios* and becomes superfluous, or, to use Agamben's term, is reduced to bare life. This is ultimately how I would like to interpret Silverman's claim that the postmodern subject survives its epistemological demise as a story: a narratable *bios* both precedes and persists beyond any epistemic function of the subject. However, as Kristeva and Cavarero note, a narratable *bios* is different from a narrated story. For Kristeva, the transformation of a narratable *bios* into narrated stories is enabled by the complex negotiations among individual and public memories, discourses (*LN*, 75–76), and, I would add, power and the politics of culture. By no means an easy task, the transformation of narratable lives into actual stories requires a judgment of *phronēsis* (*LN*, 76–77), focused on multiple particulars, rather than on the philosophical wisdom of *sophia* (*LN*, 79), concerned with universals. By establishing connections between acting, recollecting, and narrating in the context of human plurality, the judgment of *phronēsis* "adds up to a veritable politics of narration in Arendt's work" (*LN*, 75). However, we have to understand the possibilities and the limits of the politics of narration in yet another sense. As Cavarero points out, "what is intolerable" is not only the life of poverty and exclusion but also the fact "that the life-story that results from it remains without narration."[23] The narratability of life, its status as a *bios,* does not guarantee that every life will have a narrated story, because the telling/writing of such a story depends not only on the recollections of others and their willingness to narrate a story, but also on multiple, often invisible political values determining whose life stories are "worthy" of narration and memorialization in the public sphere. In the context of ever-growing circles of superfluous humanity, these value judgments about whose stories are told are eminently political, implicated in the networks of power knowledge. As Margaret Somers argues, lives deprived of narration are further denigrated and dispossessed, deprived of social significance: "Since social actors do not freely construct their own private or public narratives, we can also expect to find that confusion, powerlessness, despair, victimization, and even madness are some of the outcomes of an inability to accommodate certain happenings within a range of available cultural, public, and institutional narratives."[24] And by contrast, narration, alternative storytelling and counter histories, which challenge the dominant assumptions, values, and boundaries of the political, become all-powerful political weapons. Cavarero provides as an example women's narratives forming alternative public spaces during feminist consciousness-raising practices in the 1960s.

Despite Arendt's and Cavarero's disregard of textuality, the politics of counter-narratives brings back the question of form, or the manner of storytelling. Certainly we can recall at this point Adorno's claim that formal aspects of literary works, and in fact all artworks, are implicated in political antagonisms, which the artworks both reproduce and contest.[25] Although Arendt does not develop the politics of form, it is clear that not every story, even if it manages to be narrated, will perform a disclosure of uniqueness or safeguard a new beginning. In fact, quite the opposite seems to be the case. The politics of narration has yet another, more disciplinary and normalizing function, which manifests itself on the level of narrative form. For example, the familiar master plots in Western philosophy, religions, culture, and literature—the Oedipal plot, the Orpheus plot, the Medusa plot, the terrorist plot, the melting pot, the from rags to riches plot, the alien invasion plots (ranging from science fiction to immigration policy), the marriage plot, and so many other plots—perform such a disciplinary and normalizing function. Consequently, for a story to disclose uniqueness and to open a new beginning, these recurrent plots in the public imaginary will have to be put aside and bracketed for new ways of storytelling to be invented. And vice versa, storytelling has to be attentive to so many marks of erasure, silencing, and invisibility constitutive of the public politics of narration. By acknowledging these erasures, the politics of experimental narrative form challenge the way storytelling is entangled in the network of power/knowledge, which makes some narrative forms more readily disseminated and others—more easily disqualified. What I briefly call here a political function of narrative form,[26] and aesthetic experimentation more generally, is an ongoing formal struggle against normalization and exclusion to keep the possibility of a new beginning viable within language and culture. What these brief remarks on the politics of narration suggest is that narrative, which at first glance belongs to literature, is in fact a heterogeneous category through which politics, philosophy, and aesthetics ceaselessly confront each other to expand or shrink their limits.

In response to Silverman's argument that the postmodern subject survives its philosophical demise as a story, I have tried to sketch out the political, ontological, and narrative consequences of such a claim. My main question was that if the subject survives as a story, then what makes lives narratable? My response to this question has been inspired by the work of Hannah Arendt and her most perceptive interpreters, Kristeva and Cavarero. The engagement with their work has enabled me to propose two answers: what makes lives narratable is, first of all, the ontology of natality (rather than death), which posits action and human plurality at the center of political thought. Second, narratable lives depend upon the politics of narration. However, instead of pursuing these reflections further, I would like to end this chapter with my own brief story about Hugh Silverman, for whom this chapter is written. It is a story of just one event that perhaps will enable us to glimpse who he was. The very last event in which we participated together was a session called "Aesthetics and the Philosophy of Art" at the fiftieth anniversary of SPEP. In his lecture, "Aesthetics—Then and Now," Silverman presented his elegant reconstruction of the history of the aesthetic debates at SPEP since the inception of this organization. In a way, he was narrating a story of an organization itself of which he was one of the founding members. And he chose to finish his narrative with a more general reflection on the role of ethical responsibility and aesthetic sensibility in the formation of intellectual communities. Luckily for us, Silverman's intellectual biography of aesthetics at SPEP has been published, and I can re-create and retell it, hopefully with a different emphasis this time.

What interests me in Silverman's essay today is less the history of SPEP he reconstructed than the uniqueness of Silverman the narrator, who tells this history. And to convey this uniqueness I would like to quote a longer passage, which retrospectively sounds to me like a manifesto disclosing Hugh's own commitments to thinking and building intellectual communities embodying the principle of plurality:

> Now, the responsibilities are not just ethical or political. They enter into the practices of the artist and the philosopher; and

> how to think the responsibilities between us . . . as bringing us together in a shared community at the same time that they separate us; and how to think in an *intermedial* fashion—to think the entre nous as an event of difference, to think the *differends* as a way to respond to claims for compromise or capitulation, and for the arts to perform these various differences so that they will not simply remain "sublime" but, rather, so that they will allow each agent, each group, each set of identities to think the spaces between us—that separate us and bring us together at the same time. Can there be touching . . . at these places and events of difference? Nancy, Derrida, and Irigaray each, in their own ways, have called for a thinking of intervals, not just as a matter of theorizing but as a space of responding to each other, as a space of marking out the differences, our differences—not just their differences![27]

How to think responsibly (and not just to theorize responsibility) about intellectual inquiry, how to respond to the responsibilities between us, aesthetically, politically, and philosophically, without capitulation or easy compromise, was indeed Silverman's major concern—the key task to which he dedicated his life. One of the enduring answers he gave to these challenges was the creation of an important intellectual institution where the intellectual community could appear and flourish, namely the International Association for Philosophy and Literature. Indeed, we may read the above quotation as both Hugh's belated manifesto and the legacy of the intellectual community he created.

Notes

1. Hugh J. Silverman, "The Postmodern Subject: Truth and Fiction in Lacoue-Labarthe's Nietzsche," in *Subjects and Simulations: Between Baudrillard and Lacoue-Labarthe*, ed. Anne O'Byrne and Hugh J. Silverman (Lanham, MD: Lexington, 2015), 49. Henceforth cited as *SS*.

2. "Si ces dispositions venaient à disparaître comme elles sont apparues . . . alors on peut bien parier que l'homme s'effacerait, comme à la limite de la mer un visage de sable." Michel Foucault, *Les mots et les choses: une archéologie des sciences humaines* (Paris: Gallimard, 1966), 398; *The Order of*

Things: An Archaeology of the Human Sciences (New York: Vintage, 1973), 387.

3. J. Hillis Miller, "Narrative," in *Critical Terms for Literary Study*, ed. Frank Lentricchia and Thomas McLaughlin (Chicago: University of Chicago Press, 1990), 77–79; and Paul de Man, *Allegories of Reading: Figural Language in Rousseau, Nietzsche, Rilke, and Proust* (New Haven: Yale University Press, 1979), 205.

4. For the articulation of the constitutive relation between narrative and death, or more specifically literature and death, see Maurice Blanchot, "Literature and the Right to Death," in *The Gaze of Orpheus and Other Literary Essays*, ed. P. Adams Sitney, trans. Lydia Davis (Barrytown, NY: Station Hill Press, 1981), 21–62.

5. Michel Foucault, "Of Other Spaces," trans. Jay Miskowiec, *Diacritics* 16, no. 1 (1986): 26. Henceforth cited as *OS*. The French version is available as Michel Foucault, "Des espaces autres," *Empan* 2, no. 54 (2004): 17.

6. Ibid., 24.

7. Ibid., 25.

8. Including *The Order of Things*. See *The Order of Things*, xiv.

9. Foucault, "Of Other Spaces," 23, translation modified. "[M]ais au contraire, dans un espace qui est tout chargé de qualités, un espace qui aussi *peut être hanté de fantasme*." Michel Foucault, *Des espaces autres*, 14; italics added.

10. Foucault, *The Order of Things*, 342.

11. I still remember Hugh Silverman's discussion of Irigaray's notion of wonder at the ninth Annual International Philosophical Seminar, devoted to Irigaray's *Ethics of Sexual Difference*, Bolzano, Italy, 1999.

12. Julia Kristeva, "Life as a Narrative," in *Hannah Arendt*, trans. Ross Guberman (New York: Columbia University Press, 2001), 86. Henceforth cited as *LN*.

13. Hannah Arendt, *The Human Condition*, 2nd ed. (Chicago: University of Chicago Press, 1998), 246. Henceforth cited as *HC*.

14. For further discussion of the three meanings of natality, see Rosalyn Diprose and Ewa Płonowska Ziarek, "Time for Beginners: Natality, Biopolitics, and Political Theology," *PhiloSophia* 3, no. 2 (Summer 2013): 107–20.

15. Martin Heidegger, *Being and Time*, trans. Joan Stambaugh (Albany: State University of New York Press, 1996), 134–37 and passim.

16. Hannah Arendt, *On Revolution* (London: Penguin Books, 1963), 42.

17. Arendt links the destruction of appearance with the destruction of political subjectivity and the subsequent reign of terror in the course of the French Revolution. See Arendt, *On Revolution*, 98–107.

18. Arendt distinguishes such deadly isolation from withdrawal, most frequently associated with the most intimate and obscure of aspects of life sheltered in the private realm. As a necessary counterpart of appearing to and acting with others in public, withdrawal accompanies appearing as the mark of mystery and obscurity.

19. For further analysis of the racial and gender dimensions of political struggles, see my forthcoming essay, "Shall We Gender?," in *Genders*, as well as Ewa Płonowska Ziarek, *Feminist Aesthetics and the Politics of Modernism* (New York: Columbia University Press, 2012), 19–85.

20. For a discussion of the Oedipal answer as the philosophical answer par excellence that erases singularity, see Adriana Cavarero, *Relating Narratives: Storytelling and Selfhood*, trans. Paul A. Kottman (London: Routledge, 2000), 7–15. For a discussion of Sphinx's riddle in the context of sexual and racial difference, see Ziarek, *Feminist Aesthetics*, 180–87.

21. I disagree with two of Cavarero's claims: First, that being exposable and narratable cannot "be taken away" (*Relating Narratives*, 36), because Arendt's analysis of totalitarianism precisely shows that these aspects of the political can be destroyed. Second, I disagree that uniqueness means unity and identity.

22. "The most important of these is the arrangement of incidents, for tragedy is an imitation, not of men but of action and life . . . The purpose of action on the stage is not to imitate character, but character is a by-product of the action." Aristotle, *On Poetry and Style*, trans. G. M. A. Grube (Indianapolis: Hackett: 1989), 13–14.

23. Cavarero, *Relating Narratives*, 57.

24. Margaret R. Somers, "The Narrative Constitution of Identity: A Relational and Network Approach," *Theory and Society* 23, no. 5 (1994): 630.

25. Theodore W. Adorno, *Aesthetic Theory*, ed. Gretel Adorno and Rolf Tiedemann, trans. Robert Hullot-Kentor (Minneapolis: University of Minnesota Press, 1997), 6.

26. For further discussion of the politics of the aesthetic, see ibid., 16–39. See also Ziarek, *Feminist Aesthetics*, 11–13 and 46–49.

27. Hugh J. Silverman, "Aesthetics—Then and Now," *Journal of Speculative Philosophy* 26, no. 2 (2012): 369.

10

The Murderer, the Journalist, and the Responsibility between Us

Peter Gratton

> We certainly do experience the weight of thought. Sometimes the heaviness, sometimes the gravity of a "thought" . . . affects us with a perceptible pressure or inclination . . . But this experience remains a *limit-experience*, like any experience worthy of the name.
>
> —Jean-Luc Nancy[1]

One measures the weight of a thought as it leans on and inclines what follows, as it weighs on us, leaving indelible marks for those who take up its legacies. If this thought is produced by someone like Hugh J. Silverman, it will not be ascertainable in terms of a quantity or reducible to a given number. All the more for someone who knew Silverman going back to my undergraduate years, when I was both a philosophy and a political science major at Stony Brook and the editor of the student newspaper. Hugh and I spent countless hours discussing what most academics would think at best a running joke on most campuses, the student-run newspaper, not least because the philosophy department coverage did quite well during my era there. But Hugh was also interested in journalism and the media in general, lecturing often on "postmodern media."[2] Thus my mode of entry below into Silverman's philosophy is not esoteric, and it's notable that Silverman often wrote in the manner of the journalist: noting dates and facts relating different philosophers, while also writing in the style and cadence of simple sentences that lead to a complex conclusion.

Through an account of a certain journalistic or media "ethics," I want to bring together Silverman's long discussions of textuality, especially "autobiographical textuality," and his later, inventive elaborations of what he dubbed "the responsibility between us." The task here is to show how Silverman's oeuvre contains a vital thinking for those combating any thinking of politics or judgment looking to operate in a transcendental mode, and therefore disavowing its conditions of possibility. The questions Silverman raised in his work—in conferences, in his essays and books, and perhaps especially in his interpersonal discussions while bearing down on us with all the weight of his thought—concerned not just the "between" (how does one take the weight of a thought concerning difference and the between, that which is without substantiality?) but also a postmodern thinking of justice.

Justice to Texts

Now twenty-five years old, Janet Malcolm's *The Journalist and the Murderer* (1990) remains a touchstone for media ethicists considering the notion of "truth" as the explicit premise of the journalistic enterprise.[3] Arriving at the midpoint of Silverman's career, between his earliest texts on Sartre and existential phenomenology and his last works on "postmodernisms," *The Journalist and the Murderer* raises a plentitude of questions about the journalistic search for truth as well as the ineradicable textuality of litigation and ultimately the political itself. The title of the book refers to two litigants in a civil case eventually settled in the mid-1980s after an initial mistrial. The journalist of the title was Joe McGinniss, who gained initial fame in the 1960s with a fly-on-the-wall account of the Nixon campaign, *The Selling of the President* (1968), which practically birthed an entire genre of (tedious) books covering the internal dynamics of US presidential runs. By the 1980s, taking off from the supposed "new journalism" of Truman Capote, Norman Mailer, Joan Didion, and others of an earlier era, McGinniss was among those pumping out dubious—and quite successful—true crime novels. At first glance, Malcolm's 1990 book is a scathing indictment of not just this type of journalism, but of all forms of journalism relying on the journalist/source relationship. The first lines of the book are justly famous:

> Every journalist who is not too stupid or too full of himself to notice what is going on knows that what he does is morally indefensible. He is a kind of confidence man, preying on people's vanity, ignorance, or loneliness, gaining their trust and betraying them without remorse . . . Journalists justify their treachery in various ways according to their temperaments. The more pompous talk about freedom of speech and "the public's right to know"; the least talented talk about Art; the seemliest murmur about earning a living.[4]

While generally considered a book on the unholy and asymmetrical relation between a journalist and his or her sources, Malcolm's text arrived in a public space still fighting the supposed theory wars of the same period, taking up the prominent questions batted about at that time: whether one could reach an extra-textual real outside the play of writing and textuality, whether the self had any meaning beyond a given set of texts, and, moreover, whether deconstruction, as practiced, for example, by Hugh J. Silverman, left us ultimately in a state of irresponsibility because anything, even the most heinous of acts, can always be read otherwise. My choice of this particular journalistic text is the result of a given set of contingencies: I happened upon it again after references to it appeared in light of the HBO documentary *The Jinx* (2015), given the ethical questions raised about the relationship between the film's director and its subject,[5] while I was also revising this text on Silverman for this book. This congruence helps me here to delineate something like an "applied textualities," if I may be forgiven the term, given that Silverman himself would want to critique any opposition between a theory and practice, between textualities and their application. Textualities, for him, were events or happenings (he preferred the plural of Heidegger's *Ereignis*, *Ereignisse*, to delineate their multiplicity), not something referring to that which is extra-textual.

For Silverman, elaborating upon theories of the text from the early Foucault, Derrida, Barthes, Kristeva, and others, while inventing a textual practice all his own, textualities are disclosed through "juxtapositional deconstructive" readings (*T*, 3). The task of this kind of reading is not to reduce any given set of texts to a single signification, but to think the "place between" multiple methods, readings, and spaces. As such, both *Inscriptions* and *Textualities* explicate the "play of differences" between, within, and among texts through what Silverman dubbed a "hermeneutic semiology" operating at the "the hinge" between the science of signs and the ontico-ontological difference, between differential displacement of semiological difference and the opening of the meaning of being. (In his courses, Silverman often diagrammed his notion of difference as the happening or event at the crossing of a vertical line representing ontological difference and a horizontal line representing semiological difference.) Here Silverman summarizes his long practice of reading, though again, he did not regard reading as something extrinsic to the event of texts:

> [A] hermeneutic semiology would seek to offer a reading of the text in terms of its meaning structures as they relate to elements in the world and as they refer back not to a centered self but to the interpretive activity itself. Such a reading of meaning structures in their plurisignificational character occurs in a cultural/natural, social/individual, etc. *milieu* as a *reading* of the textuality (or textualities) of the text. (*T*, 30)

The sites of Silverman's readings in *Textualities* were examples of what he dubbed "autobiographical textualities," such as Thoreau's *Walden* and Nietzsche's *Ecce Homo*, where the self, as it were, is disseminated through a given series of texts. Rather than denouncing the self or subject as a dead theme after the various 1960s declarations of the "death of man," Silverman's abiding concern, from his 1975 article "Man and the Self as Identity of Difference"[6] to his posthumously published essay "The Postmodern Subject: Truth and Fiction in Lacoue-Labarthe's Nietzsche,"[7] was to think the differential spacing of the subject as texts and textuality while refusing to grant the self a "transcendental" position (*T*, 17).

With this in mind, we can return to the 1984 case at the heart of *The Murderer and the Journalist*, which pitted McGinniss as a defendant against Jeffrey MacDonald, who in 1979 was convicted of the murder of his pregnant wife and two children. MacDonald, raised on Long Island, where Silverman made his home for almost all of his career, was a former Green Beret who for nearly a decade after the 1970 murders was a prominent southern California doctor. He had been charged by a military court in 1970 but was acquitted given the murky evidence in the case, evidence that would not become any clearer in the years ahead. To this day, MacDonald claims the murders were committed by Charles Manson–type "hippies," an account prosecutors believe to have been invented from media depictions that year of the Manson murders, which themselves produced the true crime book *Helter Skelter* (1974) by Vincent Bugliosi. In the late 1970s, after his indictment, McGinniss befriended MacDonald, even moving in with him for long stretches and becoming a member of his defense team. In the civil case, MacDonald produced reams of letters from McGinniss that were cajoling, supportive, and all but expressive of a certain love he had for him. Upon the 1983 release of the book McGinniss wrote about the case, *Fatal Vision*, MacDonald saw just how much he had been had: his effusive friend now described him a psychotic killer of the first order, someone led by latent homosexuality and a problematic relationship with his mother to kill his wife, whom McGinniss said had become a threat to his ego when she began taking night classes in psychology. Claiming to reach beyond the texts and textuality, McGinniss argued that he could identity the truth of MacDonald, a real self lurking behind the text of his letters and the clichés of his speech patterns, a demonic evil lying beneath the surface of a banal man. This seemed to be the task for many involved in the MacDonald case over the years: lawyers, psychiatrists, and journalists alike. Just who was this self behind the various texts produced by MacDonald, and could this self have committed the 1970 murders?

The civil case itself need not detain us further in its details, though Malcolm notes the bitter irony that in the contest between the journalist and the convicted murderer, it was the convicted murderer who had the sympathy of the jury. Malcolm's book coalesces around three interrelated themes, all allied with Silverman's long investigations of textualities (always best considered in the plural): (1) the conflict of interpretations at the heart of any trial and, more widely, any judgment worthy of the name; (2) the journalistic belief that its "just the facts" approach refers to a meta-textual set of truths; and (3) the hubris of psychiatrists, lawyers, and the participants in the case to believe they could puncture a given set of texts to an extra-textual "identity" of MacDonald. Taking up the third theme for the moment, following Silverman, we could say that MacDonald was always going to be betrayed by any texts produced by or for him, with or without the malice of McGinniss. MacDonald had hoped for McGinniss to be the prosthesis for his own "autobiographical textualities," to use Silverman's terminology; that is, MacDonald had expected McGinniss to write his life by repeating his words and actions in a narrative defense, all to prove his ultimate goodness and thus his innocence. McGinniss himself meanwhile was to produce in *Fatal Vision*, his account of the trial and his own rationale for MacDonald's guilt, his own autobiographical textualities, an account of himself and his years studying the case. Every piece of purported journalism is a confession in the most classical sense: I owe you the truth of my existence, as that presence to a given set of evidence, even as that "self is dispersed into a textuality" (*T*, 92). The mistake McDonald made was to see autobiography as a nonliterary genre, to think that the author can produce the truth of one's life. Every journalistic text is a form of confession, an appeal to an impossible "I" who asserts the truth of what she has seen. As Silverman puts it, "[f]irst person singular journalistic novels . . . where the 'I' predominates, are written explicitly with devices to separate the 'I' of the text from the authorial 'I,'" that is, devices to separate the objective veridical subject at the heart of the narrative uncovering the truth and the psychological self supposedly outside the text (*T*, 93). But as Malcolm puts it:

> [T]he "I" character in journalism is almost pure invention. . . . The journalistic "I" is an overreliable narrator, a functionary to whom crucial tasks of narration and argument and tone have been entrusted, an ad hoc creation, like the chorus of Greek tragedy. He is an emblematic figure, an embodiment of the idea of the dispassionate observer of life.[8]

Yet this invention or fiction at the heart of the journalistic enterprise doesn't absolve either the author or her subjects from irreducible relations of responsibility and judgment, even as there is always a relation of autobiography to literature and vice versa: "[A]t the limit of non-fictionalization, autobiography spills over into fictionalization and at the limit of fictionalization, autobiographical textuality announces a non-fictionalization that can help the reader understand the other features of the autobiographer's experience, knowledge, and conviction" (*T*, 97). That the literary and the autobiographical are inseparable would turn out to be paramount in the case, because we presume that the journalist is out for a given truth, or indeed that a trial should excavate beneath competing narratives, beneath the various phrases in dispute, to find out the truth, for example, of the real events of the murder or the fraud alleged in the civil case. In this, McGinniss's claim at trial—to the surprise of jurors and judges alike—that he used all of the resources of literary genres is correct: it could not have been otherwise, as Silverman's *Textualities* makes clear at several crucial points.

The irresponsibility of McGinniss was to believe he could pierce through the text of "MacDonald" to some *real* self. This hubris is the effect of playing the omniscient narrator, to presume a God's power to know all up to and including the transcendental signified that would be "MacDonald." It would be, then, a claim not just to omniscience but also an ability to judge good and evil, to identify it in a given psychopathology, an updated demonology for the post-Freudian age. As Malcolm notes in passages strikingly similar to Hannah Arendt's claims in *Eichmann in Jerusalem* (1963), evil is not some intrinsic stain upon the soul, an evil genius of a sort that is inhuman, but is to be found in an all-too-human and cliché-mumbling personality. Evil is worldly, mundane, even if not banal to those treated to it. As Malcolm puts it, "The concept of the psychopath is, in fact, an admission of failure to solve the mystery of evil—it is merely a restatement of the mystery—and only offers an escape valve for the frustration felt by psychiatrists, social workers, and police officers, who daily encounter" it.[9] As in all the minutia and clichés of the Eichmann trial years before, evil is not something extra textual, but, as they say, is in the details. Texts are not something that can refer to us to some extra-textual evil, some ultimate irresponsibility, but are, as Silverman would put it, the *topoi* in which these events happen.

Textuality and Responsibility

As such, as Silverman noted time and again, there is no piercing of texts and textuality to reach some real *autos* or self, some ultimate presence beyond the play of textuality (*T*, 131–33). As Derrida noted in *Of Grammatology* in a passage important to Silverman:

> [Reading] cannot legitimately transgress the text toward *something other than it* [my emphasis], toward a referent (*a reality that is metaphysical* [my emphasis], historical, psychobiographical, etc.) or toward a signified outside the text whose content could take place, could have taken place *outside of language* [my emphasis], that is to say, in the sense that we give here to that word, *outside of writing in general*. . . . [I]n what one calls the real life of these existences "of flesh and bone," beyond and behind what one believes can be circumscribed as [e.g.] Rousseau's text, there has never been anything but writing; there have never been anything but supplements, substitutive significations which could only come forth in a chain of *differential* references, the "real" supervening, and being added only while taking on meaning from *a trace* and from an invocation of the supplement, etc.[10]

In hermeneutical terms, the text is not a meaning-object constituted by an author, but a meaning-object constituted by an interpreter, whether it is the author or a later reader. The text as textuality is both the interpreter and that which is interpreted: "There is no reader outside the text by which the meaning can be said to enter the text" (*T*, 79). In sum, there is no transcendental place from which to pronounce the meaning of a given text and end the play of texts and historicity of their meaning—the fact that each text is open to different and changing mediations and interpretations (and this is all they are). In terms of court cases and even the most prosaic of journalistic accounts, this does not mean that we posit some unreachable *an sich* beyond our interpretations, as if textualities were a semiological update of the Kantian categories. As Derrida puts it:

> [T]he concept of text or of context which guides me embraces and does not exclude the world, reality, history. Once again (and this probably makes a thousand times I have had to repeat this, but when will it finally be heard, and why this resistance?): as I understand it (and I have

> explained why), the text is not the book, it is not confined in a volume itself confined to the library. It does not suspend reference—to history, to the world, to reality, to being, and especially not *to the other*, since to say of history, of the world, of reality, that they always appear in an experience, hence in a movement of interpretation which contextualizes them according to a network of differences and hence of referral to the *other*, is surely to recall that *alterity* (difference) is irreducible.[11]

Silverman recognized this clearly, and his thinking of textuality was as the between space at the non-connective intersection of Heidegger's ontological difference and the horizontal movements of Saussurean semiological difference. Does this mean we cannot deal with the question of evil, the real evil often in our midst? Isn't this the story that we have often been told about the postmodern or indeed about postmodernisms? That it is *only* textuality and that the real has been lost in a thicket of simulacra and indecidables? And wasn't Silverman one of the prime instigators of this, arguing that "[t]extuality is the indecidability of the text," and so forth? (*T*, 85). Let me cite a bit from Silverman where he delineates the key aspects of his media theory:

> Postmodern media are not real. Postmodern media are also not unreal. Postmodern media are not true. Postmodern media are not untrue. Postmodern media operate *in medias res*. They do not constitute the real and they do not constitute the virtual. They do not deny reality. They do not create illusions. They are however lived reality. Lived reality is not a manifold of references outside of the media world. Lived reality is the media world. Lived reality is not the real as such nor is it the virtual as such. Lived reality is the textuality of postmodern media.[12]

This "textuality" is what Hugh also called the multiple events, the unpresentability in presentation itself, the *Ereignisse* of the postmodern or postmodernisms. Isn't this the ultimate antirealism, falling for the claim that all is the product of subjective and hence autobiographical texts and textuality? Or, to cite Thoreau from *Walden*, a text that Silverman cites in *Textualities* as his favorite early book, does this not provide us the belief that "the universe constantly and obediently answers to our conceptions"? (*W*, 95). Isn't this what has been challenged in recent years by the new Continental realists, who disparage work like Silverman's as belonging to a bygone age of postmodernists putting the human off in the woods of solitude, unable to think anything outside the thick nest of the downed trees of human discourse? Yet what I learned from Silverman was that the postmodernisms were not antithetical to some supposed realism—the haughty word, I should say, of those who never wanted to understand what postmodernism was in the first place, using it as a blanket phrase for everything from capitalist exploitation to kitsch to everything bad that happened after Reaganism.

Indeed, while we might hold that self-supposed realisms are perhaps more innocent as a metaphysics, even if Silverman would hold that those metaphysics are unworkable, Silverman's writing argued that metaphysical realisms are politically and ethically dangerous, because this would be to presume an "outside" from which the philosopher can speak for some identity, nature, or self, while denying the position and historicity of that very engagement. For my part, I think it best not to give up the word "real" to those metaphysicians turning back not just to before the linguistic turn, but before Kant as well, and to show how textuality itself requires a difference/deferral that is a real time/spacing itself. But Silverman was right to suggest that the turn to the textuality of philosophy signals a major shift, one that I think, despite all the hand-wringing over our postmodern condition, has yet to be taken up in political, legal, and journalistic circles, as commentary, beginning with Malcolm's book from 1990, make clear. Silverman writes (and allow me to quote at length, for this provides something of a summation, though there cannot be such a thing, of the philosophy inscribed within Silverman's autobiographical textualities):

> The textuality of philosophy marks a major shift in the understanding of philosophy in the contemporary world. It signals a reinscription of philosophy into the frameworks of textual practice. It also links up textuality with the relation between philosophy and literature. This means that philosophy cannot be understood simply as an attempt to wonder about, inquire into, reflect upon, produce arguments for, or create a system for the natural and cultural worlds in which we live. Rather philosophy must now be understood as a kind of text whose textuality spills over into a wide variety of

> domains—areas which themselves have become textualized in contemporary theory. What counts as philosophy is no longer limited to the titles of the books of Aristotle. What lies outside these names is a further domain of thought and understanding. Philosophical psychology is also a matter of philosophical autobiography, philosophical anthropology is also a matter of the cultural text, political philosophy is also the social text, philosophy of science is also the discourses of scientific practice . . . Philosophy textualizes itself in an ever disseminated, ever deployed practice.[13]

Which is to say that we deny a certain textuality and what Foucault called power/knowledge when we think that texts make transcendent claims—or better that they are more than simply *claims* to a transcendental signified. As the subtitle of Lyotard's *The Differend*, a text Silverman taught each year and referenced often, put it, there are only phrases in dispute: "a universal rule of judgment between heterogeneous genres is lacking," Lyotard argues, and the example he uses throughout is "litigation."[14] There is no third party on the scene to adjudicate these textualities not because there are only two parties, but because there is always a third, a fourth, and so on, for Silverman. There exists thus a seemingly unwinnable war between narrative and truth. Thus, for example, as Malcolm put it, the "law's demand that witnesses speak 'nothing but the truth' is a demand no witness can fulfill."[15] Where then is responsibility? After all, a trial ought to convict the guilty (leaving aside all the problems of the prison-industrial complex); a journalist ought to "get it right" and not just reproduce the narratives of the powerful; and a philosopher ought to tell us the truth of the real, even if it's simply to say that the real is not something one can give a kick to when the mood strikes. But this responsibility, for Silverman, should not mean that one presumes one has given a fixed truth, which Silverman often put under the heading of "identity" thinking:

> Making sense together—as we know from Saussurian semiology, identities are only by virtue of their differences from one another . . . Responsibility is shared—set off against and brought together at the borders that link us and separate us, that name each of our identities by virtue of the events (*Ereignisse*) of difference that delineate our anonymous ethical embodiments.[16]

In short, then, "[r]esponsibility does not happen apart from a relation, a relation of difference. . . . [T]he event of responsibility is an event of significance since it links two or more persons, two or more institutions, two or more positions of response."[17] Irresponsibility, then, would be the denial of the event of difference, producing a wrong that at the same time denies the other of entering into litigation over that wrong—murder, for example.[18] It is just toward such a thinking of textual justice that is the legacy of Hugh J. Silverman, one not just available in his many writings, but also in the numerous events of the "between" in his classrooms and in the panels of the annual IAPL. The weight of Silverman's thought is indelible, marked out in the textualities of responsibility that should help us rethink more areas of endeavor than merely philosophy and literature. This legacy is what holds together a certain community to come marked by a responsibility compelling a rethinking of these other areas of thought, including the law and journalism. Let me give the last word to Silverman:

> Responsibility can only happen in the between, in the spaces and gaps, in the chiasms and chasms that link us and separate us. As individuals, we may not feel compelled to be responsible either for what we do or for the other since responsibility does not belong to any one of us, and yet responsibility calls for a compelling, calls to be compelling. Hence, if there is to be a legacy, there will need to be a place for the responsibility that compels it. Such a place would be an interstitial place that does not belong to anyone in particular, but that nevertheless links everyone in the community in question in a web of responsibility, an enframing that encircles without being a circle, a context in which responding happens between interlocutors and members of the society—and not one built on a bundle of singularities. . . . whose response-ability resides between us . . .[19]

Notes

1. Jean-Luc Nancy, *The Gravity of Thought*, trans. François Raffoul and Gregory Recco (Atlantic Highlands, NJ: Humanities Press, 1997), 76.

2. See, for example, his "Postmoderne Medien und die Angst vor Simulationen," trans. Erik Michael Vogt, in *film denken / thinking film: Film and Philosophy*, ed. Ludwig Nagl, Eva Waniek, and Brigitte Mayr (Vienna: SYNEMA—Gesellschaft für Film und Medien, 2004), 139–48.

3. Janet Malcolm, *The Journalist and the Murderer* (New York: Vintage, 1990).

4. Ibid., 3.

5. See, for example, Rebecca Mead, "The Queasy Finale of *The Jinx*," *New Yorker*, March 16, 2015, http://www.newyorker.com/culture/cultural-comment/robert-dursts-grotesque-confession.

6. Hugh J. Silverman, "Man and the Self as Identity of Difference," *Philosophy Today* 19, no. 2 (Summer 1975): 131–36.

7. Hugh J. Silverman, "The Postmodern Subject: Truth and Fiction in Lacoue-Labarthe's Nietzsche," in *Subjects and Simulations: Between Baudrillard and Lacoue-Labarthe*, ed. Anne O'Byrne and Hugh J. Silverman (New York: Lexington Books, 2015), 47–56.

8. Malcolm, *The Journalist and the Murderer*, 159–60.

9. Ibid., 75.

10. Jacques Derrida, *Of Grammatology*, trans. Gayatri Chakravorty Spivak (Baltimore: Johns Hopkins University Press, 1976), 158.

11. Derrida, *Limited Inc.*, trans. Samuel Weber (Evanston, IL: Northwestern University Press, 1988), 137; emphasis added.

12. Silverman, "Postmoderne Medien," 140.

13. Hugh J. Silverman, "Nachwort: Über Textualität der Philosophie—Philosophie und Literature," *Über Textualität der Philosophie: Philosophie und Literature*, ed. Ludwig Nagl and Hugh J. Silverman (Munich and Vienna: Oldenbourg Verlag, 1994), 246–57. English version, http://www.hughjsilverman.com/hjs_online_texts/Silverman-TEXTUALITY%20OF%20PHILOSOPHY-Afterword%20(2004).pdf. Last accessed March 1, 2014.

14 Jean-François Lyotard, *The Differend: Phrases in Dispute*, trans. Georges Van Den Abbeele (Minnestota: University of Minnesota Press, 1988), xi.

15. Janet Malcolm, *The Crime of Sheila McGough* (New York: Vintage, 1999), 2.

16. Hugh J. Silverman, "Living On (Borderlines): The Ethics of the Event of Lived Human Relations (Merleau-Ponty/Derrida)," *Chiasmi International* 6 (2005): 282.

17. Hugh J. Silverman, "Respons-abilities—Between Three," *Archivo di Filosopfia*, LXXIV, nos. 1–3 (2006): 489.

18. Lyotard, *The Differend*, 5.

19. Silverman, "Response-abilities for Legacies," 305.

11

Postmodernisms

On a Posthumous Book

Gertrude Postl

When Hugh J. Silverman died in 2013, he left behind a book-length manuscript consisting of previously published and unpublished essays held together by the theme of "the postmodern." The prospective title of the book was *Postmodernisms: Between Ethics and Aesthetics.*[1] Given the central role postmodernism played in Hugh's overall corpus of work, especially during his later years, the present text is an attempt to offer some insights into the kind of concerns he had planned to pursue in a future that would never arrive. The manuscript consists of a collection of twenty-five essays, each highlighting a particular aspect of postmodernism, such as "Postmodern Turns," "Postmodern Temporalities," "Postmodern Ethics," "Postmodern Subjects," and "Postmodern Strangers," just to name a few. Those chapters are grouped within three large sections, "Postmodern Moments," "Postmodern Relations," and "Postmodern Arts." The introduction was supposed to be titled "Postmodern Pluralities," but it was never finished. Overall, the manuscript offers an account of Silverman's view of the postmodern in a much more comprehensive sense than the dispersed, previously published articles could have ever accomplished.

Hugh's Postmodernisms

Hugh was never deterred by claims that the debate over postmodernism would be outdated, a short-lived intellectual hype or fashionable movement. He also was not interested in relating his own view of postmodernism to the all-too-well-known accusations brought forth against it, for example, the death of the subject, its ultimate relativism, the impossibility of an epistemologically reliable notion of truth, the lack of universally binding moral principles, turning everything into a text and thus rendering it the subject of either aesthetic or semiotic analysis, in short, the charge that postmodern theory is nothing other than the permission that "anything goes." Although appropriating well-known characteristics of the postmodern, such as citationality, the blending of styles (as to be found in architecture and art), or its anti-metaphysical and anti-Enlightenment outlook (as in philosophy or cultural theory), his own "position" never wanted to be *a position*.

Hugh conceived of the postmodern in terms of a plurality. For him, there did not exist one "postmodernism" but many versions thereof, hence the plural in the title of his book: *Postmodernisms*. He furthermore insisted on distinguishing the postmodern from postmodernity, which, in his view, has been frequently misunderstood in terms of a periodization—an approach to the postmodern that he vehemently opposed. As will be shown, the postmodern cannot be understood beyond or outside the modern. And—in accordance with his rejection of a concept of identity—he refused to define or characterize postmodernisms or to summarize alleged characteristics in terms of a set of theses or tenets. Rather than defining or explaining the postmodern, his strategy throughout the text is to *demonstrate* the manifold manifestations of postmodernisms by way of—what we might call—a "reading practice" (taken in the broadest sense of the term). In Hugh's account, postmodernism is a *doing*, a certain way of approaching and interacting with contemporary as well as past theoretical and cultural developments. The goal of said "reading practice" is not to interpret a text or cultural event or—in a Heideggerian sense—to unearth a hidden truth but, rather, to bring these texts and events into an exchange with each other. Postmodernisms, for Hugh, are not just ways of deciphering texts or analyzing them in a semiotic gesture; instead, he wanted them to speak with each other.

Thus, the most striking feature of the manuscript is the overabundance of material discussed and the variety of individual works and events that are being connected and brought into an often unexpected and unpredictable discourse with each other. Theory, culture, and political and social events crisscross each other in rhizomatic fashion; are presented in their differences and interlinked by (sometimes randomly) chosen topics or themes. Philosophy, literature, films, TV shows, artworks, architecture, music (all from different time periods), but also the European Union or the new Europe, presidential elections, sport events, and the state of the university are set up within various patterns of interaction and recurring themes. None of these texts, events, or phenomena is more important than the others; there is no hierarchy or recognizable predetermined decision with respect to impact, influence, or importance. They cover a spectrum from well-known to unknown, from high culture to trashy, from well established to minor contributions. Here just some of the names discussed in the text. From philosophy: Nietzsche, Freud, Heidegger, Merleau-Ponty, Sartre, Foucault, Derrida, Lyotard, Baudrillard, Nancy, Rancière, Lacoue-Labarthe, Irigaray, Kristeva, Cixous; from literature: Greek mythologies, Shakespeare (*Hamlet* and *Romeo and Juliet*), Don Juan (in various versions), Dante, Brecht's *Threepenny Opera*, Umberto Eco; from painting: Andy Warhol, Barnett Newman, Valerio Adami, René Magritte, Anselm Kiefer, Gerhard Richter, Maria Theresia Litschauer; movies: Peter Greenaway's *The Cook, the Thief, his Wife and her Lover*, Jim Jarmusch's *Ghost Dog*, Vincent Ward's *What Dreams May Come?*, Peter Weir's *The Truman Show*, David Lynch's *Wild at Heart*, Joseph Ruben's *Return to Paradise*, Ivan Reitman's *Ghostbusters*, Robert Zemeckis' *Who Framed Roger Rabbit*, and, time and again, Quentin Tarantino's *Pulp Fiction*; from TV shows: *Twin Peaks*, and many others are mentioned; from social or political events: the European Union or the new Europe, Y2K, the 2000 presidential elections, the state of the university and the humanities in particular, the Yankees, soccer championships. Many more names, titles, and events are just mentioned or briefly discussed in passing.

There are no recognizable criteria as to which text/artwork/event is brought into contact with which other text/artwork/event and why. Many of the evoked interactions or juxtapositions seem arbitrary, some are obvious, others a little far-fetched. But what all of the discussed works or events have in common is that they are different from each other. In that everything is constituted by the difference to something else, the entire book could be described as a network of connections and juxtapositions through differences. If one were to search for a central concept at the core of Hugh's view of postmodernism, it would have to be the notion of differences. "Postmodernism articulates places of differences," he states in chapter 7, "Postmodern Ends: The Ends of Indifference" (a text that connects Gianni Vattimo's *End of Modernity*, Anselm Kiefer, and David Lynch's *Wild at Heart*).

> [T]o be in-difference is to think, to be, and to do—but differentially and not out of unity, univocity, or identity—but also not out of pure diversity, multiplicity, distinction either. To be in-difference is to think in difference . . . difference in tradition, difference in novelty, difference in beginnings, difference in ends, difference in identity, difference in difference!

Hugh does not deny or refute the respective counter-categories; he does not deny unity, identity, the subject, ethical agency, and so forth, as long as they are placed within a network of differences and approached from the perspective of multiplicity and heterogeneity. Only then will it be possible to focus on the spaces, interstices, intervals that are created through this ongoing process of differentiation—his favorite notion of the "in-between." This is to say, it is not so much the identity or unity or coherence of something that matters (of a fictional character, a person, the subject, ethical principles, etc.) but the many identities, unities, coherences that can be differentiated from each other, thereby forming a web of meaning in which the individual elements are juxtaposed with each other—joining, intersecting, but also interrupting each other. Connecting what does not seem to be connected (e.g., the ghost of Hamlet's father, the ghostlike figures in Anselm Kiefer's *Wege der Weltweisheit*, and the movie *Ghostbusters* in chapter 8: "Postmodern Returns: The Power of Ghosts") to explore the spaces that are created by differentiating it—this is what Hugh considered to be postmodern.

Subsequently, as had been stated already, Hugh did not conceive of postmodernisms in terms of a periodization, as that which comes after the modern. Rather, the modern and the postmodern have always already been intertwined. Defining the modern in terms of a search for the new (new styles, new forms, new movements, new practices, etc.), as intentionally leaving previous periods and styles behind, the postmodern becomes part of this modern but also clearly distinguished from it:

> The postmodern is inscribed in the modern . . . The postmodern comes after the modern only in the sense that it inscribes itself in the modern which is already there. But the postmodern does not refuse, reject, or replace the modern . . . The postmodern does not interrupt the modern or any of its expressions. The postmodern identifies the places of interruption, of fissure, of break of rupture in the modern itself . . . The postmodern is not a new mode of expression. The postmodern is not avant-garde. The postmodern is not a new style that comes after the modern . . . The postmodern has its place only in the modern itself. (chapter 3: "Postmodern Interruptions")

Hugh reads the modern (going all the way back to Enlightenment thought and not restricting himself to modernism in the sense of just the avant-garde) as marked by a search for coherence, identity, temporal and spatial unity, systems of thought (Lyotard's master narratives), homogeneity, the oppositions between subject and object, appearance and reality, truth and untruth, right and wrong, and so forth. Accordingly, the postmodern would be anything that interrupts, undermines, irritates, implodes the seeming coherence and order of modern thought. Comparable to what Derrida does with the center and the margins, Hugh's perspective on postmodernism can best be described in terms of the relation between identity and difference—with identity being the mark of the modern and as such to be maintained within the network of differences (rather than being replaced). His main concern is not to privilege difference over identity, but rather to open spaces in between both by highlighting differences. "The postmodern and more specifically postmodern thinking demands to think differences, to think supplementarity, indecidability, marginality. But supplements, indecidables, margins are all marked out *in modernity*" (chapter 7: "Postmodern Ends: The Ends of Indifference").

The Western philosophical and cultural tradition is arranged along a timeline of distinct historical periods and a series of canonical texts and events allegedly representative of this period. In that for Hugh postmodernism is a reading practice that interconnects and juxtaposes texts/events from different periods and genres to explore their differences, the original confinements of periodization and the canon are transgressed, and new perspectives on historically anchored canonical texts or events become possible.

This understanding of postmodernism (and of the modern) allows for a reading of clearly modernist figures, for example, avant-garde painters such as René Magritte or Barnett Newman (here following Lyotard) in terms of postmodernism. "This is not to say that Newman is a postmodern—not at all. He is still avant-garde. He is still inscribed in the history of modernism." But, according to Silverman, here following Lyotard, his paintings carry the mark of the postmodern. The zips on Newman's panels, "located in various sites across the painting, interrupting, but also bringing together the panels, constitute that which is unpresentable in the painting." These zips, read as "sites of difference" and "sublime moments," initiate an interaction between the individual panels of the painting and their disruptions. "The postmodern sites are events of difference between the panels and the zips, or between the panels when the zips interrupt the panels, or between the zips when the panels interrupt the zips." Newman's zip paintings become the "gaps, ruptures, fissures in the modern itself" and thus bring into interrelation the New of the modern and the Unpresentable of the postmodern by navigating through spaces of difference (chapter 5: "Postmodern Events: Sites of the Postmodern Sublime").

As should be obvious from this example, for Hugh, particular philosophers, painters, texts are not either modern or postmodern—postmodernism is a practice that can be applied to any philosophy, any painter, any text, any movie. Talking about Derrida's *Specters of Marx*, he claims: "Derrida reads the Shakespearean play not as a Renaissance period piece, but rather as the inscription of the postmodern in the modern, as the spectral presence of that which is not seen by most . . ." (chapter 1: "Postmodern Turns: Fin-de-siècle Crises"). The postmodern as a "spectral presence," lingering over the canonical highpoints of Western culture, ready to interrupt and disturb them any moment—just like the ghost of Hamlet's father disturbed Hamlet's meandering and self-centered thoughts. The ghostlike presence of "that which is not seen by most" can also be taken as that which has been located outside or beyond the canon, which is different from that which is seen, known, has a presence. But it is not in itself postmodern—it just is not seen, its excluded ghostly presence constituting a difference to that which is seen. Nothing is in itself postmodern—not that which comes after nor that which is outside the modern. "What links the contemporary university, the new Europe, Magritte's *Poison*, and the Minerva sign-statue[2] is in the reading of them. None is in itself postmodern" (chapter 3: "Postmodern Interruptions: Marking European Differences").

This view of the postmodern in terms of a connecting and differentiating reading practice allows for the elimination of preestablished hierarchies and categories regarding texts, authors, artists, genres, events. Marginal, unimportant, or excluded thoughts, works, genres, or events become visible by shifting the focus to the differences within the established canon but also to the differences between what is "seen by most" and what is "not seen by most." To do so, to focus on the differences and ruptures rather than the identities and coherences, unhinges the very foundation of modern thought, makes it out of joint, fragments it, disconnects it, thus opening up spaces and possibilities concealed in the seeming coherence of modern progress. And what could be more interrupting or irritating than mixing the high and the low, different academic disciplines and artistic genres, "deep" philosophical theories and second-rate films, highlights of the literary canon and TV shows? Placing next to each other—without any concern for established hierarchies or significance—not just different genres and areas but different levels of alleged importance and relevance allows for the juxtaposition and interaction of a broad spectrum of material without any hint or guidance as to which is more or less important. Oppositions such as canonical/excluded, important/unimportant, central/marginal, profound/superficial, scholarship/popular, art/entertainment, high/low, and so forth become meaningless and irrelevant. By discussing any chosen text, artwork, or event in a similar fashion well-established categories and distinctions are bypassed and intentionally ignored, thus enabling dimensions of meaning previously concealed or hidden. Reading the ghost of Hamlet's father first through a Derridean lens and then relating its spectral presence to Anselm Kiefer's painted ghostlike images of a glorious German past and to Bill Murray's attempt of ridding haunted buildings of their ghostly intruders will certainly change one's perception of Shakespeare's famous play forever.

The implications of Hugh's postmodern reading practice for traditional areas and questions in philosophy are hard to pinpoint and difficult to summarize. Thus, here are just a few sketchy traces, mostly in his own words, to illustrate just how radical a shift in perspective his understanding of postmodernisms might bring about.

Postmodern Subject

The modern tradition conceived of the subject as a—in Hugh's words—"self-same." Descartes's *Cogito*, Kant's *Ich denke*, Locke's and Hume's conception of personal identity serve as examples of a notion of the subject Hugh wants to move away from. However, contrary to many prejudices about postmodernism, Foucault's death of the subject is not the way to go either—eliminating the subject altogether would be just as limiting as the so-called "self-same." Rather, drawing upon Lacoue-Labarthe and Nietzsche, Hugh offers an altogether different avenue: "The modern subject has become—like Nietzsche's 'true world'—a fiction" (chapter 9: "Postmodern Subjects: When the Modern Subject Becomes a Fable . . ."). Embedded in a discussion of the flawed distinction between philosophy and literature, Hugh sets up the postmodern subject as a fable, thus multiplying, disseminating, decentering it; but, most importantly, replacing the metaphysical assumption of a self-same core into many narratives. The postmodern subject is not a dead subject. Rather, it seems to become a network of texts or stories.

> A fable is a fabulation, a tale told with a moral . . . To say that the postmodern subject is a fable is to say not only that it is a potential fiction, but also that each enactment will bring a different lesson, another moral, one further way of being. The postmodern subject is many tales, many moral, many lessons . . . The postmodern subject is not dead. It is not wiped from the scene. It is not despairing of its lost unity. The postmodern subject is many fables—each juxtaposed alongside the others. The postmodern subject is indeed already many subjects, many stories, many different narratives, many ways to be . . . (chapter 9: "Postmodern Subjects")

Postmodern Ethics

Discussing Irigaray's *Ethics of Sexual Difference*, Sophocles's *Antigone*, and the movie *Return to Paradise* (Joseph Ruben), Hugh sets out to apply his postmodern reading practice also to questions of ethics.

> An ethics of postmodern differences will be an ethics in which the traditional conception of an ethics of agency is overturned . . . An ethics of postmodern differences will no longer be able to rely on the autonomy of the subject, the identity of the agent, the self-determination of the ethical self. An ethics of postmodern differences will place the weight of attention on the constitution of differences between subjects, between agents, between persons." (chapter 12: "Postmodern Ethics: Giving Time and the Interval")

Employing Irigaray's concept of the "interval" (read in terms of remainders, leftovers, links, connections, relations), Hugh situates the entire ethical "transaction" in the space that is is created through the juxtaposition of differences. The ethical, though, is not just a matter of individual encounters: "(T)he interval is not just between individuals, but also between genders, cultures, traditions, religions, standards, etc." The main question in this approach is not how we should act, but rather: "Can these differences operate without having to deny the alternatives?" Talking about the conflict between Creon and Antigone, Hugh states:

> Each [of them] must choose. An ethics of postmodern differences does not claim that there is not to be a choice, rather it will understand the differences that arise in terms of the choices that are made . . . A postmodern ethics will need to recognize the differences and to install this recognition in the places where choices are made. But the differences cannot themselves become identities . . . The requirement of univocity is essential to a modernist and even pre-modernist ethics. A postmodern ethics will not require this kind of univocity . . . The question for an ethics of postmodern differences is not whether one is right and the other wrong, but how to live with the differences! (chapter 12: "Postmodern Ethics")

Postmodern Politics

Some of the themes that serve as a hinge for Hugh to discuss questions of politics are community (Nancy), stranger (Kristeva), friendship (Derrida), but also environments, or institutions; a frequently used example is the European Union. An argumentative pattern similar to the one evoked for questions of ethics emerges. Associating the modern with identity, a postmodern politics is developed out of differences—differences between states, cultures, communities, differences in relationships and between institutions—and will take place in the space that opens up in between those entities: "The modern community is built on a myth—or the modern community is constructed according to the many myths that constitute its identity . . . Postmodern Communities are those communities which have nothing in common. They . . . share their differences and ignore their identities." Being critical of Enlightenment ideals of tolerance and mere acceptance of difference and also of the demand of the nation-state for "purity" (in terms of one identifying law, custom, language, rationality), Hugh offers a blueprint for a postmodern politics:

> [A] postmodern democracy of politics will operate with modern communities in order to in-operate them, to unwork them, to think them otherwise, to establish "meetings" at the sites of difference . . . A postmodern politics builds a politics of difference by operating in the sites of differences, by thinking its textualities of difference at its internal as well as external borders—no crack will be left unturned. (chapter 13: "Postmodern Communities: European Differences and the Question of Identity")

As with respect to questions of ethics, the focus for politics, too, shifts from conceptualizing it from the perspective of one nation, community, group, citizen, to what happens between those nations, communities, groups, or citizens. What Hugh claims for friendship becomes indicative also of a postmodern rethinking of the political process: "The responsibility of friendship is not something that belongs to one friend or the other . . . there are no friends who are not responsible for what happens between them" (chapter 11: "Postmodern Friends: Just Friends and Postmodern Relationships").

To conclude: Hugh's understanding of postmodernisms is in many points still a project in the making. However, the ideas put forth in the manuscript as well as its turn toward popular culture seem forward looking and stimulating enough to warrant serious consideration. Others will have written about Hugh's usual points of reference—Heidegger, Sartre, Merleau-Ponty, Derrida, Lyotard, to just name a few. I intentionally stayed away from this well-known philosophical territory in order to highlight those aspects of Hugh's thoughts that might have occupied his future work—had this future ever arrived . . .

Notes

1. Passages quoted here are identified according to the chapter number and title as found in the unpublished manuscript. Ideas explored in the manuscript are explored throughout Silverman's final publications and presentations.
2. A sculpture outside a former bookstore in Vienna.

Part 4

Care/Time/Community

Remembering Hugh J. Silverman

12

Hugh Silverman's Cosmopolitan Hospitality

Kelly Oliver

How is Hugh Silverman to be remembered? For his philosophical writings, for his teaching of students, for his political activities, for his family relations? For "[r]emarks he made, effects on others, views expressed, statements written"? (*T*, 217) "[A]ll inscribe the life, constitute the memory, mark off the line between the man and the memory, the difference between the life and the life story. One might ask then: what is the bottom line? The answer cannot be other than: living, living on, living on in memory" (*T*, 217–18). How will Hugh Silverman live on in our memories? Through his published words, like those just quoted, taken from a discussion of Derrida's remembrances of Heidegger? Through personal relationships? Through professional connections? "The writing of memory, memory of one no longer with us," says Hugh Silverman, "makes the life 'come alive' again" (*T*, 218). How can we live up to this monumental task of making Hugh Silverman come alive again through memory and narrative? One of the many things that Hugh's work reminds us is that although there are traces of life in the text, life always takes us beyond the text, even as the text takes us beyond itself.

Hugh Silverman's work is a testament to the connections between life, memory, and writing—not just writing, but also painting, photography, architecture, film, and the aesthetic dimension of life both as we live it and as we represent it. Indeed, in his authored books, Hugh focuses on the in-between, the borders, the lines that separate one from the other. Throughout his work, he is concerned with differences, not as they divide people or cultures, but rather as they bring them together. And Hugh was an expert at bringing different cultures and different people together. Of course, the International Association for Philosophy and Literature (IAPL) is a testament to this, but so are the scores of volumes of scholarly essays that he edited, many times giving junior faculty their first published article. With friends across the globe, fluent in several languages, and well traveled, Hugh was a true cosmopolitan, a citizen of the world.

Rather than seeing differences in terms of oppositions or obstacles, through his writing and his life, Hugh explored places of difference as places of understanding (*T*, 2). Describing his own work, he says, "While *Inscriptions* identifies the places of difference—the slashes, the borders, the belonging-together of alternatives—*Textualities* reiterates the 'place between' as the locus of multiple textualities" (*T*, 2). In his books and in his life, he brought different people and traditions into dialogue; he masterfully staged encounters not only to forge understanding, but also for the greatest possible effect. That is to say, he created memories.

As the founding director of the IAPL, Hugh brought together scholars of all levels from all over the world for an experience that they would never forget. His attention to detail and his sense of place and aesthetics meant that every IAPL was an adventure and an exploration of cultural, intellectual, and artistic differences. From the IAPL pencils and tote bags to the special art installations and "field trips," Hugh made each conference unforgettable. He welcomed and greeted each participant personally with his characteristic charm and grace, his deep but soft voice distinctive even in a crowded reception area. Every IAPL regular received not only Hugh's smiling salutations, but also his playful chiding for missing a conference five years earlier or staying only three days instead of the requisite seven.

As a true cosmopolitan, Hugh had an expansive sense of time as well as place. In Hugh's presence, time was stretched and extended to the point of tearing. A meeting with Hugh could tear into your schedule. And lunch with Hugh was always leisurely. Indeed, Hugh lived the connection between life and memory. At a committee meeting, Hugh would remind you of the history of the university and place your current project in that context. Hugh's generosity with his time made you feel special, but it also made you sure to have another appointment to get to at some point in the afternoon so that lunch didn't stretch into dinner. Perhaps this is because Hugh didn't latch onto beginnings or endings but focused on the middle, the in-between. What is the time of the middle? The time of the middle, this in-between time, is the time of life. Discussing a line from Lévi-Strauss's *Tristes tropiques*—"Time, in an unexpected way, has extended its isthmus between life and myself"—Hugh says, "Time . . . is in-between" (*T*, 113). Time, then, if not the bridge or the neck that connects one part or person to another, extends the possibility of that connection. Not through the ticking of the clock as a linear progression from beginning to end, but rather as the lived time, in-between, where dwelling and encounter become possible.

In his work and in his life, Hugh took the time to carefully stage encounters. And, in both, he embraced juxtaposition. Bringing together different, even unlikely, interlocutors, Hugh enjoyed standing back to watch the fireworks, reveling in their beauty and their energy. With his charm and dogged persistence, he convinced the most prominent living philosophers, theorists, critics, and artists to speak at the IAPL. (We continued to joke about the time that one of them, Luce Irigaray, with her thick French accent, called Hugh "Ugg" throughout the conference.) He persuaded scholars in various locales across the globe to host the conference. And he welcomed everyone to participate. (Speaking of Hugh's persuasive powers, on a trip from Stony Brook to State College on our way to SPEP, I was a captive audience in Hugh's car when, for the entire five-hour journey, he explained why I should become the next chair of the Philosophy Department. That trip certainly changed the trajectory of my career.) I would hazard that many academic careers, and maybe a few marriages, were launched at the IAPL. Hugh made it a place where young scholars just starting out, and senior scholars too, could experiment and test out ideas. And before it was "politically correct" to do so, he encouraged women and others from underrepresented groups to participate and made us feel welcome.

At the conclusion of Hugh Silverman's essay on Lévi-Strauss, he quotes this telling passage: "[T]here is no place for it [the self] between us and nothing. And if, in the last resort, I opt for us . . . I only have to choose for the choice itself to signify my unreserved acceptance of the human condition" (*T*, 123). Hugh reads this as a refusal to choose either the self or nothing—rather, it is the choice of something in-between, a version of the self constructed through a text addressed to others. What Hugh does not discuss is the choice of "us" rather than either the self or nothing, a choice that affirms the human condition of intersubjectivity, intertextuality, and ultimately interpersonal relationships. Like Lévi-Strauss, Hugh chose "us" over self or nothing. He tirelessly devoted himself to bringing people together to form an "us," if only momentarily, out of disparate selves.

Although we feel the loss of Hugh Silverman and his elegant cosmopolitanism, perhaps we can find some solace in these words, his words: "Dying makes remembering possible. Remembering another is retrieving the other from obscurity, making the other live again—in memory. Marking that memory not only with a memorial, a tombstone, an epitaph, an obituary, a biography, a testimonial, a recollection, or a prayer but also with a reinscription of the line of difference between living and dying as the line of difference between dying and remembering" (*T*, 220). In this beautiful passage, Hugh Silverman reminds us that remembering is possible only because dying is part of life. "Living that was, living that should be remembered or that cannot be forgotten, living that mattered, living that meant something," says Hugh Silverman, this living "lives on in remembering" (*T*, 219).

Hugh Silverman will be remembered for many things—his writing, his teaching, bringing people together, and the way that he made everything personal. Even though Hugh the man is gone, we can still find unforgettable traces of his exceptional grace and generosity not only in our own memories, but also in our writing, teaching, and professional relationships. Indeed, Hugh has left his mark on our profession, not just philosophy or comparative literature, but the humanities generally, insofar as the reach of his writing, his teaching, and the IAPL extend across the globe and touch the lives and work of so many of us, an "us" formed in large part through Hugh's hospitality.

13

Hugh—Taking Time and Taking Care

Edward S. Casey

Hugh liked to take his time on certain things—so much so at times that he angered those whom he did not frustrate. But I want to say that, instead of being a mere "character flaw" (whatever that means), this was simply the other side of his caring for so many things and so deeply for each. I speak as a fairly dilatory person myself: I confess that I, too, anger and frustrate colleagues and students, and this often reflects my not getting things done in time, or only in the nick of time. If Hugh was the dromedary, I have been the elephant: between us, the question was not (as in the classical contest between Achilles and the tortoise) who could get to the finish line first, but who could come in last or next to last, as if this were a special distinction. Bergson's undoing of Zeno's paradox would need to take a new twist by appealing to the sheer quality of being slow: the *lenteur*, the *Langsamkeit*, the *despacio* . . . Taking one's time in short . . .

One symptom of this shared penchant for slow motion was the fact that Hugh and I preferred to talk very late at night: usually, after midnight in his office down the corridor here in Harriman Hall. The clamor of the day had dimmed, and night had gently descended. In these nocturnal talks, the topics were quite varied, but one constant was departmental politics, where we often differed but learned a great deal from our very differences. When the differences were too great—as in the period in which the department was divided into the warring camps of "P1" and "P2"—we found we couldn't talk at all: we were "not on speaking terms." But this caesura did not last long: we made up personally even as the struggle continued, and I was chosen to lead the very forces he opposed. Hugh was long-suffering in his tolerance of what he took to be the follies of his friends. Aristotle says that every virtue has its defect, but in Hugh's case the opposite was also true: his very slowness, a defect on the scales of world time, was accompanied by long-term forgiveness, a virtue in any ethics worthy of the name.

Hugh Silverman knew *how to take time*—the right time for thinking over the important things and for taking the important actions. He was persistent in his pursuit of what he took to be the right course. It took years of effort, for example, to get the Philosophy and Art certificate here at Stony Brook approved and up and running. (I, more impatient, had even given up on it, and was amazed when it finally came through.) And I don't need to detail how incredibly persistent he was in seeing that the IAPL program was just right in every detail, every year. In this major endeavor, as in many more minor ones, he combined patience with a passion for perfection, which made him at times a difficult taskmaster but at all times a person of very high accomplishment whose teaching, writing, and administration benefited countless others. If he hadn't been so persistent in his time taking, he would not have done all that he did in a career that was cut short far too soon. He was my junior in age but my senior in the range and depth of his many achievements.

To take your time also means to *take time to think*. Hugh was an admirably reflective person—*thoughtful* to the "t" of this very word. For you see: what some may have assumed was a lack of energy or even passive-aggressiveness was in fact a facet of his thinking things over—and over and over. Rather than rushing to a quick conclusion or dismissing something out of hand in a febrile impatience born from a belief that there is not enough time, he *found the time in which to think things over*. For Hugh, there was always plenty of time to think through an issue until he had analyzed it to his own satisfaction. He wasn't going to be rushed—on anything—not even if his taking more time alienated some of his friends and puzzled some of his students. I respected this side of Hugh immensely; it was not a matter of the slow labor of the negative but of the slow rumination of a thinking that takes its own time. If Aristotle's God "thinks thought itself" (*nous noesis*), Hugh, as one of us mortals, *thought things thoroughly through.* To a dromocentric age in which ever-greater velocities form the manifest image of everyday life, Hugh Silverman offered an alternative: *take the time, all the time, that is needed*: every minute of it.

All this, timely as it was (and still is for us to commemorate Hugh's life and work), was only the other side of an even more significant dimension of his character: his *caring*. Hugh only took the time he did because he cared so much about the persons or events that absorbed him. He didn't take the time he did out of any effort to slow down for its own sake. Rather: he took all this time because the caring that characterized him so deeply required patient and persistent effort, dedicated attention to detail. In short: *concerted looking.* This looking was evident in the way he looked at others—whether a family member, a student, or a colleague (he had the habit of seating himself directly across from his interlocutor in the great table in his office: looking you straight in the eye). These were outward, visible signs of his caring as it drew others into its intimate circle.

But the caring itself stemmed from a deeper place. This was Hugh's utter, unqualified respect for other human beings, whatever their rank or walk of life. From the moment I first encountered him in the late 1970s, I was struck by the way in which he treated everyone with whom he interacted in a dignified manner, whether a work-study student or a celebrated professor. For many years, he was in the habit of taking our department's administrative assistant, Alissa, out to dinner each semester—a generous gesture that he extended to very few others. He did this not from a formal sense of duty, but from the depths of his own caring for others as unique persons, whatever their station in life. He cared for people as the very human beings they are.

This caring carried with it an affectionate dimension that is rarely witnessed among men in the philosophy profession. Out of affection alone—because he genuinely *liked* so many others—Hugh bonded with countless colleagues and students, forming with them an extraordinary community of outreach that gave to everyone who was part of that community a sense of belonging to something greater than they could ever be by themselves. This was true of those active in IAPL, those in the Merleau-Ponty Circle, and many in our department. This was a *communitas* founded much more on affection than on professional advantage or advancement.

Hugh brought care to bear in the realm of time, and he brought both—care and time alike—to his enduring friendships with others.

*
* *

Care and Time belong together. There is no care where there is no time to care, no time taken for caring. And there is equally no savoring of time's durational flow except from a position of caring for how things happen, how they unfold and turn out. In Hugh Silverman, care and time converged: they merged in his own person, in a unique pattern in which both were actively co-ingredient, one supporting the other, each reflecting the other, in a single conterminous sweep.

Heidegger claims famously that "the being of human being" is Care, and he said explicitly that human "[t]emporality [is] the Ontological Meaning of Care" (in the title of Book 3, Division 2, of *Being and Time*). He introduces the Care-Structure of *Dasein* with the myth of Cura ("Care"), and in closing I cite it at length (this was, after all, a text that Hugh knew well):

> Once when "Care" was crossing a river, she saw some clay; she thoughtfully took a piece and began to shape it. While she was thinking about what she had made, Jupiter came by. "Care" asked him to give it spirit, and this he gladly granted. But when she wanted her name to be bestowed upon it, Jupiter forbade this and demanded that it be given his name instead. While "Care" and Jupiter were arguing, Earth (Tellus) arose, and desired that her name be conferred upon the creature, since she had offered it part of her body. They asked Saturn to be the judge. And Saturn gave them the following decision, which seemed to be just: "Since you, Jupiter, have given its spirit, you should receive that spirit at death; and since you, Earth, have given its body, you shall receive its body. But since "Care" first shaped this creature, she shall possess it as long as it lives. And because there is a dispute among you as to its name, let it be called "homo," for it is made out of humus (earth).[1]

Hugh's spirit passed from his body with his last breath, and his body has been received by the earth. But his caring being, which was so evident to those of us who were fortunate enough to know him while he lived and as he lived—in his time on earth—continues to exist among us, and will inform our time together and for the rest of our lives. After all, this occasion was time taking and caring—now for Hugh.

Note

1. Martin Heidegger, *Being and Time*, trans. Joan Stambaugh, rev. Dennis J. Schmidt (Albany: State University of New York Press, 2010), 191.

14

"The Silverman Network"

Gail Weiss

In his 2000 essay "Is Merleau-Ponty Inside or Outside the History of Philosophy?," Hugh J. Silverman provides a reading of Maurice Merleau-Ponty's "Everywhere and Nowhere" essay in *Signs* that beautifully captures Silverman's own expansive view of philosophy. The strong echo of Silverman in Merleau-Ponty should not be surprising, however, given Silverman's claim that "Merleau-Ponty finds in the history of philosophy what he himself has already discovered in philosophy itself, that is, what he himself has already invented in his own understanding of philosophy."[1] Just as Merleau-Ponty locates traces of his own "carnal" philosophy in Husserl's work, so too, I would argue, can we discern Merleau-Ponty's influence upon Silverman's "philosophy of the between." One notable example of Merleau-Ponty's impact on Silverman's thought can be seen in Silverman's original reading of Merleau-Ponty's claim in *Signs* that "[p]hilosophy is everywhere, even in the 'facts,' and nowhere does it have a private realm which shelters it from life's contagion."[2] According to Silverman's interpretation:

> Philosophy is public, but it is also in every nook and cranny of human life (and not just in those domains that people notice). Its business is to uncover these spaces—all of them,

> wherever they are, in whatever domain: whether it be in human society, in the natural world, in art and literature, in ideas and thoughts, in everything and everywhere.

And he continues:

> Philosophy has no "private realm," no space that is inaccessible, no safe haven away from the pain and pleasure of daily life, away from the worries and joys of human experience, away from the toil and turmoil of commerce and international exchange, away from peace and war, away from faith and conviction, away from any aspect of human experience. Philosophy is everywhere and nowhere is inaccessible to it.[3]

Like Merleau-Ponty, Silverman finds philosophy's very ubiquity and non-locatability, its grounding in an "unlimited nonprivate experiential domain," to be a positive challenge rather than a limitation. As those who knew Silverman personally can readily attest, his openness to alterity, to the presence of philosophy in "every nook and cranny of human life," the very qualities he ascribes to Merleau-Ponty, are visible in everything he did, including his research, his teaching, his conversations, his professional obligations, his mentoring of students, his friendships, and his travels.[4]

Whereas Merleau-Ponty's writings loom so much larger than Merleau-Ponty the person for the majority of Merleau-Ponty scholars, I would have to say that, for me at least, Silverman the person was an even larger presence and had a much more extensive influence on the history of philosophy and on me as a philosopher than his actual writing, though the latter is clearly a major contribution in its own right. What I am calling "The Silverman Network" is intended to mark the unique contribution that Silverman has made to philosophy, not simply through his original "manner or style of thinking" but also through his active role in creating new philosophical communities and thereby transforming the public space of philosophy into a more interesting, accessible, and hospitable place for us all.

In the final chapter of *Undoing Gender*, titled "Can the 'Other' of Philosophy Speak?," Judith Butler traces the productive movement of philosophy outside the discipline of philosophy proper, and the description she provides of the benefits of achieving some distance from the "institutionalized life of philosophy" is particularly apt, I think, in conveying Silverman's unique personal and professional contributions to the expansion of accepted styles, forms, and methods of philosophical inquiry even as he remained a well-known, full-time member of one of the top continental philosophy departments in the United States. In Butler's words:

> Much of the philosophical work that takes place outside of philosophy is free to consider the rhetorical and literary aspects of philosophical texts and to ask, specifically, what particular philosophical value is carried or enacted by those rhetorical and linguistic features. The rhetorical aspects of a philosophical text include its genre, which can be varied, the way of making the arguments that it does, and how its mode of presentation informs the argument itself, sometimes enacting that argument implicitly, sometimes enacting an argument that is quite to the contrary of what the philosophical text explicitly declares. A substantial amount of the work done in the continental philosophical tradition is done outside of philosophy departments at the current time, and it is sometimes done in especially rich and provocative ways in conjunction with literary readings. Paradoxically, philosophy has received a new life in contemporary studies of culture and the cultural study of politics, where philosophical notions both inform social and literary texts that are not, generically speaking, philosophical, but which nevertheless establish the site of cultural study as a vital one for philosophical thinking within the humanities.[5]

Unlike Butler and the other prominent scholars she mentions who no longer have homes in traditional philosophy departments, Silverman managed the delicate balancing act of keeping one foot within and one foot outside the formal discipline of philosophy throughout his career. He accomplished this not only through his professional credentials and official academic title, namely, his two doctorates in philosophy and comparative literature and his joint appointment in the Departments of Philosophy and Comparative Literature at SUNY Stony Brook, but also through the way he literally incarnated the "between" about which he so loved to speak and write in his relationships with others, not just with academics but with all the others he encountered in his yearly travels from one continent to another.

In *Inclusion and Democracy,* Iris Marion Young observes:

> It is not uncommon to hear a complaint from individuals or groups who have tried to make claims and arguments in a political discussion that they have been ignored, or worse, spoken about by others as though they were not there, deprecated, stereotyped, or otherwise insulted. No rules or formalities can ensure that people will treat others in the political public with respect, and really listen to their claims.[6]

And, she adds: "What I call greeting, or public acknowledgement, is thus a specific communicative gesture with important and not sufficiently noticed functions for democratic practice."[7] Silverman was what I consider to be the master of the art of greeting in this Youngian sense. He had a boundless interest in making new acquaintances. Hand and warm smile proffered, Hugh, as he preferred to be called, was always ready to greet the stranger, to make him or her feel at home even if, as was frequently the case, Hugh himself was not at home but merely a fellow traveler. Silverman's passionate appreciation for difference, including differences of culture, language, history, art, landscape, cuisine, and, above all, of people, was, without a doubt, the engine that drove The Silverman Network, a network that will continue to flourish and expand long after his untimely death; indeed, we are participating in it right now as we, the writers and readers of this book, commemorate Hugh J. Silverman.

Silverman's own greetings were always memorable, whether one was their direct recipient or merely an observer. Often long-winded, always hearty and enthusiastic, his greetings were rarely ever just between him and one other person. Instead, they usually included anyone else in the vicinity as Silverman invited him or her to share in what was always a unique encounter. His memory was amazing, and this was true not only for names, faces, and languages; it extended to the personal as well as the professional aspects of his interlocutors' lives. Young's capacious description of the phenomenon of greeting perfectly describes the attentiveness to the other that marked Silverman's daily interactions with others, whether they were his professional colleagues, students, strangers or friends. “Greeting,” she tells us,

> refers to those moments in everyday communication where people acknowledge one another in their particularity. Thus it includes literal greetings, such as “Hello,” “How are you?,” and addressing people by name. In the category of greeting I also include moments of leave-taking, “Good-bye,” “See you later,” as well as the forms of speech that often lubricate discussion with mild forms of flattery, stroking of egos, deference, and politeness. Greeting includes handshakes, hugs, the offering of food and drink, making small talk before getting down to real business.[8]

I find it impossible to read this passage from Young without thinking of the many instances in which I witnessed Hugh Silverman warmly proffering food and drink to newcomers during receptions at the International Association for Philosophy and Literature (IAPL) conferences he so loved, effortlessly pronouncing even the most difficult of names as he happily introduced one acquaintance to another, switching from English to French or German in mid-conversation to make sure he was greeting a new arrival in the language in which he or she was most comfortable. He was truly in his element at these annual IAPL events, fully embracing his role as the executive director responsible for bringing not only people but also ideas, disciplines, cultures, and communities together for a week of transformative engagement. Seeing Silverman in action at IAPL was an unforgettable experience that I have shared with countless faculty, graduate students, postdocs, and independent scholars from all over the world. Indeed, many of my closest friendships in the academy arose out of these annual IAPL conferences, often held overseas in fabulous international locations, and I can honestly say that I would not have developed these relationships without him. Some of these friendships, it must be admitted, were forged through shared suffering: as IAPL Executive Committee members or support staff, we dealt with the many complaints that arose because of Silverman's infamous perfectionist impulses, such as his refusal to release the conference program until he had every detail for every event and activity nailed down, no matter how many conference participants were clamoring to know on what day and time their panel was to take place!

As an IAPL Executive Committee member for six years, not only was I present for the entire conference each spring, but I also spent a very full weekend each December in Port Jefferson on Long Island, where we worked for three long days to put together the conference program, invariably begging Silverman, our taskmaster, to allow us to break for lunch or dinner as the hours dragged on. Silverman was indefatigable and mostly imperturbable during these marathon sessions, stoically and surprisingly cheerfully remaining impervious to our growing and increasingly childish chorus of complaints. It was not until they reached a crescendo that could no longer be ignored that he would finally agree that yes, we could stop for a meal break, even though he could not refrain from reminding us, as he gave into our demands, of how much more work we still had to do. As our reward, he would invariably take us out for a wonderful meal at one of his favorite local restaurants, where he would greet the owners and/or employees with his characteristic warmth, delighted to have us meet them too, happily sharing the experience of breaking bread together in his lovely hometown of Port Jefferson.

In "On Cosmopolitanism," Jacques Derrida discusses the respect due to those who "cultivate an ethic of hospitality," and his ensuing description of hospitality reminds me of the many experiences I've shared, both at home and abroad, with Hugh Silverman. "Hospitality," Derrida asserts,

> is culture itself and not simply one ethic among others. Insofar as it has to do with the *ethos*, that is, the residence, one's home, the familiar place of dwelling, inasmuch as it is a manner of being there, the manner in which we relate to ourselves and to others, to others as our own or as foreigners, *ethics is hospitality*; ethics is so thoroughly coextensive with the experience of hospitality.[9]

Silverman's own ethics of hospitability was one of his most endearing qualities. I've been introduced (and often reintroduced!) to countless individuals by him over the years, many of whom, as I previously noted, went on to become good friends. Indeed, Silverman's greatest gift, I would argue, was this gift of the other, a gift he freely gave in accordance with the "Great Law of Hospitality" that Derrida cites when discussing the continuing need for "cities of refuge" for strangers seeking asylum. In Derrida's words, it is the "Great Law of Hospitality—an unconditional Law, both singular and universal, which ordered that the borders be open to each and every one, to every other, to all who might come, without question or without their even having to identify who they are or whence they came."[10]

Silverman was committed, throughout his life, to opening up borders, to dwelling, with others, in a shared space of possibility. As he argues in *Inscriptions: Between Phenomenology and Structuralism*, "Human temporal movement is not a succession of individual meanings like the succession of frames on a film. It is projection toward what will be and what might be; it is the expectation of the manifestation of possibility" (*I*, 90). Silverman skillfully navigated not only disciplinary borders but also borders of language, geography, gastronomy, religion, history, art, and culture, embracing the unique opportunities these experiences offered for "creating new meanings in terms of the significance that one is" (*I*, 90). He not only discovered new meanings in his personal and professional relationships but also shared them through his writing, especially his writing about writing, including, most notably, his original readings of other thinkers' writings.

Silverman describes his project at the outset of *Textualities: Between Hermeneutics and Deconstruction* as a philosophical practice that "demonstrates how to 'think the between' not only by juxtaposing alternative philosophical methods and indicating how to philosophize between hermeneutics and deconstruction but also by examining various philosophical texts—bringing out the signification of the 'place between'" (*T*, 1). Bringing together the work of diverse authors, including Schopenhauer, Nietzsche, Thoreau, Lévi-Strauss, Heidegger, Barthes, Derrida, Merleau-Ponty, Blanchot, Kristeva, and Foucault, Silverman both traces and enacts a rich "philosophical textuality." This philosophical textuality, he tells us, "operates with marginalities—its capital interest lies around the frames of educational institutions, in the formulations of theoretical and scientific concerns, and in the elaboration of the very foundations of history" (*T*, 5). Silverman's own fascination with frames, margins, borders, traces, liminalities, chiasms, virtualities, rhizomes, intermedialities, layerings, edges, differences, in short, with "the between" in all of its various incarnations, was, without a doubt, the driving force that animated his own prolific textualities.

These latter were disseminated not only in his writings but also through what I am calling "The Silverman Network," namely the international community of philosophers, artists, politicians, historians, literary theorists, cultural critics, psychoanalytic theorists, architects, critical race theorists, filmmakers, feminist theorists, and public figures whom he brought together each year for his signature IAPL conferences.

As a member of the IAPL Executive Committee, it always made me smile (and I know I was not alone in this reaction!) when Silverman proudly announced the next year's IAPL conference theme, and one or the other of the "between" terms appeared prominently in the conference title. Indeed, it will come as no surprise to IAPL regulars that I generated this list of terms that Silverman so loved from a whole pile of past IAPL program booklets that I still keep on a shelf in my office (each an *objet d'art* and a labor of love and aggravation that took Silverman and the IAPL staff thousands of hours to produce)! While the local conference directors played a major role in choosing a given year's theme, one could almost always see Silverman's influence, especially his love of language, at work in each title. Titles of conferences, panels, and works mattered enormously to him, and we spent literally hours and hours discussing them in our IAPL sessions, going over each word and phrase to be sure it was aesthetically, philosophically, and politically pleasing, eloquently opening up inquiry rather than closing it down.

Silverman concludes *Textualities* with a series of reflections on the "reasons" that propel philosophical inquiry and the production of philosophical texts; these reasons, he suggests, challenge the hegemony of reason within philosophy because they exceed the carefully guarded borders of rationality that seek to delimit and thereby circumscribe the domain of philosophy "proper." "Philosophy," he tells us,

> has its reasons for wanting to know beyond, across, and between what it itself is and what it is not. Philosophy has its reasons for examining its own foundations as well as those of everything else. Philosophy has its reasons for being itself as well as being *other* than what it is. These are the reasons that make up the text of philosophy. They are the reasons that reason doesn't know about; *car la philosophie a ses raisons que la raison ne connaît point*—philosophy has its reasons which reason doesn't know at all. (*T*, 240)

Silverman, like each of us, and in accordance with his description of philosophy above, always had his reasons for pursuing the paths that he did, reasons that defied reason, and that we will never know. One of these reasons concerned why he chose to keep as silent as possible about his serious illness during the final year of his life, his decision not to share details of his condition with most members of his vast network of colleagues, students, and friends. For such a public persona (for it was rare to find someone at any of the conferences he regularly attended who didn't know or at least know of him, including not only IAPL, but also the Society for Phenomenology and Existential Philosophy (SPEP), the American Philosophical Association (APA), the International Merleau-Ponty Circle, and so many others), Silverman chose, in the end, to keep his health issues private; though many of us knew that he had undergone surgery for prostate cancer in the fall of 2012 and that his recovery was proceeding very, very slowly, necessitating his absence from his regular autumn conferences, the news of his sudden death in spring 2013 was a shock that continues to reverberate in and outside the Stony Brook community, the discipline of philosophy, and all of the other communities that Silverman participated in and brought together.

The beauty of a healthy network, however, is that even if the center is no longer able to perform its usual function of tying everything together, other parts of the network can perform this role instead. The textual network that Hugh helped to build throughout his life, through his work, his conferences, his leadership, his speech, and his deeds, cannot help but continue to proliferate after his untimely death. This volume itself constitutes a new extension of The Silverman Network and provides abundant proof that, even in his absence, Hugh J Silverman continues to be a vital intellectual presence.

In the introduction to his edited collection, *Writing the Politics of Difference,* Silverman states: "Continental philosophy is in its adolescence. Its future(s) will doubtless be rich and rewarding; its past is inscribed within a variety of traditions that still remain to be reread; its present is one of many differences."[11] Silverman's in-depth knowledge of the interconnections and disjunctions among the variety of traditions and scholars within continental philosophy never ceased to impress me, and I always enjoyed hearing his colorful anecdotes about his personal interactions with major continental figures. His reading, his writing, his teaching, his conferences, his conversations, and his good fellowship have offered those of us who have been fortunate enough to experience them new ways of engaging with this tradition; an exposure to novel perspectives, authors, works, theories, places, and cultural encounters that we might not have had otherwise.

Extremely attentive to the subtle theoretical, political, aesthetic, literary, historical, linguistic, sexual, rhetorical, racial, class, cultural, and practical differences that, emerging out of the past, create unique possibilities in the present that can open up new futures, Hugh Silverman never stopped looking for new ways to express and share his passion for difference with others. In addition to sharing this passion through his published work, conference presentations, and lively conversations, his incessant picture taking at IAPL functions and his mastery of the newest computer technologies to improve the processing and communication of information to and from IAPL members provide further examples of the ever-proliferating "Silverman Network" in action.

Never one to squander an opportunity for engagement, Silverman was always on the move at conferences in his trademark hat, dark jacket, and, of course, those distinctive sideburns! It was very hard to miss him, and he almost never missed me. Typically (and I know that this experience was shared by the other contributors to this volume as well as many of its readers) he would spy me from across a crowded room and call me over to meet a graduate student or old colleague, adroitly finding a way to weave me into the interrupted discussion. The Silverman Network was always operating at full force not only at IAPL and at all the other conferences he regularly participated in but also during Silverman's many travels. Even if a newcomer hadn't yet met Hugh Silverman personally, it usually didn't take long before the necessary introduction took place, often through Silverman's own initiative. He simply loved people and loved sharing new experiences with them. He was never content to simply enjoy what was already known, comfortable, and familiar, but actively sought out and delighted in the places and spaces of difference that underpin not only our most exotic but also our most mundane experiences. He was most happy functioning at the center of whatever activity he was engaged in, and though his legendary perfectionism was undoubtedly irritating at times, his goal, whether he served as the official or unofficial "master of ceremonies," was always to create a stimulating, intersubjective, intercorporeal experience that was truly meaningful, aesthetically pleasurable, and genuinely enjoyable for all.

How can we best advance this rich network of good philosophy, good fellowship, good food, and good places that Hugh J. Silverman has bequeathed to us? This volume is itself a start, a gift that he would surely have loved, and I'm sorry he isn't alive to read firsthand these accounts of the significant impact his life and work has had on so many of us. His unexpected death in spring 2013 when he was fully immersed in so many different projects means that the gargantuan task of completing them has fallen to his wife, Gertrude Postl, a burden with which numerous colleagues and friends in the profession, including the editors of this volume are helping her.

Very few philosophers have a fellow philosopher as our life partner, and though Postl and Silverman always pursued their own research, teaching, and professional interests and have always been affiliated with different institutions, they have also been a well-known couple both in and outside our profession. Not only were they both publicly as well as privately supportive of one another's work, but they also were fortunate to have a very wide circle of friends throughout the world who can confirm how much fun they were to hang out with! Thus, one of the losses that I am mourning with his sudden death is the loss of future opportunities to enjoy spending time with the wonderful couple that was Hugh and Gerda. Whether we were spending a day visiting Petworth and the Royal Pavilion at Brighton or seeing a Shakespeare play at Stratford during the Brunel IAPL conference, visiting a twelfth-century church and medieval village at the end of IAPL in Cypress, going on an end-of-conference winery tour in Melbourne, hanging out at SPEP, or even having dinner in Port Jefferson the final night of our IAPL Executive Committee meetings (the only time that Hugh, at my urgent request, let Gerda join us, namely after our work was done!), I have always treasured the shared experiences we have enjoyed together.

Hugh Silverman, as conference participants would readily agree, had a knack for planning exciting, fun, and intellectually stimulating activities during IAPL that promoted the forging of new relationships and, ultimately, new friendships. As I mentioned earlier, he loved nothing better than bringing together mutual acquaintances who hadn't yet met. And, as his wife, IAPL Executive Committee members, and IAPL staff can unanimously confirm, he spent countless hours taking care of all of the innumerable details that would culminate in the memorable experiences we shared in unique venues throughout the world. Whether we were having a reception at a former palace in Strasbourg, getting a guided tour of a current exhibit at the Basel Art Museum, meeting the town mayor at the historic City Hall in Freiburg (and this all took place at a single IAPL conference!), hearing Stephen Hull give a presentation at and about the fabulous art museum he designed in Helsinki, or hearing Jacques Derrida present an incredible lecture on Artaud as one of the plenary speakers at UC Irvine, it was Hugh's mission to exceed the expectations of the conference participants each year, and he almost always succeeded, even though his minute attention to every detail drove his local conference directors, his Executive Committee, and his staff absolutely crazy!

Though I was unable to attend IAPL in Singapore the month after Silverman died, practically the first thing I thought of when I heard of his passing was "What will happen to his beloved conference?," especially because it was scheduled to take place a few weeks later. Knowing how long it took him to publicly release the IAPL program each year, because he would not relinquish it to the publisher until every single item in the more-than-100-page booklet was exactly the way he wanted it, I knew that there was no way it could have been ready to go yet no way that Silverman would allow the conference to not take place. He was, as I have been indicating, the consummate master of ceremonies, and this meant that when Silverman was in charge the show always went on, even if making it happen required resolving several crises behind the scenes. His plans were always so ambitious for IAPL that we were surprised each year when he succeeded, against the odds, to find another willing victim—that is, host—to serve as conference director and procure the necessary funding to make the conference happen. Little did most conference directors know exactly what would be involved in advance, namely, that Silverman would micromanage every event taking place during the conference, down to the most minor of details. On his annual pre-conference trips, he would visit every single conference venue personally, including meeting with chefs and waiters at restaurants where meals would be taking place, getting to personally know the staff at the hotels where we would be staying, making the acquaintance of important town or city officials, as well as using his charm to wheedle even more resources out of the university administrators at the host institution than the local director had managed to obtain. In the midst of this whirlwind of activity, Silverman would also be continually pulling out his camera to shoot his infamous pictures of every venue, both large and small, to post on the IAPL Web site, part of his own one-man publicity campaign to generate more excitement about that year's conference.

Hugh, you drove most of us who worked closely with you nuts at least half of the time, but you succeeded along the way in fostering a wonderful international community of interdisciplinary scholars, artists, politicians, and above all friends that I am and always will be proud to be part of. My hope is that we will find new ways to build upon this amazing legacy, to keep The Silverman Network alive and flourishing, even in Silverman's own absence. I have no doubt that he will continue to play a major role in these endeavors, even though he is no longer with us, his influence manifesting itself not only in the past, but also in the futures of the organizations and institutions he loved so well. Nonetheless, I will miss his idiosyncratic presence, and, for the countless others who knew him, including those of us whom he irritated on more than one occasion, I expect you will too.

Notes

1. Hugh J. Silverman, "Is Merleau-Ponty Inside or Outside the History of Philosophy," in *Chiasms: Merleau-Ponty's Notion of Flesh*, ed. Fred Evans and Leonard Lawlor (Albany: State University of New York Press, 2000), 139.

2. Maurice Merleau-Ponty, *Signs*, trans. Richard C. McCleary (Evanston, IL: Northwestern University Press, 1964), 130. Quoted in Silverman, "Is Merleau-Ponty Inside or Outside," 139.

3. Silverman, "Is Merleau-Ponty Inside or Outside," 139.

4. Ibid.

5. Judith Butler, *Undoing Gender* (New York: Routledge, 2004), 234–35.

6. Iris Marion Young, *Inclusion and Democracy* (Oxford: Oxford University Press, 2000), 57.

7. Ibid.

8. Ibid., 57–58.

9. Jacques Derrida, "On Cosmopolitanism," in *On Cosmopolitanism and Forgiveness*, trans. Mark Dooley and Michael Hughes (New York: Routledge, 2001), 16–17.

10. Ibid., 18.

11. Hugh J. Silverman, "Introduction," *Writing the Politics of Difference* (Albany: State University of New York Press, 1991), ix.

Afterword

15

The Final Between—Being Inbetween Self

Epigrams Inbetween Epigraphs and Epitaphs

Lee Silverman

My thoughts "endpaper" this book of my brother's life—remembering him through myself because so many of his colleagues spoke out about my similarity to him. In the beginning was the word and in the end is the word. Between, epigrams and inscriptions demarcate how we develop ideas. As a youth, Hugh J. Silverman (my brother) inscribed a book for me with this George Santayana quote: "Those who do not remember the past are condemned to repeat it."[1] Before this, I was always looking forward—believing that if I ignored the past, then I would be unique in all that I did. I learned from this small inscription one of the most vital lessons of my life.

In an epitaph, we attempt to wrap our loved ones' lives with one short phrase on a headstone (or many more words in a memorial service). Some epitaphs become ironic, such as Mel Blanc's at Hollywood Memorial Park in California: "That's All Folks!" This epigraph expresses the essence of the "Man of a Thousand Voices." Hugh was a man of one voice and a thousand languages. Accents were precise for him, and he could read an individual's past by his or her intonation and dialect. This appears genetic, as I have it too. "Transcription" is the conversion of speech into written text. I create poetry by voicing the sound of words and then writing them down. The sound dominates, and this creates the sound between the text. In a personal portmanteau, I conflate the titles of Hugh's two books, *Inscriptions* and *Textualities*, into "Transcriptions." "Transcription" is the first stage of gene expression where a particular segment of DNA is copied into RNA. From that inscription that Hugh wrote to me as a teenager to the day of his death, I seem to replicate him and his mind in many ways. This became obvious when I met many of his colleagues and former students at the September 2013 Silverman Memorial Symposium at Stony Brook University.

"Epigrams," "epitaphs," and "epigraphs" all share their root with "ephemeral" and "epiphany." Importantly, this root also relates to the study of knowledge in the word "epistemology." Here I hope that I can spotlight the fence posts of my memories of Hugh through a series of vignettes. Like fence-post holes that must be dug deep, these end points must be solid enough to carry the strength and weight of both inscription and engraving—the core of epigraph and epitaph. Among Shakespeare's many sonnets, Sonnet 76 highlights how epigrams may reincarnate a well-chosen epitaph: "*Why, with the time, do I not glance aside / To new-found methods . . . / That every word doth almost tell my name, / . . . So all my best is dressing old words new.*"[2] From this, we understand that, in dressing up old words, a book's *fancy endpapers* are an expression of the texts that mark our lives with milestones and end in an epitaph. I am comfortable with the finality of death—the respectful nonexistence—leaving behind only words.

The texts that define our lives are varied and many. Two that I will remember best are the epigraph above that my brother inscribed in a book and one that I will never know, my very own epitaph. My brother, Hugh J. Silverman, has no headstone. His words are left in other texts that define him—he spent his life writing his own epitaph. His lasting impression through word and voice and reading has been left with all whom he touched with his mind, by his presence. Many epitaphs speak by their omission of "the whatever else" about the person. Perhaps something like William Faulkner's phrase "The past is not dead. It is not even past." They read what is absent, the parts one would never say about a person. Hugh J. Silverman has no epitaph carved. The words that I choose here reveal what remains for me after much introspection and reflection on the parts of my life that overlapped with those of my brother. Although this paper sits in an academic compendium, let this essay be what I would write on an electronic headstone for my brother, Hugh. Please pardon my need to call him Hugh rather than Silverman. As much as it personalizes the piece, it also allows me to distinguish him from myself, which is the theme of this paper—not the "self" in Philosophy, but the very self that defines his and my personalities.

On Being Inbetween: Man and Mind

The similarities are unmistakeable; the differences may be hard to find for the casual observer. After Hugh's death, I read my presence at the HJS Symposium at Stony Brook in 2013 in this way. I became the standard bearer of his voice, his diversity of thought, his care of time and disregard for timeliness. Here I hope to refine who Hugh was through my own vision of our similarities and differences. This chapter occupies a space that represents our shared thought attributes (not voice, not complexity, and not time). As Hugh's brother, I share many genes, of course, but seemingly I also share a range of mental tendencies far beyond the scope of genetics. Through my viewing of persistent topics such as "self," between texts and semiotics, I hope to read insight into Hugh's thinking by extension of my own mind.

Hugh was staunchly respectful of himself. Viewing his Wikipedia page is a lodestone about him—it is clear, detailed, and formally correct in grammar, syntax, and academic style, yet it misses the human, caring, and deeply loving person that he was. I have done and accomplished many important things in my career of forty years, but I struggle often to fill a page with my accomplishments; Hugh's curriculum vitae is 120 pages, and I cannot even find the real title of his doctoral dissertation in it. This paper gives the human side to Hugh; not the philosopher and cultural theorist (as on Wikipedia), but the person that I knew. As a way to define the gap between Hugh and me, I attempt a "disentangling"[3] of the word "inbetween" to typify this difference.

The Lithe Line between Time

The inbetween, the line between, whether a space or a place, is infinitely thin; it is lithe and agile. For this essay, the inbetween has become a lifeline. Whether it is a simple wrinkle at the base of the hand, a striped lifesaver on a boat's cabin, a repelling line off a cliff face, or a ripcord in a parachute, we need a visualization to express how we live our lives and predict the future remembering the past. Yes, the "inbetween" occupies no space, but it provides the gap between the between. The very thinness of this imaginary line tells the story of our future based on our past. There are sciences (including mathematics) and philosophies around this concept. An actuary does this forecast through numbers; a psychic does this through some form of prescience; meteorologists do this through analytics and historical data. In some way, we all do this prediction through our own observation. By absorbing our past, we predict what may be a future outcome by remembering the results of previously like occurrences.

In the *Structure of Scientific Revolutions*, Thomas Kuhn's predictive view is that scientific prescience causes a paradigm shift, the movement of a field toward a revolution when the gap inbetween what is known and what is believed becomes too great. Searching for the potentially unknowable is the essence of Kuhn's "shift." This is what I think new movements in philosophy try to achieve. I, like Hugh, have been enamoured with the unknown, the unknowable, and the power of exploration to discover what we previously did not understand. This, more than any other attribute, is the characteristic that binds my way of living to how Hugh did his research, his discovery, and his written texts. Exploring the unknowable is done most conveniently with words and texts—these are the dancing bears in our minds that sit somewhere between the reader and the author. They compose the text between the communication and the communicated, between the space and the place of expression. With new words, defined terms, and the freedom gained by knowing many fields and several languages, Hugh was able to juxtapose concepts and hold our attention with his words that remain. While his exploration may not have uncovered a paradigm shift, the journey took us places that none would have envisioned. Most ventures into the unknowable never produce the outstanding result that we seek, yet that does not lessen their impact on a field continuously charting new waters (despite how self-referential they may be).

After thirty-five years in computer graphics, I know that animation employs a concept called "inbetweening." "Tweening," as it is known, interpolates extra frames between the key frames that have been created by the animator; this is perhaps the clearest expression of the inbetween. What is not created by an expert animator in traditional animation or by a human (program, potentially) is the computer animation "inbetween." The inbetweens are the frames expressed in time by animation, but in the space of the mind these can occupy a place unwittingly unconscious of how the reader and the writer create the known. Inside and outside or between the frame, as expressed by Lawlor, this could be the core concept that links time and space and may even resolve the perplexing distinction between the space or place between. I only attempt to describe those attributes of Hugh and myself that are merely nuances of difference between two personalities so similar in kind, in kindness, and in the will to understand other humans through their voice, their expression, and through their "texts."

Space between and inbetween distance or time makes for a fundamental notion to explore here. Between the between is the inbetween. That is the space that I describe to merit how Hugh and I are so alike in our method of thinking and yet wildly different. For me, the inbetween is a tool to distinguish why his academic rigor had the chinks in the armour in the evolution of his thinking. The tool of language and its ambiguity is the device for the humanities that makes exactness of thought impossible. Commerce has gaping holes that have allowed me to excel with gaping holes in my thinking within the far less disciplined normal standard in commerce. One gets away with this in commerce because so few people are reading you over again along with students (unless of course you have the number of users of a Microsoft or of a Google). Here I am merely "authoring" a poetically sculpted reading of my own mind through the life and work of my brother, Hugh, exposing the differences between our career paths.

Inbetween Nuance and the Between

This paper intends to create a notional space for all three aspects noted of my similarity to Hugh—voice, thought, and time—by creating a notion of the "Inbetween" via reflection on Hugh's inquiry into the Between. For me, the thin existential space between two betweens is the "inbetween." As Hugh's brother, the similarities were deeper than I previously knew until after his death, and for this reason alone I needed to define a concept from the "between," namely, the "inbetween," to convey the inexplicable urge not just to discover language in all its variants, but also to create it. In spite of being a businessman rather than an academic, I have had this urge (like Hugh) all my life. The "Inbetween" here creates a virtually, infinitely thin space, a conceptual, semipermeable membrane between the similarities and differences between Hugh and his brother. Through this "text" I too have learned the surprisingly subtle nuances between Hugh's mind and my own.

Another great "inbetween" that marks our lives is the inbetween of "city" and "country" (not the suburbs). I learned their difference when I moved from one to the other, but I also learned their sameness. This is a trite apposition, but one apropos of how Hugh defined himself. The beauty of the country against the backdrop of the cultured city has inspired us not in a pastoral sense, but in its appositions. Hugh could never decide whether to be a shepherding intellectual or an intellectual shepherd. I could never decide whether to be a cowboy or a technologist, but at some point my father's engineering instincts took over, and I left behind the dream of riding a horse and wearing a tall Stetson.

Between Mondegreens and Difference

As a child, I languished in the enjoyment of hearing "God in three persons, blessed internally" instead of "eternally." I still bathe in appreciation of the mondegreen, the mishearing and misinterpretation of a phrase or lyric (as a result of near-homophony). The mondegreen gives new meaning to the author's intention—it is the very definition of text. From my youth, I disavowed authorship and the attribution of owning a written piece by pinning my name to it as "author." Hugh espoused this idea in text, but not in his work. Amazingly, I published many authors and artists in my high school literary magazine without ever attributing ownership to their pieces. Barthes states:

> To give a text an Author is to impose a limit on that text, to furnish it with a final signified, to close the writing . . . [However] by refusing to assign a "secret," an

> ultimate meaning, to the text (and to the world as text), liberates what may be called an anti-theological activity, an activity that is truly revolutionary since to refuse to fix meaning is, in the end, to refuse God and his hypostases—reason, science, law.[4]

Hugh spent his life discoursing on texts and "the death of the author." On the other hand, he resolutely refused to pin his own work with the anonymity of "text." He was adamantly academic in attributing ownership to everything that he wrote. In contrast to me, Hugh tried to reconcile homophony as well. His essay on the distinction between "intension" and "intention" is a clear example of this.

Landes states, "Silverman was a master of *disentangling* rather than of *deciphering*. He was an explorer, not a code breaker."[5] I, on the other hand, am most prone to entangle in order to encode. It is a computer thing related to security, perhaps. But as a poet, I never attempted to make myself clear as long as it sounded gorgeous. I always replaced the cacophony of meaning with euphony and sonorous sounds. My poetry still thrives on its sound; meaning is secondary sometimes to aural aspects such as alliteration, rhythm, homophony, euphony, of assonance and sibilance. I have learned the import of clarity of communication in my day job, where it is integral for legal and commercial purposes to convey what is agreed upon. My poetry and Hugh's philosophy have no such rules. This is the freedom of responsibility or the responsibility of freedom, as Hugh expressed it.

Nuance makes for massive differences. Differences between meaning and intention are the nuance that I enjoy. I am so much like Hugh and yet so massively different. He cared to define the distinction and intention of "intension" and "intension", I simply rest at peace in their homophony. Mondegreens have modeled my life, in a way. Perhaps this is why I always voiced the claim that Hugh's doctoral dissertation was titled "The Ambiguity of Ambiguity." Only a decade ago, when rifling through a collection of memorabilia in storage at our mother's last home, did I discover a copy of it and learn something entirely different.[6] Hugh worked all his life to refine distinctions. One might even say that he was obsessed by differences, like Derrida. I have blurred them—enjoying the newness, the play, and the nuance of sound without regard to certainty. I am most at home when the nuance of taste and sound wobble in an unusual way.

Hugh was, from the age of nineteen, a Francophile. By the time Hugh was twenty, the average Parisian could not distinguish him from a native. I remember how much he would "mondegreen" in his own way, not with words and lyrics, but with sounds and smells. Two vignettes of this occurred when I reconnected with him in August 1998, when he and Gerda were living with us in Sydney, Australia. He had stopped drinking wine then, but I had recently become deeply engaged in it. I was enjoying an Australian Shiraz, which he wanted to smell, although he wouldn't drink it. He said it smelled like fine French Bordeaux, but I knew from my preference for heavier styles of wine that this was not possible. Another repeatedly pleasing occurrence of one of his dissonant mental mondegreens occurred when we went out to dinner most evenings and a waiter or waitress asked for our order. Upon hearing his or her accent, Hugh would ask whether he or she were from Ireland or France or Italy. The waiters and waitresses were mostly backpackers on short-term visas in Australia, and because the overlay of the Australian accent that they learned there impinged on their native accent, Hugh was almost always wrong in his assumptions. We both have had masterful ears for accents. I could guess effectively what suburb around Boston someone was from when we were growing up; Hugh could usually pick someone's nationality most often by his or her non-Australian English-speaking accent. But the Australian overlay tricked him almost every time, and it became quite humorous when he would ask a Serbian if he was from Ireland or such. It is just another mental mondegreen—an aural one, while the wine "mishearing" was an olfactory one.

Swords into Symbols

For Hugh and for me, words are our greatest (if not our only) weapons. We beat ploughshares into words so we could joust with our opponents or maim our combatants. We form(ed) words into poetic and philosophical expressions intending to leave meaning sometimes ambiguous, like a yet unformed strategy. Deeply versed in how to delve into semantics, he used words as tools to shape all the fields of study—phenomenology, semiology, hermeneutics, poststructuralism, deconstruction, and the rest. I know not where this list ends, but for me these words have been the tools to understand and capture technology.

Computer programming is partially about numbers, but it is much more about syntax and normalized semantics in the specific languages created for programming. I never designed a computer programming language, but I have had students who did. In my day, I learned many different programming languages—each had its own style and method. I always felt most at home with Lisp, with its distinctive and completely parenthesized Polish prefix notation. It is the syntax of parentheses within parentheses that makes so much sense to me. It is the way that I would write English, if I could be understood—each term defined into an ever-deepening nest. Reverse Polish notation also makes the most sense to me. I think of the operation before the object. It is almost the reverse of German—instead of the verb at the end of the sentence—it is right at the start ready to process whatever subject or object that you throw at it. It may seem surprising that, as much as I relish ambiguous grammar, when I want to be precise, I want it to be very precise—much more so than English allows. Lisp (and its dialect of Scheme), based on the deconstruction of words and phrases into parenthetical groups with many layers of nesting, allows precise usage and absolutely unambiguous clarity of meaning. It is known as an interpretive computer programming language, which means it does not necessarily have to be run through a compiler. This also means it must make sense at runtime, so the interpretation is nonambiguous. It simply will not work if its syntax is not clear—a far cry from the Romance and Germanic languages that we love so well.

This is what written language is for me (when I am not writing poetry, which is the diametric opposite)—the ability to nest deeply into words and phrases to get to the very essence and therefore the detailed meaning. Hugh did this with philosophy; I do it with computers. Hugh mastered more languages than I ever will, but the very poor German, Dutch, and French that I speak reminds me every time of how expert Hugh became in so many modern languages. We both had our roots in learning Latin, but neither of us learned Spanish—although that would have been by far the easiest to acquire.

Semiotics and Sound

I began this essay in China over Christmas. There I was reminded of a snippet that Hugh once said when he first returned from Taiwan:

"I have never been in a place where I could not read the signs." I am paraphrasing here, as I do not remember the exact words, but they would have been quite important. What I understood that he meant was that even in Greece or Norway, the symbols (letters, if you will) on signs had notional familiarity to him to be able to string together a root or a sound or a semblance of verbal-linguistic hooks to hang upon, or even attempt to voice (if you had sufficient background in the Greek alphabet), but with Chinese characters, there was none of that. Since then, my wife has begun to learn Mandarin, and she is enthralled by the characters and sees them as the source of her visual rather than verbal memory by which to learn the language.

What my brother said when he returned from Taiwan suggests why, when he could not recognize the symbols as words, he felt so isolated. It was through *words* and *semiotics* that he saw the world; he spoke to people in their native tongue and wanted to understand the origin of their accent. People fascinate me because of the way they speak, the places from which they come that made them speak that way, and the source of their accent that may have been modified by life. Do I want to know the individual, or do I want to classify him or her in my mental file cabinet of how people from Limerick speak? Do I want to know the person or understand the people? These are the questions that, to this day, I cannot answer. Hugh was, as I am, a linguistically curious animal. We both hungered constantly to interact with the locals in their local language, however minimally, and relish in the culture, food, and history of their language. Like Hugh, words and symbols fascinate me; especially when they intersect or overlay. This is why Chinese characters and their history hold the same fascination as cave drawings for me. I read the dictionary as a child, and over time I began to use symbols in photography to convey stories.

Time and Enemies

As Ed Casey relates: "Hugh Silverman knew how to take time—the right time for thinking over the important things and for taking the important actions. He was persistent in his pursuit of what he took to be the right course."[7] In this manner, time was both a friend and foe to my brother. Yes, he took time (as much as he would like), but he also took great care—the careful steps of his rhythmic words. Casey makes the clear point that somewhere between time and care is an extreme sense of quality that was devoted to all that Hugh did. I've always known this to be true, and it was proven in one of his last years when he rebuilt his own driveway, brick by brick.

We all miss key moments and junctures in our life because we care more about time than about timeliness. We care about time, but not about timing. Jokes require timing; thinking requires time. Timing makes the man or woman, and time makes the mind. While my brother was rarely on time, he certainly took the time to think and consider. One might say unreservedly that both Hugh and I took time, even when it was not offered (as I did with this chapter), and never let a good deadline get in the way of the quality of our work. It is a piece of magic to say, as the Rolling Stones did, that "time is on our side," but, as we know, death seems to disprove that notion, and time then wins for the other side. Time is our friend and our enemy. The ephemeral and the temporal make time both friend and foe. Hugh knew, as Chaucer wrote, that "time and tide wait for no man." As we all sense from birth, our choices drive our care for and our abuse of time. Forever, time will be an enemy and a friend to those who care. Hugh was without a doubt one of those beings who could, and would, care about people; for me, nothing brings more value than caring about people, and that is the simple aspect of Hugh that I loved beyond all else.

When time wins, there is the "never." When we sit between, we are nowhere. When humans beat time, they are alive. "All and never" sounds so simple an algorithm, yet it is forever sitting between the inbetween.

The Philosopher's Knot

My glancing blows with philosophy have meant that I know the language but not the history or the concepts—a dangerous place in this compendium. Thanks to my brother, Hugh, I am comfortable around the academic field of philosophy and, in fact, majored in it as an undergraduate. While I find philosophical inquiry rewarding and engaging, now in my later years I find it more like learning to tie a knot—if you can do it well, it works like magic; if you get it slightly wrong, it completely unravels.

The concept of the "self" is so reflexive that I never carried it through to its philosophical conclusion in my studies. It is no surprise that the "self" and ambiguity are where Hugh began his philosophical inquiry. My best understanding of the field of philosophy is like the field of knotting, where infinite terms are created both in the composition of the knot (such as bight or tail) and the various types of knots (such as a stopper knot or a bitter end). Knotting, like philosophy, becomes a place where texts leave the second wrap of the knot unfinished (such as an undressed knot). Knots and seamanship fascinated Hugh. In particular, he sought to know how to make knots, and I now understand why.

This corpus will unravel. It should be seen as text—unfinished and missing crucial understanding. We would prefer to leave earth without untied ends, but it never works out that way. Perhaps this work will tie up my reflections on Hugh J. Silverman, philosopher and brother. I hope my perceptions of the man, the mind, and the thinking of Hugh will highlight a person while others reflect on his oeuvre in this compendium. Perhaps a human context will spotlight the genesis of his corpus through the inner workings of a mind quite like his—mine. To be tied up in pure ideas, one can miss the essence of "self."

The Book's Fancy Endpapers

Let us finish with the space between all hardbound books—the fancy endpapers. Without text (unless inscribed), these papers occupy the space inbetween the cover and the text. Words reincarnate the book's endpapers in an essay—words around our life—epigraphs and epitaphs—whether inscriptions or transcriptions. I know of the importance, if not the necessity, of defining and sometimes making up words—I learned this from my brother. Here I have worked the inbetween to distinguish the between. By defining the nuance, the difference, and the inbetween of Hugh and myself, I have placed the forever thinning line between who Hugh was and what I have been.

I do not intend to decode, decipher, or even discourse on the lineage of the concepts in philosophy that other authors do here; I purely tried to paint the space between Hugh and myself with a series of sketches drawn to fill spaces with the shading and painted words.

I trust that this adds to the reflections of the genuinely able authors elsewhere in this book. As Landes states, "[i]f the between marked Silverman's Philosophy, then he is one of a rare breed of philosophers whose life and work shared in a single authentic style. He relished the between, relished in the between, and had the courage to linger there." Perhaps, as I am less organized in my external life than my brother, I relish and languish in the inbetween—and see no need to define or clarify that any further. It is the attribute that distinguishes Hugh from me—a place in the Inbetween to compare how Hugh's thinking is more diligent than my own; as Casey says, "he combined patience with a passion for perfection." Casey continues:

> Hugh's spirit passed from his body with his last breath . . . But his caring being, which was so evident to those of us who were fortunate enough to know him while he lived and as he lived—in his time on earth—continues to exist among us, and will inform our time together . . . or the rest of our lives.[8]

This essay is a lasting memory that serves as both an epigraph and an epitaph to my brother. If I could, then I would inscribe Hugh's books—*Inscriptions* and *Textualities*—virtually with an epigraph of my own: *Please let the book's endpapers reflect themselves internally forever as a text.*

Notes

1. George Santayana, *The Life of Reason or the Phases of Human Progress* (New York: Charles Scribner and Sons, 1954), 82. (Note, I am referring to the one-volume edition of this book).

2. William Shakespeare, "Sonnet 76," in *The Complete Works of William Shakespeare* (Ware, UK: Wordworth, 1996), 1234.

3. Donald A. Landes's essay "Between Inscriptions: Intertextuality as Philosophical Method" (chapter 3 in this volume) explains that Hugh Silverman disentangles rather than decodes. This is an expression to say Hugh was an explorer rather than a decipherer. How does one man present himself and his ways of discovery? We are unique, but we also fit molds—I too am an explorer or, as we say in business, "a hunter," not a "farmer."

4. Barthes, *DA*, 147.

5. See Donald A. Landes, "Between Inscriptions: Intertextuality as Philosophical Method," in this volume.

6. [Editor's note: Hugh's dissertation, defended at Stanford University in 1973, was titled *Existential Ambiguity: A Phenomenology of Human Nature.*]

7. See Edward S. Casey, "Taking Time and Taking Care," in this volume.

8. Ibid.

Selected Bibliography of Published Writings by Hugh J. Silverman

Compiled by Kathleen Hulley

Books

Inscriptions: Between Phenomenology and Structuralism. New York: Routledge, Kegan and Paul, 1987.

Inscriptions: After Phenomenology and Structuralism. 2nd ed. Evanston, IL: Northwestern University Press, 1997; translated into Korean by Ho-Byeong Young (Seoul: So-myong, 2011).

Textualities: Between Hermeneutics and Deconstruction. New York: Routledge, 1994; translated into German by Erik Michael Vogt (Vienna: Turia + Kant, 1997); into Arabic by Hassan Nadhem and Ali Hakim Salih (Beirut, 2002); into Italian by Paolo Cappelletti and Valentina Grimaldi (Milan: Spirali, 2003); and into Korean by Ho-Byeong Young (Seoul: So-myong, 2009).

Edited Books

Jean-Paul Sartre: Contemporary Approaches to his Philosophy. Coedited with Frederick A. Elliston. Pittsburgh: Duquesne University Press and Harvester Press, 1980.

Piaget, Philosophy and the Human Sciences. Atlantic Highlands, NJ: Humanities Press; Sussex, UK: Harvester Press, 1980; translated into Spanish by

Juan Jose Utrilla (Mexico City: Fondo de Cultura Económica, 1989); also appears as *Piaget, Philosophy and the Human Sciences.* Evanston, IL: Northwestern University Press, 1997.

Continental Philosophy in America. Coedited with Thomas Seebohm and John Sallis. Pittsburgh: Duquesne University Press, 1983.

Descriptions. Coedited with Don Ihde. Selected Studies in Phenomenology and Existential Philosophy 11. Albany: State University of New York Press, 1985.

Hermeneutics and Deconstruction. Coedited with Don Ihde. Selected Studies in Phenomenology and Existential Philosophy 10. Albany: State University of New York Press, 1985.

The Horizons of Continental Philosophy: Essays on Husserl, Heidegger and Merleau-Ponty. Coedited with Algis Mickunas, Theodore Kisiel, and Alphonso Lingis. Dordrecht: Kluwer, 1988.

Philosophy and Non-Philosophy Since Merleau-Ponty. Continental Philosophy I. London and New York: Routledge, 1988; also appears as *Philosophy and Non-Philosophy Since Merleau-Ponty.* Evanston, IL: Northwestern University Press, 1997.

Postmodernism and Continental Philosophy. Coedited with Donn Welton. Selected Studies in Phenomenology and Existential Phenomenology 13. Albany: State University of New York Press, 1988.

Derrida and Deconstruction. Continental Philosophy II. New York: Routledge, 1989; translated into Korean by Ho-Bye Youn (Seoul, 1998).

Postmodernism: Philosophy and the Arts. Continental Philosophy III. New York: Routledge, 1990; translated into Korean by Ho-Bye Youn (Seoul: Koreaone Press, 1992).

The Textual Sublime: Deconstruction and Its Differences. Coedited with Gary E. Aylesworth. Contemporary Studies in Philosophy and Literature 1. Albany: State University of New York Press, 1990.

Gadamer and Hermeneutics. Continental Philosophy IV. New York: Routledge, 1991.

Writing the Politics of Difference. Selected Studies in Phenomenology and Existentialism 14. Albany: State University of New York Press, 1991.

Texts and Dialogues: On Philosophy, Politics, and Culture by Maurice Merleau-Ponty. Coedited with James Barry Jr. Amherst, NY: Humanities Press, 1992; revised edition, 1996.

Questioning Foundations: Truth/Subjectivity/Culture. Continental Philosophy V. New York: Routledge, 1993.

Textualität der Philosophie: Philosophie und Literatur. Coedited with Ludwig Nagl. Wiener Reihe 7. Vienna and Munich: R. Oldenbourg, 1994.

Cultural Semiosis: Tracing the Signifier. Continental Philosophy VI. New York and London: Routledge, 1998.

Philosophy and Desire. Continental Philosophy VII. New York: Routledge, 2000.
Lyotard: Philosophy, Politics and the Sublime. Continental Philosophy VIII. New York: Routledge, 2002.
Derrida und die Politiken der Freundschaft. Coedited with Erik M. Vogt and Serge Trottein. Vienna: Turia + Kant, 2003.
Über Žižek: Perspectiven und Kritiken. Coedited with Erik M. Vogt. Vienna: Turia + Kant, 2004.
Subjects and Simulations: Between Baudrillard and Lacoue-Labarthe. Coedited with Anne O'Byrne. Lanham, MD: Lexington, 2015.

Articles and Book Chapters

1974

"Artistic Creation and Human Action." *Mosaic: Literature and Ideas* 8, no. 1 (Fall 1974): 157–64.

1975

"Man and the Self as Identity of Difference." *Philosophy Today* 19, no. 2 (Summer 1975): 131–36.

1976

"Dufrenne's Phenomenology of Poetry." *Philosophy Today* 20, no. 1 (Spring 1976): 20–24.
"Re-Reading Merleau-Ponty." *Telos*, no. 29 (Fall 1976): 106–29.
"The Self in Husserl's 'Crisis.'" *Journal of the British Society for Phenomenology* 7, no. 1 (January 1976): 24–32.

1977

"Heidegger and Merleau-Ponty: Interpreting Hegel." *Research in Phenomenology* 7 (1977): 209–24.
"Thinking and Being: The Essential Relation." *Philosophy Today* 21, no. 3 (Fall 1977): 241–49.

1978

"A Cross-Cultural Approach to the De-Ontological Self Paradigm." With David A. Dilworth. *The Monist* 61, no. 1 (January 1978): 82–95.

"*Dasein* and Existential Ambiguity." In *Heidegger's Existential Analytic*, edited by Frederick Elliston, 97–108. New York: Mouton, 1978.

"Heidegger and Merleau-Ponty: Interpreting Hegel." In *Radical Phenomenology: Essays in Memory Of Martin Heidegger*, edited by John Sallis, 209–24. Atlantic Highlands, NJ: Humanities Press, 1978.

"Imagining, Perceiving, and Remembering." *Humanitas* 14, no. 2 (May 1978): 197–207.

"Jean-Paul Sartre versus Michel Foucault on Civilizational Study." *Philosophy and Social Criticism* 5, no. 2 (September 1978): 160–71.

"Sartre and the Structuralists." *International Philosophical Quarterly* 18, no. 3 (September 1978): 241–58.

"Self-Decentering: Derrida Incorporated." *Research in Phenomenology* 8 (1978): 45–65.

1979

"Biographical Situations, Cognitive Structures and Human Development: Confronting Sartre and Piaget." *Journal of Phenomenological Psychology* 10, no. 2 (Fall 1979): 119–37.

"For a Hermeneutic Semiology of the Self." *Philosophy Today* 23, no. 3 (Fall 1979): 199–204.

"Merleau-Ponty's Human Ambiguity." *Journal of the British Society for Phenomenology* 10, no. 1 (January 1979): 23–38.

"Merleau-Ponty on Language and Communication (1947–1948)." *Research in Phenomenology* 9 (1979): 168–81.

"Michel Foucault's Nineteenth Century System of Thought and the Anthropological Sleep." *Seminar* (Journal of the Philosophical Seminar, University College, Cork) 3 (April 1979): 1–8.

1980

"Autobiographizing" (Review of *Between Existentialism And Marxism* and *Life/Situations* by Jean-Paul Sartre). *Partisan Review* 47, no. 1 (January 1980): 142–46.

"Un égale deux ou l'espace autobiographique et ses limites." Translated by Françoise Marin. In *Le Deux*, edited by Marc Le Bot. *Revue d'esthétique*, nos. 1–2 (1980): 279–302.

"From Utopia/Dystopia to Heterotopia: An Interpretive Topology." *Philosophy and Social Criticism* 78, no. 2 (1980): 170–82.

"Merleau-Ponty and the Interrogation of Language." *Research in Phenomenology* 10 (1980): 122–41.

"Phenomenology." In "Philosophy: An Assessment." Edited by Peter Caws. Special issue, *Social Research* 47, no. 4. (Winter 1980): 704–20.

"Sartre's Words on the Self." In *Jean-Paul Sartre: Contemporary Approaches To His Philosophy*, edited by Hugh J. Silverman and Frederick A. Elliston, 85–104. Pittsburgh: Duquesne University Press, 1980.

1981

"The Autobiographical Space and its Limits." *Eros: A Journal of Philosophy and Literary Arts* 8, no. 1. (June 1981): 95–115.

"The Autobiographical Textuality of Nietzsche's *Ecce Homo*." *Boundary 2: A Journal of Postmodern Literature* 9/10, nos. 3/1 (Spring–Fall 1981): 141–51.

"The Limits of Logocentrism (On the Way to Grammatology)." In *Heidegger and Language*, edited by David Wood, 51–70. Coventry, UK: Parousia Press, 1981.

"Merleau-Ponty and the Interrogation of Language." In *Merleau-Ponty: Perception, Structure, Language*, edited by John Sallis, 122–41. Atlantic Highlands, NJ: Humanities Press, 1981.

"Prolegomena to a Theory of Literature." *Journal of the British Society for Phenomenology* 12, no. 1 (January 1981): 29–40.

1982

"Autobiographical Textuality: The Case of Thoreau's *Walden*." *Semiotica* 41, nos. 1–4 (1982): 257–76.

"Beckett, Philosophy and the Self." In *The Philosophical Reflection of Man in Literature*, edited by Anna-Teresa Tymieniecka, 153–60. Analecta Husserliana 12. Dordrecht: D. Reidel, 1982.

"Cézanne's Mirror Stage." *Journal of Aesthetics and Art Criticism* 40, no. 4 (1982): 369–79.

"Communicability." In *Interpersonal Communication: Essays in Phenomenology and Hermeneutics*, edited by Joseph J. Pilotta, 109–24. Washington, DC: University Press of America, 1982.

"Jean-Paul Sartre." In *Contemporary Literary Criticism* 20, edited by Sharon R. Gunton. Detroit: Gale Research, 1982.

"Merleau-Ponty's New Beginning: Preface to *The Experience of Others*." In "Merleau-Ponty and Psychology." Special issue, *Review of Existential Psychology and Psychiatry* 18, nos. 1–3 (1982–1983): 25–31.

"The Philosopher's Body and the Body of the Photograph." *Journal of the British Society for Phenomenology* 13, no. 3 (October 1982): 256–66.

"The Time of Autobiography." In *Time and Metaphysics*, edited by David Wood and Robert Bernasconi, 39–65. Coventry, UK: Parousia Press, 1982.

1983

"The Continental Face of Philosophy in America." *Philosophy Today* 27, no. 4 (Winter 1983): 275–80.

"Writing (on Deconstruction) at the Edge of Metaphysics." *Research in Phenomenology* 13 (1983): 97–111.

1984

"The Limits of Logocentrism (On the Way to Grammatology)." *Man and World* 17, nos. 3–4 (1984): 347–59.

"Oriëntatie: Continentale filosofie in Amerika." Translated by Adriaan Peperzak. *Wijsgerig Perspectief op Maatschappij en Wetenschap* 25, no. 4 (1984–1985): 133–35.

"Phenomenology: From Hermeneutics to Deconstruction." *Research in Phenomenology* 14 (1984): 19–34.

1985

"The Autobiographical Textuality of Nietzsche's *Ecce Homo.*" In *Why Nietzsche Now?*, edited by Daniel O'Hara, 141–51. Bloomington: Indiana University Press, 1985.

"The Limits of Logocentrism (On the Way to Grammatology)." *Phenomenology and the Human Sciences*, edited by J. N. Mohanty, 107–19. The Hague: Nijhoff, 1985.

"The Self in Question." In *Phenomenology in Practice and Theory*, edited by William S. Hamrick, 153–60. Dordrecht: Martinus Nijhoff, 1985.

"Textuality and the University." In "Humanism and the University. Vol. II: The Institutions of Humanism." Special issue, *Boundary 2* 13, nos. 2–3 (1985): 123–32.

1986

"Hermeneutics and Interrogation." *Research in Phenomenology* 16 (1986): 87–94.

"Interrogation and Deconstruction." In *Studien für neueren französischen Phänomenologie: Ricœur, Foucault, Derrida*, edited by Ernst Wolfgang Orth, 113–27. Phänomenologische Forschungen 18. Freiburg: Verlag Karl Alber, 1986.

"Le lieu de l'histoire: Sartre et Foucault." *Études Sartriennes* II–III (1986): 151–56.

"Literature/Text." In *Sartre: An Investigation of Some Major Themes*, edited by Simon Glynn, 127–46. Aldershot, UK: Gower, 1986.

"Postmodernism, Language, and Textuality, Part I." *Phenomenology + Pedagogy* 4, no. 1 (1986): 3–8.

"What Is Textuality? Part II." *Phenomenology + Pedagogy* 4, no. 2 (1986): 54–61.

"Who Signs This Poem? On the Institution of Poetry." *Rivista di estetica "filosofia e poesia"* 26, no. 22 (1986): 101–06.

1987

"Afterthoughts." In *Phenomenology: Descriptive or Hermeneutic?: The First Annual Symposium of the Simon Silverman Phenomenology Center*, 85–92. Pittsburgh: Duquesne University/Simon Silverman Phenomenology Center, 1987.

"Phenomenology: From Hermeneutics to Deconstruction." In *Phenomenology: Descriptive or Hermeneutic?: The First Annual Symposium of the Simon Silverman Phenomenology Center*, 21–38. Pittsburgh: Duquesne University/Simon Silverman Phenomenology Center, 1987.

"Philosophy Has Its Reasons . . ." In *Deconstruction and Philosophy: The Texts of Jacques Derrida*, edited by John Sallis, 21–32. Chicago: University of Chicago Press, 1987.

1988

"Textuality and the Origin of the Work of Art." In *The Horizons of Continental Philosophy: Essays on Husserl, Heidegger, and Merleau-Ponty*, edited by Hugh J. Silverman, Algis Mickunas, Theodore Kisiel, and Alfonso Lingis, 153–67. Dordrecht: Kluwer/Nijhoff, 1988.

1989

"Derrida, Heidegger, and the Time of the Line." In *Derrida and Deconstruction*, edited by Hugh J. Silverman, 149–63. Continental Philosophy II. New York: Routledge, 1989.

"Philosophical Passages: An Essay in Self-Presentation." In *American Phenomenology: Origins and Developments*, edited by Eugene F. Kaelin and Calvin O. Schrag, 374–83. Analecta Husserliana. Dordrecht: Kluwer, 1989.

"Textuality and the Ends of Modernity." *Differentia*, nos. 3–4 (1989): 321–28.

1990

"Concerning *Differentia.*" *Quaderni d'italianistica* XI, no. 1 (1990): 136–39.

"Filming: Inscriptions of *Denken.*" Coauthored with Wilhelm S. Wurzer. In *Postmodernism–Philosophy and The Arts*, edited by Hugh J. Silverman, 173–86. Continental Philosophy III. New York: Routledge, 1990.

"Merleau-Ponty and Derrida: Writing on Writing." In *Ontology and Alterity in Merleau-Ponty*, edited by Galen A. Johnson and Michael B. Smith, 130–41. Evanston, IL: Northwestern University Press, 1990.

1991

"Interpreting the Interpretative Text." In *Gadamer and Hermeneutics*, 269–76. Continental Philosophy IV. New York: Routledge, 1991.

"The Text of the Speaking Subject: From Merleau-Ponty to Kristeva." In *Merleau-Ponty Vivant*, 183–94. Albany: State University of New York Press, 1991.

1992

"Between Merleau-Ponty and Postmodernism." In *Merleau-Ponty: Hermeneutics and Postmodernism*, edited by Thomas W. Busch and Shaun Gallagher, 139–47. Albany: State University of New York Press, 1992.

"The Inscription of the Moment: Zarathustra's Gate." *International Studies in Philosophy* 24, no. 2 (1992): 53–61.

1993

"Cézanne's Mirror Stage." In *The Merleau-Ponty Aesthetics Reader: Philosophy and Painting*, edited by Galen A. Johnson, 262–77. Evanston, IL: Northwestern University Press, 1993.

"*Foucault/Derrida: Ursprünge der Geschichte.*" Translated by Erik Vogt. In "Klios Texte." *Österreichische Zeitschrift für Geschichtswissenschaften* 3 (1993): 492–503.

"The Philosophy of Postmodernism." In *Contemporary Philosophy of Art*, edited by John W. Bender and H. Gene Blocker, 74–77. Englewood Cliffs, NJ: Prentice Hall, 1993.

"Traces du sublime: La visibilité, l'expressivité et l'inconscient." Translated by Carol Richards. "Esthétiques en chantier." Special issue, *Revue d'esthétique* 24 (1993): 83–92.

"*Visibilität und Textualität: . . . ein nahezu vollkommener Chiasmus . . .*" Translated by Anke Müller. In "Geschriebene Bilder: Das Theater der Repräsentation," edited by Herta Wolf and Michael Wetzel. *FRAG•MENTE: Schriftenreihe für Kultur-, Medien- und Psychoanalyse*, no. 41 (1993): 115–28.

1994

"French Structuralism and After: de Saussure, Lévi-Strauss, Barthes, Lacan, Foucault." In *Continental Philosophy in the Twentieth Century*, edited by Richard Kearney, 390–408. Routledge History of Philosophy Series 8. London: Routledge, 1994.

"Nachwort: Über Textualität der Philosophie—Philosophie und Literatur." Translated by Erik Vogt. In *Textualität der Philosophie und Literatur*, edited by Ludwig Nagl and Hugh J. Silverman, 246–57. Wiener Reihe 7. Vienna: Oldenbourg, 1994.

"Postmodernism and Contemporary Italian Philosophy." *Man and World* 27, no. 4 (1994): 343–48.

"Textualität der Postmoderne: Lyotard, Ereignis, Erhabenes." Translated by Erik Vogt. In *Textualität der Philosophie und Literatur*, edited by Ludwig Nagl and Hugh J. Silverman, 236–45. Wiener Reihe 7. Vienna: Oldenbourg, 1994.

"Visibilität und Textualität: . . . ein nahezu vollkommener Chiasmus . . ." Translated by Anke Müller. In *Der Entzug der Bilder: Visuelle Realitäten*, edited by Michael Wetzel and Herta Wolf, 37–46. Munich: Wilhelm Fink Verlag, 1994.

1995

"The Child's New Logic (Derridean Choreographies)." In *Joyful Wisdom: Zarathustra's Joyful Annunciations*, edited by David Goicoechea and Mark Zlomislić, 86–101. Studies in Postmodern Ethics 4. Port Colbourne, ON: Thought House, 1995.

"Lyotard en het postmoderne sublime." In *Lyotard Lezen: Ethiek, Onmenselijkheid en Sensibiliteit*, edited by Richard Brons and Harry Kunneman, 80–88. Amsterdam: Boom, 1995.

"The Mark of Postmodernism: Reading *Roger Rabbit*." *Cinémas: Revue d'études cinématographiques/Cinémas: Journal of Film Studies* 5, no. 3 (printemps 1995): 151–64.

1996

"Modernism and Postmodernism." In *Encyclopedia of Philosophy* (Supplement), edited by Donald M. Borchert, 253–54. New York: Macmillan, 1996;

now available as "Modernism and Postmodernism." Vol. 6 of *Encyclopedia of Philosophy*. 2nd ed., edited by Donald M. Borchert, 316–19. Detroit: MacMillan (Gale Virtual Reference Library), 2006.

"Traces of the Sublime: Visibility, Expressivity, and the Unconscious." In *Merleau-Ponty: Difference, Materiality, Painting*, edited by Véronique Fóti, 128–36. Atlantic Highlands, NJ: Humanities Press, 1996.

" 'Wenn ich Fremder bin, gibt es keine Fremden:' Reflexionen über postmoderne Fremde." Translated by Daniel Weidner. "Psychoanalyse und Philosophie." *Mitteilung des Instituts für Wissenschaft und Kunst, Wien* 51, no. 1 (1996): 10–16.

1997

"Nietzsche's Italics: Chiasmatic Inscriptions—Between the Sheets/Nietzsches Cors(iv)o: Chiasmatische Inschriften/Einschreibungen—Zwischen den Tafeln." In Maria Theresia Litschauer, *Nietzsche in Italien: Text–Bild–Signatur (Ein Cross-Over von Kunst und Philosophie)*, 68–101. Vienna: Graphische Kunstanstalt Otto Sares, 1997.

"Postmodernismi Ja Elokuva: Roskaelokuvissa Econ ja Derridan kanssa." Translated by Anita Seppä. *Synteesi: Taiteidenvälisen Tutkimuksen Aikakauslehti* [Finland] (1997): 89–97.

"Reading Postmodernism as Interruption (between Merleau-Ponty and Derrida)." In *Écart & Différance: On Seeing and Reading in Merleau-Ponty and Derrida*, edited by M. C. Dillon, 208–19. Atlantic Highlands, NJ: Humanities Press, 1997.

1998

"Befindet Merleau-Ponty sich innerhalb oder außerhalb der Geschichte der Philosophie?" In *Krise der Wissenschaften—Wissenschaft der Krisis? Wiener Tagungen der Phänomenologie*, edited by Helmut Vetter, 141–55. Frankfurt am Main: Peter Lang, 1998.

"The Sign of the Rose: Filming Eco." In *Cultural Semiosis: Tracing the Signifier*, edited by Hugh J. Silverman, 167–77. Continental Philosophy VI. New York: Routledge, 1998.

1999

"Continental Philosophy on the American Scene: An Autobiographical Statement." In *Portraits of American Continental Philosophers*, edited by James R. Watson, 186–202. Bloomington: Indiana University Press, 1999.

"Kontinentalphilosophie auf der amerikanischen Szene: Eine autobiographische Aufzeichnung." In *Amerikanische PhilosophInnen in Selbst-*

darstellungen, edited by James R. Watson, 265–86. Translated by Erik Michael Vogt. Vienna: Turia + Kant, 1999.

"Markierungen der Postmoderne: Eine Lektüre von *Roger Rabbit*." Translated by Erik Vogt. In *Filmästhetik*, edited by Ludwig Nagl, 229–43. Vienna: Oldenbourg and Akademie Verlag, 1999.

"Maurice Merleau-Ponty." In *A Companion to the Philosophers*, edited by Robert L. Arrington, 397–404. Blackwell Companions to Philosophy. Oxford: Blackwell, 1999.

"La scrittura avanti lo scrivere." Translated by Alessandro Carrera. *Intersezioni: Rivista di storia delle idee* XIX, no. 3 (December 1999): 417–20.

2000

"Is Merleau-Ponty Inside or Outside the History of Philosophy?" In *Chiasms: Merleau-Ponty's Notion of Flesh*, edited by Fred Evans and Leonard Lawlor, 131–43. Albany: State University of New York Press, 2000.

2001

"Andy Warhol: Chiasmatic Visibilities." In *Impossible Presence: Surface and Screen in the Photogenic Era*, edited by Terry Smith, 193–207. Sydney: Power Publications; Chicago: University of Chicago Press, 2001.

Forward to *Ritual Thinking: Sexuality, Death, World*, by Mario Perniola, 9–14. Translated by Massimo Verdicchio. Amherst, NY: Humanity Books, 2001.

"Le postmodernisme comme modernité 'fin de siècle' (ou: Le posmodernisme aux fins de l'indifférence')." Translated by Arnaud Villani. In "Philosophie américaine contemporaine." Special issue, *Revue de Metaphysique et de Morale*, no. 4 (octobre–décembre 2001): 67–78.

2002

"Jacques Derrida." In *Postmodernism: The Key Figures*, edited by Hans Bertens and Joseph Natoli, 110–18. Malden, MA: Blackwell, 2002.

"Jean-Francois Lyotard—Between Politics and Aesthetics." In *Lyotard: Philosophy, Politics and the Sublime*, edited by Hugh J. Silverman, 1–19. New York: Routledge, 2002.

"Lyotard and the Events of the Postmodern Sublime." In *Lyotard: Philosophy, Politics and The Sublime*, edited by Hugh J. Silverman, 222–29. New York: Routledge, 2002.

"Philosophy has its reasons . . ." In *Derrida: Critical Assessments of Leading Philosophers*, edited by Zeynep Direk and Leonard Lawlor, 64–74. New York: Routledge, 2002.

2003

"Merleau-Pontys Gespenster in der amerikanischen Kontinentalphilosophie." In *Was heißt Kontinentalphilosophie in den USA? Eine internationale Debatte über Hermeneutik, Dekonstruktion, Feminismus*, edited by Erik M. Vogt, 57–74. Vienna: Turia + Kant, 2003.

"Rechte Freunde: Die Ethik der (postmodernen) Beziehungen." In *Derrida und die Politiken der Freundschaft*, edited by Erik M. Vogt, Hugh J. Silverman, and Serge Trottein, 19–42. Vienna: Turia + Kant, 2003.

2004

"Foreword: Perniola's Postmodern Shadows." In *Art and its Shadow*, by Mario Perniola, vii–xiii. Translated by Massimo Verdicchio. New York: Continuum, 2004.

"Postmoderne Medien und die Angst vor Simulationen: Die Leiden des jungen Truman." Translated by Erik Michael Vogt. In *film denken/thinking film: Film and Philosophy*, edited by Ludwig Nagl, Eva Waniek, and Brigitte Mayr, 139–48. Vienna: SYNEMA—Gesellschaft für Film und Medien, 2004.

"Über 'Being postmodern': Žižeks tückische Subjekte." Translated by Erik M. Vogt. In *Über Žižek: Perspektiven und Kritiken*, edited by Erik M. Vogt and Hugh J. Silverman, 27–38. Vienna: Turia + Kant, 2004.

2005

"Living On (Borderlines): The Ethics of the Event of Lived Human Relations (Merleau-Ponty/Derrida)." *Chiasmi International* 6 (2005): 273–84.

2006

"Lyotard and the Events of the Postmodern Sublime." In *Jean-Francois Lyotard: Critical Evaluations*. Vol. 1, *Aesthetics*, edited by Gregg Lambert and Victor E. Taylor, 241–50. New York: Routledge, 2006.

"Merleau-Ponty and the Interrogation of Language." In *Merleau-Ponty: Critical Assessments of Leading Philosophers*. Vol. 2, *Perception and Expression*, edited by Ted Toadvine, 177–94. New York: Routledge, 2006.

"Respons-abilities—Between Three." *Archivio di Filosofia /Archives of Philosophy* LXXIV, nos. 1–3 (2006): 479–89.

"Specters of Merleau-Ponty." *Interrogating Ethics: Embodying the Good in Merleau-Ponty*," edited by James Hatley, Janice McLane, and Christian Diehm, 311–25. Pittsburgh: Duquesne University Press, 2006.

"Zwischenzonendenkforschung als Interventionsforschung ohne Intervention." In *Klagenfurter Beiträge zur Interventionsforschung*. Vol. 4, *Beiträge zur Interdisziplinären Ringvorlesung Interventionsforschung*, edited by Peter Heintel, Larissa Krainer, and Ina Paul-Horn, 59–66. Klagenfurt: Fakultät für Interdisziplinäre Forschung und Fortbildung, 2006.

2007

"Can the Globalized World Be in-the-World?" In *Weakening Philosophy: Essays in Honor of Gianni Vattimo*, edited by Santiago Zabala, 110–16. Montreal: McGill-Queens University Press, 2007.

"La Continental Philosophy sulla scena culturale americana. Una riflessione autobiografica." Translated by Sarah F. Maclaren. *Ágalma: rivista di studi culturali e di estetica*, no. 13 (March 2007): 68–79.

"Response-abilities for Legacies: Jacques—on vous suit à travers vos texts." "Following Derrida: Legacies." Special issue, *Mosaic: A Journal for the Interdisciplinary Study of Literature* 40, no. 2 (June 2007): 297–306.

"Tracing Responsibility: Levinas between Merleau-Ponty and Derrida." *Journal of French Philosophy* 17, no. 1 (2007): 81–96.

2008

"Art and Aesthetics." In *Merleau-Ponty: Key Concepts*, edited by Rosalyn Diprose and Jack Reynolds, 95–108. London: Acumen Publishing, 2008.

"Die Grenzen der Aufklärung und das Ereignis der Grenze: Derrida und Adorno." Translated by Gertrude Postl. In *Derrida und Adorno: Zur Aktualität von Dekonstruktion und Frankfurter Schule*, edited by Eva L.-Waniek and Erik M. Vogt, 70–82. Vienna: Turia + Kant, 2008.

"Excessive Responsibility and the Sense of the World (Merleau-Ponty and Nancy)." *Chiasmi International* 10 (2008): 305–17.

"°.°: Rückkehr der Postmoderne: Die Macht der Gespenster." Translated by Sabine Malicha and David Ender. In "Specters°.° Gespenster." Special issue, *Corpus* 11 (October 2008). http://www.corpusweb.net/dd1-rehr-der-postmoderne.html.

2009

"Chiasmatic Intersections: The Installation-Events of Inhwan Oh" (in English and in Korean). Translated by Kisoo Kim. In *Inhwan Oh: Artworks*, 12–25. Seoul: Samsuo, Space for Contemporary Art, 2009.

2010

"Justice and the Art of Technicity: The Aporetic Responsibility Between Us" [in English]. *The Korean Society of Aesthetics and the Science of Art* (proceedings) (2010): 245–58;

"Justice and the Art of Technicity: The Aporetic Responsibility Between Us." Translated into Korean by Kisoo Kim. *The Journal of Aesthetics and the Science of Art* (published by the Korean Society of Aesthetics and Science of Art, Seoul, Korea) 32 (2010): 167–96.

"The Limits of the Timeless: Kristeva's Intimate Re-Volts." In "Philosophy, Language, Literature." Edited by Robin M. Muller. Special issue, *Graduate Faculty Philosophy Journal* 31, no. 1 (2010): 91–107.

"Malabou, Plasticity, and the Sculpturing of the Self." *Concentric: Literary and Cultural Studies* 36, no. 2 (2010): 89–102.

"Repetition-Juxtaposition-Difference: Warhol, Merleau-Ponty, and the Chiasmatic Inscriptions of Postmodern Events." *Studies in the Humanities* (published by the Institute of Humanities, Catholic University of Daegu, Gyeongbuk, Republic of Korea), 13 (June 2010): 119–36.

"Repetition-Juxtaposition-Difference: Warhol, Merleau-Ponty, and the Chiasmatic Inscriptions of Postmodern Events." Translated into Korean by Kisoo Kim. *Sculpture* Journal (S. Korea), (Summer 2010): 69–75.

2011

"Derrida, *code enforcement* und Religionswahl." Translated by Artur Boelderl. In *Die Tradition einer Zukunft: Perspektiven der Religionsphilosophie,* edited by Florian Uhl, Sylvia Melchardt, and Artur R. Boelderl, 349–64. Graal-Müritz, Germany: Parerga, 2011.

"*Ereignisse* of the Postmodern: Heidegger, Lyotard, and Gerhard Richter." In *Postmodernism. What Moment?*, edited by Pelagia Goulimari, 38–49. Manchester: Manchester University Press, 2011.

"Just Friends: Ethics of (Postmodern) Relationships" [in Chinese]. *Intergrams: Studies in Languages and Literatures* 11, no. 2 (2011): 1–12.

"Metaphorizing Abysses and the Archaeologies of Vision." *JTLA: Journal of the Faculty of Letters, University of Tokyo, Aesthetics* 36 (2011): 13–26.

"Postmodern Turns—*Fin de siècle* Intermedialities." In *Intermedialities: Philosophy Arts Politics*, edited by Henk Oosterling and Ewa Płonowska Ziarek, 15–25. Lanham, MD: Lexington Books, 2011.

2012

"Aesthetics—Then and Now." *Journal of Speculative Philosophy* 26, no. 2 (2012): 361–69.

"Just Friends: The Ethics of (Postmodern) Relationships." In *Critical Communities and Aesthetic Practices: Dialogues with Tony O'Connor on Society, Art, and Friendship*, edited by Francis Halsall, Julia Jansen, and Sinéad Murphy, 181–93. Contributions to Phenomenology 64. Dordrecht: Springer, 2012.

2014

"Literature." In *The Cambridge Foucault Lexicon*, edited by Leonard Lawlor and John Nale, 263–69. Cambridge: Cambridge University Press, 2014.

2015

"The Postmodern Subject: Truth and Fiction in Lacoue-Labarthe's Nietzsche." In *Subjects and Simulations: Between Baudrillard and Lacoue-Labarthe*, edited by Anne O'Byrne and Hugh J. Silverman, 47–56. Lanham, MD: Lexington Books, 2015.

Translations

Translated Books

Consciousness and the Acquisition of Language, by Maurice Merleau-Ponty. Translated with a preface. Evanston, IL: Northwestern University Press, 1973.

Translated Articles

"The Experience of Others," by Maurice Merleau-Ponty. Translated with Fred Evans. In "Merleau-Ponty and Psychology." Special issue, *Review of Existential Psychology and Psychiatry* 18 (1982–1983): 33–63.

"Philosophy and Non-Philosophy Since Hegel," by Maurice Merleau-Ponty. In *Philosophy and Non-Philosophy Since Merleau-Ponty*, edited by Hugh J. Silverman, 9–83. Continental Philosophy I. New York: Routledge, 1988.

Works Cited

Adorno, Theodore W. *Aesthetic Theory*. Edited by Gretel Adorno and Rolf Tiedemann. Translated by Robert Hullot-Kentor. Minneapolis: University of Minnesota Press, 1997.

Arendt, Hannah. *The Human Condition*. 2nd ed. Chicago: University of Chicago Press, 1998.

———. *On Revolution*. London: Penguin Books, 1963.

Aristotle. *On Poetry and Style*. Translated by G. M. A. Grube. Indianapolis: Hackett, 1989.

Barthes, Roland. "The Death of the Author." In *Image–Music–Text*, translated by Stephen Heath, 142–48. New York: Hill & Wang, 1977.

———. "From Work to Text." In *Image–Music–Text*, translated by Stephen Heath, 155–64. New York: Hill & Wang, 1977.

———. *Roland Barthes*. Translated by Richard Howard. New York: Hill & Wang, 1977.

Beauvoir, Simone de. *The Second Sex*. Translated by Constance Borde and Sheila Malovany-Chevallier. New York: Alfred A. Knopf, 2010.

Blanchot, Maurice. "Literature and the Right to Death." In *The Gaze of Orpheus and Other Literary Essays*. Edited by P. Adams Sitney. Translated by Lydia Davis, 21–62. Barrytown, NY: Station Hill Press, 1981.

Butler, Judith. *Undoing Gender*. New York: Routledge, 2004.

Cavarero, Adriana. *Relating Narratives: Storytelling and Selfhood*. Translated by Paul A. Kottman. London: Routledge, 2000.

Cavell, Stanley. *Little Did I Know: Excerpts from Memory*. Stanford: Stanford University Press, 2010.

———. *Philosophy the Day after Tomorrow*. Cambridge: Belknap Press of Harvard University Press, 2005.

———. *A Pitch of Philosophy: Autobiographical Exercises*. Cambridge: Harvard University Press, 1994.

Colapietro, Vincent. "Striving to Speak in a Human Voice: A Peircean Contribution to Metaphysical Discourse." *The Review of Metaphysics* 58, no. 2 (December 2004): 367–98.

Derrida, Jacques. *L'autre cap*. Paris: Minuit, 1991.

———. *Limited Inc.* Translated by Samuel Weber. Edited by Gerald Graff. Evanston, IL: Northwestern University Press, 1988.

———. *Marges de la philosophie.* Paris: Minuit, 1972.

———. *Margins of Philosophy.* Translated by Alan Bass. Chicago: University of Chicago Press, 1982.

———. *Of Grammatology.* Translated by Gayatri Chakravorty Spivak. Baltimore: Johns Hopkins University Press, 1976.

———. "On Cosmopolitanism." In *On Cosmopolitanism and Forgiveness*, translated by Mark Dooley and Michael Hughes, 1–24. New York: Routledge, 2001.

———. *The Other Heading: Reflections on Today's Europe.* Translated by Pascale-Anne Brault and Michael B. Naas. Bloomington: Indiana University Press, 1992.

———. *The Politics of Friendship.* Translated by George Collins. London: Verso, 1997.

———. *Positions.* Translated by Alan Bass. Chicago: University of Chicago Press, 1981.

———. *The Post Card: From Socrates to Freud and Beyond.* Translated by Alan Bass. Chicago: University of Chicago Press, 1987.

———. *Speech and Phenomenon: And Other Essays on Husserl's Theory of Signs.* Translated by David B. Allison. Evanston, IL: Northwestern University Press, 1973.

———. " 'This Strange Institution Called Literature': An Interview with Jacques Derrida." Translated by Geoffrey Bennington and Rachel Bowlby. In Jacques Derrida, *Acts of Literature*, edited by Derek Attridge, 33–75. New York: Routledge, 1992.

Derrida, Jacques, and Geoffrey Bennington. *Jacques Derrida.* Translated by Geoffrey Bennington. Chicago: University of Chicago Press, 1993.

Diprose, Rosalyn, and Ewa Płonowska Ziarek. "Time for Beginners: Natality, Biopolitics, and Political Theology." *PhiloSophia* 3, no. 2 (Summer 2013): 107–20.

Foucault, Michel. "Des espaces autres." *Empan* 2, no. 54 (2004): 12–19.

———. *Les mots et les choses: une archéologie des sciences humaines.* Paris: Gallimard, 1966.

———. "Nietzsche, Genealogy, History." In *The Foucault Reader*, edited by Paul Rabinow, 76–100. New York: Pantheon Books, 1984.

———. "Of Other Spaces." Translated by Jay Miskowiec. *Diacritics* 16, no. 1 (1986): 22–27.

———. *The Order of Things: An Archaeology of the Human Sciences.* New York: Vintage, 1973.

Heidegger, Martin. *Being and Time.* Translated by Joan Stambaugh. Albany: State University of New York Press, 1996.

———. *Being and Time*. Translated by Joan Stambaugh. Revised by Dennis J. Schmidt. Albany: State University of New York Press, 2010.

———. "Letter on 'Humanism.'" Translated by Frank A. Capuzzi. In *Pathmarks*, edited by William McNeill, 239–76. Cambridge: Cambridge University Press, 1998.

Irigaray, Luce. *Marine Lover of Friedrich Nietzsche*. Translated by Gillian C. Gill. New York: Columbia University Press, 1991.

Kristeva, Julia. "Life as a Narrative." In *Hannah Arendt*, translated by Ross Guberman, 3–99. New York: Columbia University Press, 2001.

———. *Revolt She Said*. Translated by Brian O'Keeffe. New York: Semiotext(e), 2002.

Kronick, Joseph G. "Philosophy as Autobiography: The Confessions of Jacques Derrida." *MLN* 115, no. 5 (December 2000): 997–1018.

Landes, Donald A. *Merleau-Ponty and the Paradoxes of Expression*. London: Bloomsbury, 2013.

Lawlor, Leonard. *This Is Not Sufficient: An Essay on Animality and Human Nature in Derrida*. New York: Columbia University Press, 2007.

Lyotard, Jean-François. *The Differend: Phrases in Dispute*. Translated by Georges Van Den Abbeele. Minneapolis: University of Minnesota Press, 1988.

Malcolm, Janet. *The Crime of Sheila McGough*. New York: Vintage, 1999.

———. *The Journalist and the Murderer*. New York: Vintage, 1990.

Man, Paul de. *Allegories of Reading: Figural Language in Rousseau, Nietzsche, Rilke, and Proust*. New Haven: Yale University Press, 1979.

Mead, Rebecca. "The Queasy Finale of *The Jinx*." *New Yorker*, March 16, 2015. http://www.newyorker.com/culture/cultural-comment/robert-dursts-grotesque-confession.

Merleau-Ponty, Maurice. *Phenomenology of Perception*. Translated by Donald A. Landes. New York: Routledge, 2012.

———. "Philosophy and Non-Philosophy Since Hegel." Translated by Hugh J. Silverman. In *Philosophy and Non-Philosophy Since Merleau-Ponty*, edited by Hugh J. Silverman, 9–83. Continental Philosophy I. New York: Routledge, 1988.

———. *Signs*. Translated by Richard C. McCleary. Evanston, IL: Northwestern University Press, 1964.

———. *Texts and Dialogues: On Philosophy, Politics, and Culture*. Edited by Hugh J. Silverman and James Barry Jr. Amherst, NY: Humanities Press, 1992.

———. *The Visible and the Invisible*. Translated by Alphonso Lingis. Evanston, IL: Northwestern University Press, 1968.

Miller, J. Hillis. "Narrative." In *Critical Terms for Literary Study*, edited by Frank Lentricchia and Thomas McLaughlin, 66–79. Chicago: University of Chicago Press, 1990.

Nancy, Jean-Luc. *The Gravity of Thought*. Translated by François Raffoul and Gregory Recco. Atlantic Highlands, NJ: Humanities Press, 1997.

Nietzsche, Friedrich. *Beyond Good and Evil: Prelude to a Philosophy of the Future*. Translated by Walter Kaufmann. New York: Vintage, 1989.

Plato. *Symposium*. Translated by Alexander Nehamas and Paul Woodruff. In *Plato: Complete Works*, edited by John M. Cooper, 457–505. Indianapolis: Hackett, 1997.

Poulet, George. "Phenomenology of Reading." *New Literary History* 1, no. 1 (October 1969): 53–68.

Santayana, George. *The Life of Reason or The Phases of Human Progress*. New York: Charles Scribner and Sons, 1954.

Saramago, José. *Small Memories: A Memoir*. Translated by Margaret Jull Costa. Boston: Mariner Books, 2012.

Shakespeare, William. *The Complete Works of William Shakespeare*. Ware, UK: Wordworth, 1996.

Silverman, Hugh J. "Aesthetics—Then and Now." *Journal of Speculative Philosophy* 26, no. 2 (2012): 361–69.

———. "Autobiographical Textuality: The Case of Thoreau's *Walden*." *Semiotica* 41, nos. 1–4 (1982): 257–76.

———. "Cézanne's Mirror Stage." In *The Merleau-Ponty Aesthetics Reader: Philosophy and Painting*, edited by Galen A. Johnson, 262–77. Evanston, IL: Northwestern University Press, 1993.

———. "Continental Philosophy on the American Scene: An Autobiographical Statement." In *Portraits of American Continental Philosophers*, edited by James R. Watson, 187–202. Bloomington: Indiana University Press, 1999.

———. "Excessive Responsibility and the Sense of the World (Merleau-Ponty and Nancy)." *Chiasmi International* 10 (2008): 305–17.

———. "Existential Ambiguity: A Phenomenology of Human Nature." PhD diss., Stanford University, 1973.

———. *Inscriptions: Between Phenomenology and Structuralism*. New York: Routledge, Kegan and Paul, 1987.

———. "Is Merleau-Ponty Inside or Outside the History of Philosophy?" In *Chiasms: Merleau-Ponty's Notion of Flesh*, edited by Fred Evans and Leonard Lawlor, 131–43. Albany: State University of New York Press, 2000.

———. "Living On (Borderlines): The Ethics of the Event of Lived Human Relations (Merleau-Ponty/Derrida)." *Chiasmi International* 6 (2005): 273–284.

———. "Man and the Self as Identity of Difference." *Philosophy Today* 19, no. 2 (Summer 1975): 131–36.

———. "The Mark of Postmodernism: Reading *Roger Rabbit*." *Cinémas: Revue d'études cinématographiques/Cinémas: Journal of Film Studies* 5, no. 3 (printemps 1995): 151–64.

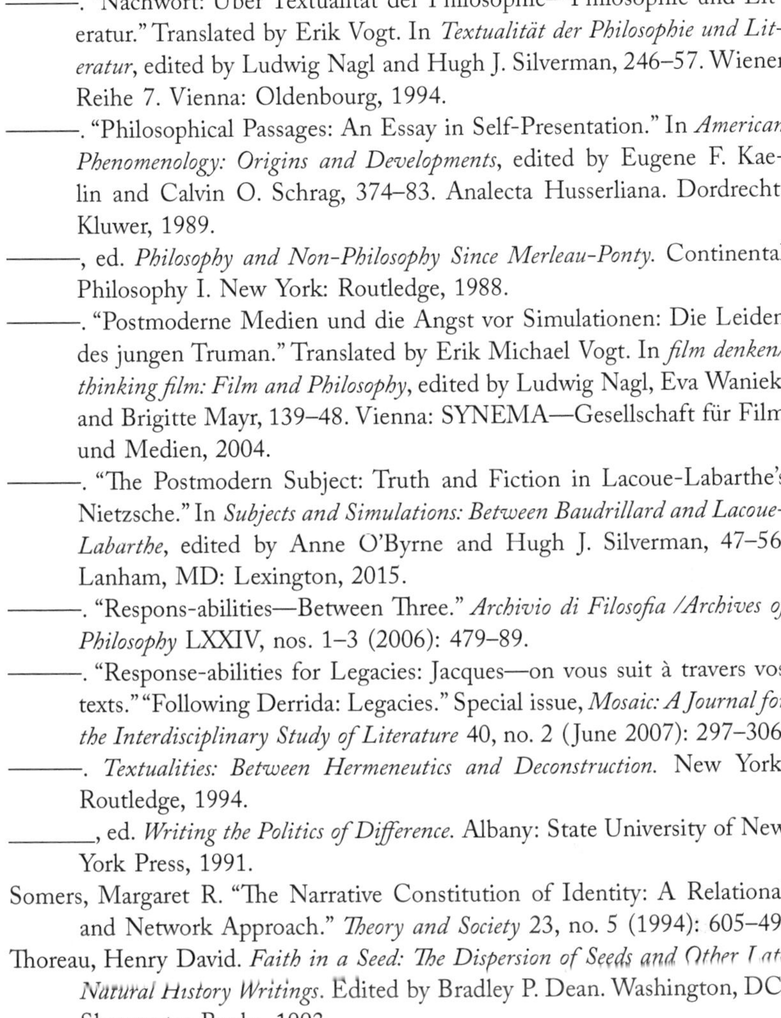

———. "Nachwort: Über Textualität der Philosophie—Philosophie und Literatur." Translated by Erik Vogt. In *Textualität der Philosophie und Literatur*, edited by Ludwig Nagl and Hugh J. Silverman, 246–57. Wiener Reihe 7. Vienna: Oldenbourg, 1994.

———. "Philosophical Passages: An Essay in Self-Presentation." In *American Phenomenology: Origins and Developments*, edited by Eugene F. Kaelin and Calvin O. Schrag, 374–83. Analecta Husserliana. Dordrecht: Kluwer, 1989.

———, ed. *Philosophy and Non-Philosophy Since Merleau-Ponty.* Continental Philosophy I. New York: Routledge, 1988.

———. "Postmoderne Medien und die Angst vor Simulationen: Die Leiden des jungen Truman." Translated by Erik Michael Vogt. In *film denken/thinking film: Film and Philosophy*, edited by Ludwig Nagl, Eva Waniek, and Brigitte Mayr, 139–48. Vienna: SYNEMA—Gesellschaft für Film und Medien, 2004.

———. "The Postmodern Subject: Truth and Fiction in Lacoue-Labarthe's Nietzsche." In *Subjects and Simulations: Between Baudrillard and Lacoue-Labarthe*, edited by Anne O'Byrne and Hugh J. Silverman, 47–56. Lanham, MD: Lexington, 2015.

———. "Respons-abilities—Between Three." *Archivio di Filosofia /Archives of Philosophy* LXXIV, nos. 1–3 (2006): 479–89.

———. "Response-abilities for Legacies: Jacques—on vous suit à travers vos texts." "Following Derrida: Legacies." Special issue, *Mosaic: A Journal for the Interdisciplinary Study of Literature* 40, no. 2 (June 2007): 297–306.

———. *Textualities: Between Hermeneutics and Deconstruction.* New York: Routledge, 1994.

_______, ed. *Writing the Politics of Difference.* Albany: State University of New York Press, 1991.

Somers, Margaret R. "The Narrative Constitution of Identity: A Relational and Network Approach." *Theory and Society* 23, no. 5 (1994): 605–49.

Thoreau, Henry David. *Faith in a Seed: The Dispersion of Seeds and Other Late Natural History Writings.* Edited by Bradley P. Dean. Washington, DC: Shearwater Books, 1993.

———. *Walden.* Edited by Jeffrey S. Cramer. New Haven: Yale University Press, 2004.

Ulmer, Gregory L. "The Post-Age." *Diacritics* 11, no. 3 (Autumn 1981): 39–56.

Young, Iris Marion. *Inclusion and Democracy.* Oxford: Oxford University Press, 2000.

Ziarek, Ewa Płonowska. *Feminist Aesthetics and the Politics of Modernism.* New York: Columbia University Press, 2012.

Contributors

Gary E. Aylesworth is professor of philosophy and former chair of the philosophy department at Eastern Illinois University. He also serves as codirector of the International Philosophical Seminar. His publications include *The Textual Sublime: Deconstruction and Its Differences*, coedited with Hugh J. Silverman, and translations of Martin Heidegger's *Basic Concepts* and *The Heidegger-Jaspers Correspondence*. He has also published articles on postmodernism, Heidegger, Nietzsche, hermeneutics, deconstruction, and other topics in contemporary continental philosophy.

Debra Bergoffen is professor emerita of Philosophy at George Mason University and the Bishop Hamilton Philosopher in Residence at American University. Her writings include *The Philosophy of Simone de Beauvoir: Gendered Phenomenologies, Erotic Generosities*; *Contesting the Politics of Genocidal Rape: Affirming the Dignity of the Vulnerable Body*; and the coedited anthology *Confronting Global Gender Justice: Human Rights, Women's Lives*. Her essays, dealing with sexual violence in armed conflict, human rights, Simone de Beauvoir, Nietzsche, and Lacan, have appeared in numerous edited collections and journals. She is currently working on a book titled *Antigone After Auschwitz*.

Edward S. Casey is distinguished professor of philosophy at Stony Brook University. Past president of the American Philosophical Association, Eastern Division, he is the author of *Getting Back into Place* (2nd ed., 2009), *The Fate of Place* (2nd ed., 2010), *Remembering* (2nd ed., 2000), and *Imagining* (2nd ed., 2000). He has published *The World at a Glance* (2007), a companion volume to which he is now completing: *The World on Edge* (forthcoming, 2016). With Mary Watkins, he has written *Up Against the Wall: Re-Imagining the U.S.-Mexico Border* (2014).

Peter Gratton teaches at The Memorial University of Newfoundland. He has published in political, continental, and intercultural philosophy and is the author of *The State of Sovereignty: Lessons from the Political Fictions of Modernity* (State University of New York Press, 2012) and *Speculative Realism: Problems and Prospects* (Bloomsbury, 2014). Series editor of the new Edinburgh University Press book series New Perspectives in Ontology, Gratton has also coedited four books: *Traversing the Imaginary: Richard Kearney and the Postmodern Challenge* (Northwestern University Press, 2007), with John Mannousakis; *Jean-Luc Nancy and Plural Thinking: Expositions of World, Politics, Art, and Sense* (State University of New York Press, 2012), with Marie-Eve Morin; *The Meillassoux Dictionary* (Edinburgh University Press, 2014), with Paul Ennis; and *The Nancy Dictionary* (Edinburgh University Press, 2015), with Marie-Eve Morin.

Galen A. Johnson is Jane C. Ebbs Professor of Philosophy at the University of Rhode Island and former general secretary (executive director) of the International Merleau-Ponty Circle. He has been a recent recipient of fellowships from the National Endowment for the Humanities (NEH) and American Philosophical Society (APS). He is editor of *The Merleau-Ponty Aesthetics Reader: Philosophy and Painting* (1993, 1998) and author of *The Retrieval of the Beautiful: Thinking Through Merleau-Ponty's Aesthetics* (2010). His coauthored book *Merleau-Ponty's Poets and Poetics* is forthcoming from Fordham University Press. His current research interests include the art and writings of Paul Klee and a study of the sublime and the baroque in Merleau-Ponty's late writings.

Donald A. Landes is professeur adjoint (assistant professor) of philosophy in the *Faculté de philosophie*, at Université Laval in Québec City. He is the author of *Merleau-Ponty and the Paradoxes of Expression* (Bloomsbury, 2013), which won the 2014 Book Prize for an Outstanding Book in Phenomenology from the Center for Advanced Research in Phenomenology. He is also the author of *The Merleau-Ponty Dictionary* (Bloomsbury, 2013) and the sole translator of Merleau-Ponty's *Phenomenology of Perception* (Routledge, 2012). He coedited with Azucena Cruz-Pierre *Exploring the Work of Edward S. Casey: Giving Voice to Place, Memory, and Imagination* (Bloomsbury, 2013) and has published articles in contemporary continental philosophy, ethics, and the history of philosophy. Landes received his PhD in philosophy from Stony Brook University in 2010, where his dissertation was codirected by Hugh J. Silverman and Edward S. Casey.

Leonard Lawlor received his PhD in philosophy from Stony Brook University in 1988. He is Edwin Erle Sparks Professor of Philosophy at Penn State University. He is the author of seven books: *Early Twentieth Century Continental Philosophy* (Indiana University Press, 2011); *This Is Not Sufficient* (Columbia University Press, 2007); *The Implications of Immanence* (Fordham University Press, 2006); *Thinking Through French Philosophy* (Indiana University Press, 2003); *The Challenge of Bergsonism* (Continuum, 2003); *Derrida and Husserl* (Indiana University Press, 2002); and *Imagination and Chance* (State University of New York Press, 1992). Lawlor is currently working on a new book titled *Violence against Violence* (for Edinburgh University Press).

Eduardo Mendieta is professor of philosophy at Penn State University. He is the author of *The Adventures of Transcendental Philosophy* (Rowman & Littlefield, 2002) and *Global Fragments: Globalizations, Latinamericanisms, and Critical Theory* (State University of New York Press, 2007). He is also coeditor with Craig Calhoun and Jonathan VanAntwerpen of *Habermas and Religion* (Polity Press, 2013) and with Stuart Elden of *Reading Kant's Geography* (State University of New York Press, 2011) He recently finished a book titled *The Philosophical Animal,* which will be published by State University of New York Press

Michael Naas, a graduate of Stony Brook University (PhD, 1990), is currently professor of philosophy at DePaul University in Chicago. He works in the areas of Ancient Greek philosophy and contemporary French philosophy. His most recent books include *Miracle and Machine: Jacques Derrida and the Two Sources of Religion, Science, and the Media* (Fordham University Press, 2012) and *The End of the World and Other Teachable Moments: Jacques Derrida's Final Seminar* (Fordham University Press, 2014). He is a cotranslator of several works by Jacques Derrida, including *The Other Heading*, *Memoirs of the Blind*, *Rogues*,

The Work of Mourning, and *Athens, Still Remains*. He also coedits the *Oxford Literary Review*.

Kelly Oliver is W. Alton Jones Professor of Philosophy at Vanderbilt University. She was professor of philosophy at Stony Brook University from 1998 to 2004 and chair of the Philosophy Department from 2001 to 2004. She is the author of more than one hundred articles and more than twenty books, including *Hunting Girls* (forthcoming); *Earth and World: Philosophy After the Apollo Missions*; *Technologies of Life and Death: From Cloning to Capital Punishment*; *Knock Me Up, Knock Me Down: Images of Pregnancy in Hollywood Film*; *Animal Lessons: How They Teach Us to Be Human*; *Women as Weapons of War: Iraq, Sex and the Media*; *The Colonization of Psychic Space: A Psychoanalytic Theory of Oppression*; *Noir Anxiety: Race, Sex, and Maternity in Film Noir*; *Witnessing: Beyond Recognition*; *Subjectivity Without Subjects: From Abject Fathers to Desiring Mothers*; *Family Values: Subjects Between Nature and Culture*; *Womanizing Nietzsche: Philosophy's Relation to "the Feminine"*; and *Reading Kristeva: Unraveling the Double-Bind*. She has also edited or coedited several books.

Gertrude Postl is professor of philosophy and women's and gender studies at Suffolk County Community College in Selden, New York. Her publications focus on feminist theory (in particular Luce Irigaray, Julia Kristeva, and Hélène Cixous), philosophy and literature, and aesthetics. She currently works on issues regarding the interrelation between body and language in feminist theory, on theories of subversion, and on the political implications of reading/writing. Her most recent publication is the coedited volume *Hélène Cixous. Das Lachen der Medusa zusammen mit aktuellen Beiträgen* (Vienna: Passagen Verlag, 2013).

Lee Silverman is a serial entrepreneur who lives in Melbourne, Australia. Lee has founded seven companies and is currently the CEO of a group of technology companies in Australia. Lee began his career teaching at universities around Boston, Massachusetts. At MIT, he was coordinator of the Visible Language Workshop from 1980 to 1985, where he taught, researched, and produced software and hardware for the digital blending of words, images, and graphic ideas into various media from print to long-distance transmission to large-scale billboards. The work done then, at what became the MIT Media Lab, was seminal to the realization of what today we know as the most expansive publishing medium ever—the World Wide Web. In addition to his career in technology development, Lee has continued to pursue ideas around the integration of words, images, and graphics as a means to create artists' books, computer graphic art, photographs, as well as several other forms of printmaking and video. Like his brother, Hugh, Lee has always been fascinated by language, accents, and people's/peoples' histories that have led them to today.

Gail Weiss is professor of philosophy and human sciences at The George Washington University in Washington, DC. She is the author of *Refiguring the Ordinary* (Indiana University Press, 2008) and *Body Images: Embodiment as Intercorporeality* (Routledge, 1999), the editor of *Intertwinings: Interdisciplinary Encounters with Merleau-Ponty* (State University of New York Press, 2008) and coeditor (with Debra Bergoffen) of the Summer 2011 Special Issue of *Hypatia: A Journal of Feminist Philosophy* on "The Ethics of Embodiment," vol. 26, no. 3. She is also the coeditor of three anthologies: *Feminist Interpretations of Maurice Merleau-Ponty* (Pennsylvania State University Press, 2006); *Thinking the Limits of the Body* (State University of New York Press, 2003); and *Perspectives on Embodiment: The Intersections of Nature and Culture* (Routledge, 1999). Other publications include journal articles and book chapters that employ a feminist phenomenological methodology to explore fundamental issues concerning human embodiment.

Ewa Płonowska Ziarek is Julian Park Professor of Comparative Literature at the University of Buffalo. She is the author of *Feminist Aesthetics and the Politics of Modernism* (Columbia University Press, 2012); *An Ethics of Dissensus: Postmodernity, Feminism, and the Politics of Radical Democracy* (Stanford University Press, 2001); and *The Rhetoric of Failure: Deconstruction of Skepticism, Reinvention of Modernism* (State University of New York Press, 1995). She is the coeditor of, among others, *Revolt, Affect, Collectivity: The Unstable Boundaries of Kristeva's Polis* (State University of New York Press, 2005); *Time for the Humanities* (Fordham University Press, 2008) and *Intermedialities: Philosophy, Art, Politics* (Rowman & Littlefield, 2010). Her interdisciplinary research interests include feminist political theory, modernism, continental philosophy, ethics, and critical race theory.

Index